Michael Green is the author of twenty-two books and plays, including the perennially popular series that began with *The Art of Coarse Rugby.* A stage version of *The Art of Coarse Acting* transferred from the Edinburgh fringe to London's West End, while *The Art of Coarse Moving,* devoted to the horrors of buying a new home, became a TV series on the BBC.

Michael Green broadcasts regularly on radio and TV, acts in his one-man show based on *Coarse Acting,* and contributes to a wide variety of newspapers and magazines. He is unmarried and lives in West London, where he has declared his garden a nature reserve to save cutting the lawn.

Other books by Michael Green

The 'Coarse' Series

The Art of Coarse Rugby
The Art of Coarse Sailing
Even Coarser Rugby
The Art of Coarse Acting
The Book of Coarse Sport
The Art of Coarse Golf
The Art of Coarse Drinking
The Art of Coarse Moving
The Art of Coarse Cruising
Even Coarser Sport
The Art of Coarse Sex
The Art of Coarse Office Life

Novels

Don't Print My Name Upside Down
Squire Haggard's Journal

Plays

Four Plays for Coarse Actors
The Coarse Acting Show Two
The Third Great Coarse Acting Show

Others

Tonight, Josephine
Don't Swing from the Balcony, Romeo
Rugby Alphabet
Stage Noises and Effects

The Boy Who Shot Down an Airship

The first part of an autobiography

by

MICHAEL GREEN

BANTAM BOOKS

TORONTO · NEW YORK · LONDON · SYDNEY · AUCKLAND

THE BOY WHO SHOT DOWN AN AIRSHIP
A BANTAM BOOK 0 553 17620 X

Originally published in Great Britain by William Heinemann Ltd

PRINTING HISTORY

William Heinemann edition published 1988
Bantam Books edition published 1989

Copyright © Michael Green
Cover art copyright © Robin Jacques

Bantam Books are published by Transworld Publishers Ltd.,
61-63 Uxbridge Road, Ealing, London W5 5SA, in Australia by
Transworld Publishers (Australia) Pty. Ltd., 15-23 Helles
Avenue, Moorebank, NSW 2170, and in New Zealand by Transworld
Publishers (N.Z.) Ltd., Cnr. Moselle and Waipareira Avenues,
Henderson, Auckland.

Made and printed in Great Britain by
The Guernsey Press Co. Ltd., Guernsey, Channel Islands.

CONTENTS

ILLUSTRATIONS

FOREWORD

The great Dr Samuel Johnson said: 'In lapidary inscriptions a man is not on oath.' That was when they criticised him for his epitaph on Oliver Goldsmith's tomb, which rather overdid the praise. Neither is a man on oath when writing an auto-biography. So, although I have tried to be as accurate as possible, I apologise for any accidental errors in detail such as names or dates. This is an impression of my early life, not an official history of my old regiment or school.

Sometimes incidents have been slightly altered to protect those involved. In the same way, although I have used real names where possible, they have been altered where it might cause distress to innocent people.

Michael Green

CHAPTER ONE

My grandfather might have nearly bowled W. G. Grace

I shall begin with grandfather. That's not the right way to do it, of course. These days you're supposed to start an auto-biography with the present day, preferably something salacious, and work backwards, so the author's birth is described on page 256 while his sex life begins at the start of Chapter One. Thus: 'I was driving through Somerset the other week with my fourth wife and her children and as we passed a field near Glastonbury I saw a naked girl sunning herself in the grass. And my mind went back to those days long ago when I had romped trouserless with the village girls in those same fields. . .' etc., etc. This cleverly brings in a hint of uninhibited sexual revelations if the reader will go on.

But I always planned to start with grandfather because he loomed large in my early life and because he is one of the few members of the family to have any claim to fame. Family legend says he once nearly bowled W. G. Grace, the Great Cricketer. For years I planned to call this book

MY GRANDFATHER NEARLY BOWLED W. G. GRACE

which was the title of my first radio broadcast in 1963. In it I described how difficult it was to sustain the burden of being descended from such a hero, especially when you're not much good at cricket. My moment of glory came, however, when a rude person at a posh and very boring cricket club dinner held at the House of Commons asked, 'Why on earth have they invited you to speak?' and I replied firmly, 'Because my grandfather might have nearly bowled W. G. Grace.' The BBC must have been as impressed by grandfather as I was, because they reprinted the broadcast in a collection recently.

However, when it came to publishing this book there were second thoughts. I worried that people might believe it was all about cricket and sport, which it isn't. Cricketers would buy and be disappointed. Non-sportsmen would look at the cover and put it back on the shelf. So the title was altered but I'm still going to start off with grandfather, since he began it all.

The family called him Grampy, the traditional West Country term, but his real name was Will Smeath. His old house is still there in Cobourg Road, Montpelier, Bristol, but the front wall's been torn down for a parking space and the house divided into flats. As with all legends, there were about five different versions of his great encounter with the world's most famous cricketer. The most striking said that about 1890 Grampy was practising at the county ground nets in Bristol (he was a pal of Mr Spry, the groundsman, and allowed to use them). Dr Grace was there, limbering up for a county match with Gloucestershire, and called on Grampy to bowl to him. He obliged with a ball of hurricane force which tore the Doctor's stumps clean out of the ground. Another version, much favoured by an uncle, was that Grampy called out, 'I'll give you one of they new twisty 'uns, Doctor,' and delivered a spinner of such cunning that Grace was left vainly smiting empty air as his wicket tumbled. 'The Doctor said he'd never seen bowling like it,' my uncle used to say. A further variation had Grampy running through the streets of Bristol waving the ball and shouting, 'I just bowled the Doctor! I just bowled W. G. Grace!' before reaching home and placing it carefully in a box labelled BALL WITH WHICH I BOWLED W. G. GRACE.

But there was no doubt about the authenticity of the ball. It was passed down as a family heirloom and came into mother's possession while Grampy was still alive. I was allowed to look at it as a child and no matter how desperate the shortage of those old cork cricket balls on the local playing-fields, we were

2

never allowed to use Dr Grace's conqueror. It was something of a disillusionment years later when mother confessed she didn't think Grampy actually bowled the doctor. It was the *ball* which had bowled Grace, not Grampy. The groundsman had given it to him as a souvenir. But that didn't alter its value. It is still there, on my mantelpiece, salvaged from a drawer after mother died, looking rather brown and battered and disappointingly ordinary. It is next to another, more modern ball, on a plinth with a plaque recording I was awarded it for being top of the bowling averages in the *London Evening Star* editorial cricket team in 1956. Typical of Fleet Street. They couldn't even add up. It was the *batting* averages I topped, not the bowling, but still, I'm proud of it, even though it's small beer compared with Grampy's feat.

The Victorians, of course, had an obsession about souvenirs of the famous. They worshipped anything an important person had even touched. An elderly friend of the family used to keep what looked like a small dog turd under a glass dome on his mantelpiece. It was proudly labelled: 'Cigar butt thrown away by His Royal Highness the Prince of Wales outside the Café Royal, London, November 14, 1893', and visitors were allowed to smell it. The owner had snatched it off the pavement after HRH had passed.

Grandfather must have been about 70 when I first remember him, as a toddler in the early thirties. By then he'd given up cricket for bowls, but his legend was still strong, fed by numerous aunts and uncles. Grandfather searching for a gas leak with a naked candle, and somehow surviving the subsequent explosion; grandfather going out in a horse-drawn wagonette for the annual wayzgoose, or printers' outing, and being propped up against the front door on their return (his comrades fled when they heard grandmother coming); grandfather riding a bucking mule at a Bristol fair and only coming off when the desperate proprietor stuck a pin in its backside to stop him winning the prize; grandfather playing rugby on Clifton Down.

There seemed nothing grandfather wouldn't tackle. He was also a racing cyclist and mother used to describe how he tore round Bristol on a penny-farthing. People associate the ludicrous penny-farthing cycles with old codgers, but in reality they were a sportsman's bicycle, the mount for the racing man, and with their enormous height it took a bold one to ride them fast, sitting six feet off the ground. The reason for the strange design, with the huge front wheel, was speed. A large wheel was the simplest way of getting most leverage from the pedals, which were directly attached to the hub.

When Grampy was born in Exeter about 1860, slavery was still in force in America and world statesmen included such historic figures as Lincoln, Gladstone, Bismarck and Garibaldi. His father ran a livery stable but Grampy started work as a compositor (printer) on the Bristol morning newspaper and stayed there for the rest of his life. Their cricket team used the old county ground and that was how he got to tangle with W. G. Grace. Typesetting was done by hand when he started, the lead letters being picked out from a case divided into compartments and like all the other men Grampy kept his snuff in the 'Z' compartment, which was rarely used. He received 35 shillings a week, which compared favourably with the journalist's wages, as they averaged around 25 shillings and had to provide their own top hats as well. Towards the turn of the century hand-setting of type was superseded by Linotype machines, which functioned mechanically, with a keyboard. A quarter of the printers were sacked but Grampy was kept on at an increased wage of 39 shillings a week. It was a bad time to be out of work. My mother remembered a friend of the family who walked from Exeter to Bradford in search of a job. He stayed overnight at grandfather's before resuming the long march.

Among grandfather's achievements, he was a crack shot, and frequently won prizes at local fairs. A sergeant in the Volunteers, forerunners of the present Territorial Army, he'd volunteered for service in South Africa in the Boer War of 1900 but they turned him down because he had a family. 'But that's why he was going, because he had a family,' one of my uncles used to remark cynically. Mother remembers the whole family going down to Avonmouth Docks to see the soldiers march away. As the artillery passed, a woman ran from the crowd and flung her arms round a man's neck, sobbing bitterly. Queen Victoria came down to bid the troops farewell.

'She was tiny, just like a little doll,' said mother.

Grandmother was a teacher in one of the new Board Schools, which established the first universal free education. I remember her as a little old lady who always dressed in black with a 'choker' round her throat. She dressed the same way for 70 years. She bore grandfather four children in the draughty house in Montpelier, my mother, two brothers, George and Will, and another girl, my Aunt Nan. Auntie was the last of the line and rumour said that she hadn't been wanted because there wasn't enough money in the house, at least not enough to support four children and Grampy's social activities.

From what mother and aunts and uncles told me, life in Coburg Road was typical of Victorian lower middle-class existence. It was lively but home-centred and strict. On Sundays the children all had to change their clothes twice – once after morning church for the afternoon walk, and again for evening service. The great Dr Grace was no stranger to the district and mother saw him go by in his pony and trap. Indeed, the mother of her best friend Amy, at Fairfield High School (fees, fivepence a week), was a patient of The Great Cricketer, when he could spare time from the game.

Mother was christened Winifred Jane. On leaving school, she got a job in the education office of Bristol Corporation as a 'lady typewriter', as they were sometimes known in those days. She could do shorthand, too, so she was one of the early girl secretaries. Mother had many admirers before she finally fell for father, although they were granted few favours. 'I was not fast, like some girls,' she used to say.

One boy-friend was a Welsh rugby player in the Newport team. He caught the train from Bristol every Saturday to play, but always spent Saturday mornings with mother.

'That's the only way I can keep off the beer, Win,' he told her. 'I know you won't let me drink.'

That was true enough. Like so many of her generation, mother had a horror of the strong stuff and her children's liking for it was to prove a source of friction later. Another admirer was so distressed when mother rejected him that he went to Africa on safari and sent her back the skin of a tiger he'd shot. Or so she said. We had the skin at home in Leicester, its glass eyes glaring balefully up from the floor and a long tear by the neck stitched up.

Most of her boy-friends disappeared in the holocaust of World War One, like the rest of their generation. One called Dick got drunk at a twenty-first birthday party in a Bristol restaurant and whirled mother round in a mad dance. Shy and frightened, she ran home to Cobourg Road. Some hours later my Aunt Nan (always the larky one of the family) arrived home with the now helpless young man, who was smuggled into the house and left unconscious on a downstairs sofa. He had originally been taken home in a cab but his father, true to the standards of that generation, had refused to have him in the house and Aunt Nan took pity on him. A year or two later he was killed in Flanders.

One man who paid court to mother was a German count. 'He was a real Von,' said mother wistfully as she plunged her hands into the washing-up water. 'He used to bow and click his heels. He had a moustache which he waxed to make it pointed. But of course I saw through him. He was a German spy, investigating Bristol docks. He disappeared just before the outbreak of war in 1914.'

Mother's beauty, which photographs confirm, must have suffered a blow when they took all her teeth out. There was nothing wrong with them but there was a craze at the time for removing teeth as a source of infection. The doctor decided mother was potentially consumptive and out they came in her early twenties, to be replaced by grinning tombstones made from porcelain. She lived to be 90 so it seems the diagnosis was somewhat exaggerated.

Not all of mother's contemporaries were as respectable as her. She often spoke of a girl at school who became the mistress of Gordon Selfridge, the millionaire founder of the London store. 'He gave her a carriage of her own and kept her on the Isle of Wight,' mother used to say. 'Of course, nobody would speak to her when she came back to Bristol.' Another school friend was wooed by a full-blooded regular army colonel, married him and bore two children, only to discover too late that he was already married. Mother always spoke of these experiences as confirming her suspicion of men. 'I kept them all at arm's length until your father came along.'

When mother did eventually fall in love, it was in a fashion that makes the great romances of fiction pale into prosaic insignificance. In 1916, when World War One had already been raging two years and hospitals were full of wounded men from France, a friend of mother's (my honorary Auntie Gwen in later years) who was a VAD nurse at Southmeads Hospital, Bristol, asked her to play the piano for wounded soldiers. Sometimes men who were dying would ask mother for a special piece of music and when she came next evening their beds were empty. All her life she talked about one terribly wounded boy who begged her to play the intermezzo from *Cavalleria Rusticana* for him. When she looked up from the piano they were putting the screens round his bed. She remembered the story a few weeks before she died in 1981 and tears still came to her eyes as she recalled it.

One patient at Southmeads was a 28-year-old corporal in the Canadian army. Jack Green had emigrated to Canada from Leicester in 1910 and joined the Canadian army the day war broke out in August 1914. He survived until 1916 when his right arm was shattered by shrapnel from a shell and later amputated at Southmeads. I know every detail of how father lost his arm, which is not surprising because as children we heard it once a week. Father and some men from his unit, the City of Toronto Regiment, were resting behind the line and harmonising 'The Old Rustic Bridge by the Mill' in barber-shop style. Father, who had a pleasant, light voice, took the tenor part. When the song finished, orders came to return to the front line, where they joined in an attack which captured some German trenches. The Germans retaliated with a fierce bombardment and a shell burst immediately over father's head. As he flung up his right arm to protect himself, shrapnel shattered it and pierced his left wrist, and he flopped down in the bottom of the trench, holding the remains of his arm.

'A stretcher-bearer came along, took one look at me, and another at the shelling, and said I'd better stay where I was, the cowardly toad,' father used to say (he always referred to people he disliked as either toads or dogs). 'He said the bombardment was too fierce to leave the trench. There wasn't any cover on the way back, you see, because we were now in the captured German front-line and no communication trenches had been dug. So I sat there, holding my arm and bleeding to death, with the whizz-bangs* thudding into the earth behind me, the Jack Johnsons* bursting in front and the Minnewherfers* coming down all the time.'

Father was saved by a comrade called Bob Kerr, one of his machine-gun grew, who dragged him out of the trench and back to the support line through the bombardment, splashing water from shell-holes into his face every time he collapsed. Another friend, Cy Young, took over and helped him back to the dressing-station.

They didn't immediately amputate his arm but shunted him back to England amid the horrors of the hospital train, which stopped every so often to unload dead soldiers into makeshift mortuaries along the line. At Bristol, an over-optimistic surgeon nearly killed him by trying to save the shattered arm. 'The bones were all in little pieces,' father used to say. 'It had shrunk to half its normal size. I told them it'd have to come off but they insisted on trying to preserve it. But after three days it got poisonous and turned black and swelled up so much the stitches burst and they had to take it off at once. And only just in time, too. It would have been gangrenous in another 24 hours. The surgeon said it was the worst arm he'd ever amputated.'

Ironically, father need never have lost his arm. He'd already been wounded once when shrapnel pierced his nose, leaving a hole which stayed for the rest of his life and made him snore in a strange manner. Then he was ruptured and they sent him

---

* Various German projectiles. The Whizz-bang was a field-gun shell, the Jack Johnson a heavy calibre howitzer and the Minnewherfer a large mortar. Most children of my generation would know what he meant from reading war stories and listening to grown-ups' conversation.

back to England for an operation and there he could have stayed. 'But I got fed up with parade-ground soldiering, my boy. Like a fool I wanted to get back in the trenches with the boys,' he said in later years.

So there he was, one arm amputated, the other pierced by shrapnel, his whole being twisted by the torment he had undergone, when mother met him. It was love at first sight. 'After I met your father, I never thought of any other man,' said mother. Father, too, was taken by the tall, slim girl with pretty legs who played the piano, and asked her to the pictures. Mother, shy as always, said she wouldn't go alone so they fixed up a foursome, my 'Auntie' Gwen and a wounded sergeant who'd lost a leg in France. It was one of those early silent Chaplin films. Afterwards they all went to Auntie Gwen's house near Clifton Down and father and the sergeant returned after lights out. To avoid the sentry they helped each other climb the hospital wall and sneaked back into the ward, despite having only six limbs between them.

'It was typical of your father,' mother always said proudly. 'He was afraid of nothing.'

They carried on the relationship when father went back to Leicester, where his father ran a hardware and furniture business. Dad was employed in the firm. Mother gave him a photo of herself and a lock of her golden hair which he carried for the rest of his life. I found them still in his wallet after he died in 1971. Every day they were apart, father wrote to mother, letters written in great savage strokes as he struggled to learn to write with his left hand. To the end of his life letter-writing was an agony which left the whole house in an uproar as father tried to fill his fountain pen with one hand or found the paper slipping away despite a host of paperweights. But in 1920 they were married at St Andrew's Church, Montpelier, Bristol.

CHAPTER TWO

The day the R101 flew over

My parents had two children. Brother Roger was born in 1921 and I came along on Sunday, 2 January 1927, at 'Henleaze', Baden Road, Leicester, a small semi-detached in the suburbs, built two or three years before. The name of the house came from the district in Bristol where Aunt Nan lived. I just missed being born in a council house, as father and mother lived in one at Humberstone, Leicester, the first council estate built in the city, after they got married and Roger was born there. This was a pity, because in the fifties and sixties middle-class people used to compete with each other in proving how working-class they were. Many a dreary hour I spent with teachers and BBC staff all boasting of proletarian origins and habits. I lost the chance of saying, 'But I tell you I was actually born in a council house.' As it was I had to be content with 'I was almost born in a council house,' which is rather like Grampy's boast that he nearly bowled W. G. Grace.

Mother, on the contrary, was not proud of having lived in a council house. 'Lots of nice people had to do it after the Great War,' she used to say defensively. 'There were some very respectable people on that estate.' Like most people of the time, my parents were highly class-conscious. Well aware of their backgrounds (Grandpa Green had started as a shop assistant), they struggled to maintain a lower middle-class position. A milk bottle on the table was a cardinal sin; sugar was picked up with plated silver tongs; fish could only be eaten with the special knives they got as a wedding present. We were never allowed to forget that on father's side of the family an ancestor had once been Mayor of Leicester and there was a tablet to his memory in the cathedral. He also founded an almshouse for decayed descendants called The Consanguinitarium and it is still there, in what is now a very run-down area. Recently I passed it and an old man with a grey beard peered from a window at me. Odd to think he was probably a distant relative.

The care lavished on modern mothers-to-be was scorned by mother. 'I saw the doctor once when I was pregnant and the next time I saw him was when you were born,' she said. I was delivered in the front bedroom by Dr Jackson, who always wore a black coat and a wing collar. After I was born, father, who had been waiting downstairs, gave Dr Jackson a large whisky and soda.

'I'm glad it's a boy, doctor, because I've no time for women,' he told him.

At least that is mother's story. Father denied it, but the sentiments were not foreign. He distrusted most women except mother, including her sister, Aunt Nan, who was rather forceful in her opinions. Father's attitude to the female sex was summed up by the way he addressed mother. Usually he called her simply 'mother'. If he felt particularly affectionate he called her 'Winnie' or 'Winifred Jane'. If annoyed, it was 'woman' ('Woman, I know what I'm doing, I tell you'). In fairness to him, both the attitude and form of address were common at the time.

The house is still there, occupied by an Indian family now. It was a small three-up and two-down with no garage and I can still see scratches on the bricks by the porch made by our bicycles when we propped them there. I doubt if the Indian children use the hall, which had a stone floor, for roller-skating, as we did on rainy days.

The first thing I remember strongly is the doomed R101 airship passing over Baden Road. I have earlier, more vague recollections – my mother singing me to sleep in a cot, Brother Roger leering at me through the bars (or perhaps it was his normal expression), being wheeled in a folding pushchair down Baden Road, but these are glimpses. The R101 is a sharply-etched episode. It crashed in 1930 so I would have been about three. It was the last word in airships, quite literally in fact, because they stopped building them in this country after it came down in France on the maiden flight, killing almost all on board. In 1930 the airship was going to be the transport of the future, the Concorde of that decade. Aircraft range was limited but the airship could fly the Atlantic with ease. They were to link the British Empire with a network of services, starting with the brightest jewel in the King's crown, India. Like Concorde, the R101 generated enormous interest and, like Concorde, the cost soared and the snags escalated. Unlike Concorde, though, at one point they stuck in an extra bit in the middle to make it bigger. There is a graphic account of the doomed project in Neville Shute's autobiography *Slide Rule*.

Shortly before the R101 left on its maiden voyage from Cardington, in Bedfordshire, to India, it flew over Leicester, which was only fifty-odd miles from its base. I was sitting in my wooden high chair eating mashed potatoes and gravy (a favourite dish then, as now), when a neighbour knocked on the front door, shouting, 'Mrs Green, come quick, the R101's going over!' Mother grabbed me and ran into the road. The street was already crowded with people staring upwards and waving. Mother held me up and there was the great, silver, ponderous cigar gently lumbering over. It was huge – about two hundred yards long – and travelled slowly, so it appeared to blot out the whole sky. I have never seen anything so big in the sky in my life, nor anything that made such an impression. It was like seeing the Town Hall fly overhead. Because of its slow speed it was a minute or two before it disappeared from view and we stood watching in the middle of the road until the huge sausage vanished.

A day or two later it set off for India and crashed in bad weather into a hill in Beauvais, France, killing 43 passengers and crew. Only five survived the crash and the fire which followed. Among those killed was the Air Minister, who'd gone on the trip as a gesture of government confidence in the project.

The disaster sent a thrill of horror through the whole country, but we had extra reason to be appalled in Baden Road. Tony English, the ten-year-old brother of one of my playmates up the road, had shot at the airship as it passed over with his air rifle, a powerful weapon already proved deadly to birds. When he heard the news he took his air rifle and buried it at the bottom of the garden, convinced the shot had proved fatal. He told my brother, 'I saw the slug go in and start a tear in the gasbags. I expect it was a slow leak and all the gas ran out when it got to France.'

For days Tony crept about with a frightened face. Whenever a policeman cycled down the road on some routine errand he ran indoors and hid. But as time passed without arrest he became bolder and boasted of what he'd done. The buried gun was exhumed and exhibited with pride. 'Only a Webley could have done it,' was the verdict of older boys.

Just before the R101 crashed my paternal grandfather died. I cannot remember him. My Leicester grandparents never meant the same to me as my mother's parents in Bristol. To start with, Grandpa Green had never bowled W. G. Grace and he died before I knew him, whereas Grampy lived until I was 22. I do know that Grandfather Green was a man who loved life and enjoyed food and drink, especially the latter. He was also reputed to be a bit 'awkward', a trait he passed down to his son and grandson, and refused to attend the wedding of his daughter, my Aunt Mabel, on some obscure grounds, although she was marrying a perfectly respectable chemist. Father gave her away. His taste for good living is recalled in his enormous pocket flask, holding nearly a pint, which stands on my sideboard. He also left a pipe with a silver band which I smoked in my youth, and a box of the finest Cuban cigars. Father, who had given up smoking, used to smoke one a year, every Christmas, and it took him 20 years to clear them all. What they tasted like at the end, heaven knows.

One of grandfather's peculiarities, father told me, was that he would never drink singles. 'I can't stand that miserable smear in the bottom of the glass,' he said. 'Don't buy me a whisky by all means, but if you insist, then make it a double.'

Unfortunately, one of his best friends, a clergyman in East Leicestershire, was teetotal. When they visited him grandfather would say, 'It's a dry shop there, mother,' and make extensive preparations. These consisted of getting together a sort of travelling liquor store, which he set up in their bedroom at the vicarage. Whenever chance came, grandfather made an excuse to leave the company and hopped upstairs for a double Scotch. The clergyman frowned on smoking, too, so grandfather smoked his cigars lying down in front of the bedroom fireplace, wafting the smoke up the chimney with his bowler hat. Forty years after he died I was to use the legend as the basis for a character in my books, the jovial Uncle Walter of *The Art of Coarse Drinking* and other volumes.

After his death, grandmother lived on alone in the old family home, a large red-brick double-fronted house in Tichborne Street, a respectable inner suburb at the end of the nineteenth century. By the sixties, with grandmother long dead, the house became a brothel. I shall never forget father's horror when he read in the *Leicester Mercury* that a West Indian had been stabbed in a brawl there and the proprietor jailed. 'What would your grandfather have said, my boy?' he asked. Indeed, I shudder to think. Probably, 'Pass the Scotch.'

Grandfather's firm had a hardware shop and a wholesale business in Highcross Street, in the centre of Leicester, and dad was employed as manager. It was a strain for a maimed man, shattered by the war and struggling to keep up with other people. He drove the firm's van one-handed. It had no special controls, but fortunately Fords produced a model with a foot gear-change. When it broke down in a remote Leicestershire village, father took off the carburettor and cleaned it in the pouring rain, using only his one hand and teeth. Struggling with something difficult like this he would go red in the face and breathe heavily and the useless stump of his right arm would twitch and flap violently and he cursed and swore at the frustration of it all.

No wonder grandfather left the business to be sold when he

died in 1929 and the money was put in trust for grandmother, my aunt and father. The income and a corporal's disability pension from the Canadian army were just enough. In common with many of his generation, father never revealed his income to mother, or indeed anyone, but it was probably not much less than a sales rep or teacher and by intense economy he could keep his respectability. The fact the firm was put up for sale instead of being left in the family increased his bitterness but the war shattered him so badly he could not have coped. Even the burdens of everyday life were a nightmare.

He would not compromise and insisted on doing everything for himself, wearing a shirt with cuff-links and a separate, stiff collar. We could hear him groaning and cursing upstairs as he struggled with cuff-links and studs and the black tie he always wore. Yet he could be incredibly adept and often pottered round the house with a mouthful of nails doing odd jobs. When there was a sudden fall of snow he built a wooden sledge for us boys in one afternoon, mother holding the nails and screws for him. He would spend hours bowling to me in the garden with a tennis ball to teach me cricket. Yet he was inordinately sensitive about his arm. Swimming on holiday he would plunge into the sea and quickly surge away from the beach, moving with remarkable speed for a one-armed crawl. When he came back mother ran down the beach with a towel and put it over his shoulders to conceal the remains of his right arm and stop people staring.

Thrust back on his own bitterness, he spent hours muttering in the bathroom or bedroom, pacing the floor as he fought World War One over again or brooded on the past. As I played with my Hornby trains I'd hear, 'Look out, they're in the trench!' or 'Get the stretcher-bearers!' It could be embarrassing if we had guests. Many a visitor would be startled to hear a shout of 'Look out, the bastards are coming over!' emanating from the bathroom. But there were few visitors. My parents preferred, as they put it, 'to keep ourselves to ourselves'.

It was a strange era to grow up in, a kind of betwixt and between, with the Victorian age dying hard and lingering well into the twentieth century. My parents' generation were born before most of the inventions which transformed the world were familiar. Mother often used to describe a ride in one of the first motor cars in Bristol. It broke down and had to be towed home behind a horse and cart. She was 25 before she even saw an aeroplane. My generation are different. Almost every invention of modern life – aircraft, radio, cars, electronics – was in use when we were growing up. Yet in many ways our lives were no different from those of our Victorian parents.

Milk, for instance, still came round in a pony and trap (a milk float they called it for some reason) from Elms Farm, Evington, a village about a mile away, although we were under two miles from the city centre. Curly, the milkman, dressed in boots and riding breeches, ladled it out of the churn with a big, metal dipper. Groceries were delivered by Mr Freeman, who was too poor even to own a horse and used a handcart. Later, when business prospered, he bought a horse and cart but he always gave the horse a day off at bank holidays and used the old handcart. 'The horse needs a holiday like you and me, mum,' he told mother. She liked him and gave him a cup of tea or cocoa every time he called. He would sip it from a saucer noisily, his ill-fitting false teeth slipping in and out all the time.

Father, meanwhile, peered out of the front-room window, hoping the horse would have a shit and he could collect some manure for the back garden. The passage of every horse down the road was marked by the scraping of shovels as residents gathered the precious substance, often while it was still steaming. We kept a special manure shovel in the coal shed. Alas, poor Mr Freeman. He collapsed when giving his horse yet another day off and died from a heart attack in Leicester Royal Infirmary. They said it was overwork.

Even more Victorian was the delivery of coal by Leicester Co-operative Society. It came in a steam lorry, clanking its way up Evington Drive and into Baden Road in a cloud of smoke and vapour, a great fire blazing beneath. It was an awe-inspiring sight like the last scene of *Götterdämmerung*. From each side a blackened head stuck out crying 'Coal! Coal!' and people ran into the road and stopped it if they wanted any, but we had ours from a horse and cart run by two little men.

On Saturday nights the road was visited by a man and woman in a pony and trap who sold tripe. We had a pound most Saturdays in the winter, mother running out to collect some in a bowl. This was cooked with onions and carrots in a white sauce for father's supper. None of the rest of the family would touch the slimy mess but years later, when I was about 12, I had some and got the taste. I have loved tripe ever since.

Sometimes tramps called, asking for a bit of food. Mother was good to them and gave out bread and cheese and a slice of cake, perhaps remembering Grampy's friend who walked to Bradford for work. Chimney-sweeps were always wheeling their barrows past, their eyes a startling white in their black faces. When the sweep called, the whole house was covered in white sheets to protect the furniture, and evacuated. I would be taken outside to see the moment when his brush emerged from the chimney and he gave it a triumphant twirl. All the tradesmen whistled, from the baker to the greengrocer, usually the latest popular hit such as 'The Isle of Capri' or something traditional like 'Colonel Bogey'. Nobody whistles today. Is it because modern pop music is so hideously untuneful?

There were lots more door-to-door salesmen then and they didn't just vanish, they kept coming back. Mother got her disinfectant from a man who came round once a month and she replaced household brushes from the Kleeneezee man perhaps twice a year.

The road was lit by gas. A lamp outside 'Henleaze' was lighted every evening by a man in black uniform with a waistcoat with metal buttons. He cycled round igniting the lamps by a long pole with a flame on the end, like a huge cigarette-lighter. Many people still cooked on coal-fired kitchen ranges and we had one ourselves, but it wasn't normally used except for heating the water and drying firewood, until a bomb in the war stopped the gas. We rented a cooker from the local gas company, run by the City Council, who also ran the electricity works. A mile away, on East Park Road, trams thundered along. Built in the grand manner just after Victoria's death, they had magnificent cut-glass windows and splendid arching brass lampholders inside. A favourite game was to put halfpennies on the line so a tram passed over them. They emerged bent into a strange shape and hot with the friction of the wheels. With luck, the tram would stop and the conductor shout abuse. The railway, too, had not changed since Victoria. Totally dependent on steam, little branch lines meandered all over Leicestershire. The city itself had five stations, all now demolished except one. West Bridge Station was the original terminus of one of the first railways in the world, the Leicester to Swannington line of 1836. It was still used for goods until the sixties.

Leicester had a reputation as a clean city and a prosperous one, despite the recession. Its history went back to Roman times and the remains of a Roman market-place were preserved not far from grandfather's former shop. On the outskirts of the city was Leicester Abbey where Cardinal Wolsey died. there were also many dignified large houses dating from the early nineteenth century and the imposing County Assembly Rooms, designed 200 years ago by my ancestor commemorated in the cathedral. The city had the air of a county town with its market-place and the high-class grocery store, Simkin and James, which the gentry and upper-classes patronised. Yet the overwhelming impression of Leicester then was still redbrick.

Ours was a mixed sort of road, a frontier area between town and country. Half a mile away, Victorian Leicester began with line after line of classic redbrick terraces, with no front gardens, aspidistras glaring in the windows and the front steps scrubbed spotlessly white every morning by working-class wives. Half a mile in the other direction, cows were milked. In Baden Road, there were several redbrick villas, perhaps fifty years old then, built when the area was still fields, some vacant land and half-a-dozen semis, of which our house was one. Opposite, frowned a row of large terrace-houses, taking up almost the whole side of the street. Where they finished was a row of lock-up garages, although only two people in the street owned cars. It was forbidden to leave unlit cars in the street and when Uncle Will visited he had to leave his Ford at a petrol station a mile away and walk back. Once, the garage was shut and he left the car outside the house until a policeman knocked on the door and insisted he put the lights on. Will did so, and arose at 4 a.m. to put them out and conserve his six-volt battery.

There were no houses with a garage, except the four corner houses, which were detached and grander than the rest, but they strictly belonged to Evington Lane and Evington Drive, the adjoining roads. One corner house belonged to Dr Somerville, our local GP and another to Mr Price, whose daughter and I played mothers and fathers when we were about five. Mr Price wore plus-fours and drove a big Riley with tin GB plates. He was a class above the rest of us.

The road was split by strange feuds. Mr Lister next door to us wouldn't talk to Mr Hetherington two doors away. Both worked on the L.M.S. railway, Mr Lister as a clerk and Mr Hetherington as a guard, and Mr Lister didn't forgive him for working in the General Strike of 1926. Opposite, Mrs Martin, whose son Dick was my brother's best friend, was the subject of a weird rumour. A distant relative was supposed to have been a German spy during the First World War.

'He was out in his car signalling with his headlights to the Zeppelins the night they bombed Loughborough Station,' ran the rumour. Even as a child this seemed ludicrous to me but the story stuck.

We also had our mystery. Mrs ——, who had a daughter with whom I sometimes played, lived with a bald-headed elementary schoolteacher who always wore black boots. The exact nature of their relationship is still something of a puzzle, but they did not adopt the usual euphemism of calling him a lodger. He was described as the daughter's 'guardian'. No mention was ever made of the husband.

There was little traffic and we played freely in the road, traditional games such as hopscotch, tops and marbles or a strange game called 'touch-finger lurkey'. It was, like most of our sports, a variation of chasing somebody madly up the street. And there were endless games of soccer or cricket with a tennis ball in front of the lock-up garages while the mad, old spinster opposite beat vainly on her window and called on us to stop.

A good example of the contradiction of the age was the telephone. By the thirties the telephone had been invented for more than fifty years. But only two people in Baden Road had one. I don't think anyone in the road had a refrigerator or an electric iron when I was born. But the radio, or wireless as we called it, was coming. Long poles sprouted in suburban gardens to catch the squeaky transmissions from Daventry or Droitwich, although we didn't get our first wireless until 1935.

My parents were old-fashioned even by the standards of the time and stuck rigidly to the way they had been brought up. Although there was a perfectly good lavatory in the bathroom upstairs they always used a chamber-pot in their bedroom during the night. Each had their own pot, with floral decoration, parked under their side of the bed, and mother emptied them down the lavatory every morning. When I got older I taxed my parents about the absurdity of this arrangement and they replied it was hygienic. They were distressed that my brother and I scorned chamber-pots and insisted on going to the bathroom. 'Why do you want to go to all that trouble when you have a perfectly good chamber-pot?' they argued. Even in the 1970s, my mother always asked for a chamber-pot in a hotel and was surprised when she couldn't get one.

It's appropriate my first memory was of the R101 airship, because it was above all the air age, just as today is the space age. Ordinary people didn't travel by air, any more than they travel in space today, but everybody believed man's future lay in the air, for good or bad. If war came, it was predicted Leicester would be laid waste by bombs, its inhabitants blown to pieces or choked by poison gas. If the fragile peace survived, what was vaguely referred to as 'the aviation era' was expected to be ushered in. Strange aircraft flew over the city. Besides the R101 I saw an autogyro, a primitive form of helicopter in which the rotor blades had no power of their own but were driven by the machine's forward speed. Two helmeted figures in leather overcoats crouched in the cockpit as it buzzed low over the city. Sometimes a Flying Flea would lurch across the sky. This was to be the People's Plane. Powered by a motor-cycle engine and looking like a large moth, it was built at home from a kit. They were so badly designed most of them never got off the ground and those that did staggered about at dangerously low heights. Later they were condemned as unsafe.

People believed in the air as if it was some magic restorative which would put the world right. Leicestershire had its own fanatic in Sir Lindsay Everard, of the brewing family, who had a private aerodrome (as it was called then) by his house at Rearsby, a few miles from the city. When I was older I cycled out to see it. There was a tiny control tower, about the size of a sentry box, and when Sir Lindsay's airborne guests left, he would get in, open a window, thrust out his arm and fire a Very pistol as a signal for take-off. Unfortunately, this once ignited the dry grass on the field and his friends took off in a sea of flame.

Much nearer home we had our own daring aviator, Cyril Hurst, who lived a hundred yards away, down Evington Drive. He'd been a pilot in World War One and carried his passion for flying into civilian life. He was the epitome of the go-ahead thirties man with his plus-fours, long scarf and Lagonda car with a leather strap round the huge bonnet, not to mention the long leather overcoat and cloth cap which he sometimes exchanged for a leather flying helmet. He smoked St Bruno, lit his pipe with Swan Vestas and drank Worthington or draught Bass copiously. Cyril owned a small aircraft and frequently took his wife and childen on trips. Sometimes these ended in disaster. The *Leicester Mercury* published a picture of Cyril standing proudly in a field, pointing to the wreckage of his machine, hanging in a tree. The family were with him and they featured on the front page under a heading something like

ANOTHER ESCAPE FOR LEICESTER AVIATOR

Mrs Hurst, a small, blonde woman, bore it all with considerable courage, much to the astonishment of my own mother, who was terrified of flying (she never flew in her life, although father was quite keen and treated us boys to a joy-ride when Leicester Aerodrome opened in 1936). I always hoped Mr Hurst, who made a living by running a series of small businesses with varying success, would make one of his forced landings in our road but he never obliged. His son Billy, the middle of three brothers, was one of my first pals. We often argued about whose father had the best war record ('And my dad killed more Germans than your dad'). But however gallant Cyril had been – and he was reputed to have survived a dogfight with Baron von Richthofen, the great German air ace – he had emerged unscathed. This is surprising, since he fought without a parachute. The authorities would not allow them, as they were believed to encourage cowardice. However, the evidence of father's martyrdom was plain to see as he strode down Evington Drive, muttering to himself and breaking off to raise his bowler hat courteously to a woman neighbour (despite his mistrust of the female sex he was invariably polite to women).

At 4 I went to school, a small private establishment for infants, called Micklefield School, about half a mile away. It was little better than a Dame school, since it had a staff of only three, including the headmistress, a Miss Cowdell. 'Michael is a strange child,' she once told my mother. Thirty years later, it would transpire she was the godmother of my literary agent, but not knowing this at the time I did not hold it against her. The nearest state school (or elementary school as it was called) was 1½ miles away and without a car the distance was prohibitive at the age of 4. Not that mother and father would have sent me there.

I was taught by a tall, dark, slim lady called Miss Grafton who looked incredibly old to me and who was about 22. Later she would marry and her husband be killed in World War Two. I learned to read and write with unusual speed, a facility the book-buying public would regret forty years later. There was no nonsense of the look-and-learn method. We chanted the alphabet and wrote it until we knew it and then put the letters into syllables and short words. For a few weeks I couldn't fathom it and then my brother went through the alphabet with a picture book in bed one night (we slept together until I was six) and the mists cleared. Next day I could recite the whole alphabet. I was so proud I went around chanting it until they told me to shut up. I'm still repeating it, only now they pay me for doing so. 'With my twenty-six soldiers of lead I will conquer the world,' said one of the founders of printing, and writing is just a question of arranging those 26 soldiers.

Literacy was highly-prized and my parents encouraged us to read 'good books' (some of which, such as *Robinson Crusoe*, would be condemned today by left-wing zealots). Every Sunday evening father read to Roger and me in bed, usually extracts from Grimm's fairy-tales, playing all the parts himself and getting carried away until mother shouted up that supper was ready and he would twitch his stump and call, 'All right, woman, I know, I know.'

With no job, father tried to fill time as best he could. His problem was not so much physical as emotional. The shell which shattered his arm had wrecked his ability to cope with life and he withdrew into himself. Although he'd never ridden he loved horses and sometimes went racing. These expeditions were not successful and filled him with a horror of gambling, not surprising since he once saw a man put money on five horses in a six-horse race and the sixth horse won.

'How anyone can risk money on those stupid, unintelligent creatures is beyond me,' he used to say. 'It only needs a scrap of paper blowing across the course and they will panic and run wild or refuse a fence. How can people put their life savings on something so irrational?' His dislike of gambling was almost obsessional and forty years later, towards the end of his life, he would say, 'How are you off for money, my boy? I hope to God you haven't been backing the gee-gees. Keep off the gee-gees, whatever you do.' Despite denials he was always suspicious I was secretly betting and repeated the advice at monthly intervals.

As for father's own secret love of the turf, he sublimated it by placing imaginary bets on horses, going through the *Daily Mail* in the mornings and ticking off likely winners. If he lost he would proudly announce, 'I cheated the bookies of five pounds today, my boy. That's one fiver the dogs won't get off the public.' This pleased him more than winning, the thought

23

that he had actually deprived a bookmaker of money. As he rarely picked winners, he got that satisfaction often.

He transferred his interest to hunting, of which there was a surplus in Leicestershire, whose county symbol is a fox. He followed on foot, a popular local pastime. Usually he walked to town and caught a train to a village station for the meet. Those were the days when for a few shillings they would add a horse-box to a local train at a village station and many riders travelled that way. Sometimes father was given a lift by Mr Bilston from Evington Drive in his Morris Cowley. This meant Mr Bilston had to be invited to tea under the rigid laws of suburban hospitality and would tell his story. It went on for ever and concerned the time he was gathering wild fruit on land belonging to Lord Nutting, who owned most of the Melton Mowbray area in those days. Old Bilston was caught red-handed by Lord Nutting himself, who angrily demanded, 'What the devil do you think you're doing? I'm Nutting, I tell you.'

'And I'm blackberrying,' replied Mr Bilston innocently, a remark which apparently gave the noble lord apoplexy. At this point in the story Bilston would cough and choke over his bread-and-butter and fishpaste, and shake with mirth. Mother gave a wan smile and father tried to force a grin. The first half-dozen times I heard the tale I drummed my little heels but then it began to pall. Old Bilston never forgot it, though. Fifteen years later, when I was home on leave from the army, I met him down the Drive and he grabbed my arm and said, 'Here, young Mick, did I ever tell you of the time I went scrumping on Lord Nutting's land . . .?' and out came the old story.

Father took me hunting when I was a little older. I have always loved animals, especially dogs, to the point of senti-mentality, but luckily the hunts were so incompetent they rarely killed anything except themselves. The famous five-barred gates of Leicestershire are designed to be lifted off their hinges and used as stretchers for hunting casualties and every so often father would return with a graphic description of some local aristocrat breaking his neck. Or her neck. The hunting women of the county were formidable Amazons, riding side-saddle in long black skirts, although the younger women were taking to wearing breeches. Father took me to see the Cottesmore Hunt, which was meeting at a village in East Leicestershire. As we stood in the road watching them scour a distant covert, father whispered, 'Look over there in the churchyard.' I turned and saw a fox sitting on a grave, licking its paws like a cat. It gave us a grin and loped off. Below, in the valley, the trumpeting and howling increased to a crescendo as the hunt set off on some false scent.

Most foxes in Leicestershire had been hunted so often they knew the routine better than the hunt. It was said some knew the time of the meets and used to turn up to watch from behind a hedge. Or perhaps they read about it in the *Leicester Mercury* which gave a weekly list of hunting dates. Apart from the hunt they were quite safe. No country person would have shot a fox, especially if Lord Nutting had been his landord.

After hunting, father always came home to the same supper, two huge and evil-smelling duck-eggs, purchased from Leicester market, the meal rounded off with raw onions and great hunks of red Leicestershire cheese or rotting Stilton (also a local cheese, made near Melton Mowbray, although the village of Stilton is in Herts). In those days we did not know that eating duck-eggs gives you arsenic poisoning, or so scientists say. However, father lived to be 82, a tribute to the healthy properties of arsenic.

Leicester was an important boxing centre in the thirties and sometimes father went to the big fights at the Granby Halls. Once he brought back a signed photograph of Larry Gains, the British Empire light-heavyweight champion, covered in the champion's own blood. This brought me much renown with my friends. Larry was our local hero. He lived only two or three streets away, behind my friend Billy Hurst's house. A West Indian, although born in Canada, he was a courageous fighter and much admired, although like many boxers desperately poor. 'Mrs Gains said she couldn't afford anything for dinner except bread and dripping,' I overheard a neighbour tell mother when Larry was on a losing streak.

Father hated boxing promoters and managers for robbing the fighters, who were gullible about finance. 'No wonder Larry Gains is starving, my boy,' he said. 'He is being robbed by the scum of the earth, men who think more of a guinea than their right arm. Show me a boxing manager and I will show you a toad, my boy.' Anyone father hated would be called a toad or a dog. These animals could range from the government to a rugby side which defeated Leicester. Thus he might say, 'The dogs have raised the tax on beer,' or 'The dogs scored three penalty goals.' Sometimes it was difficult to decipher his meaning. When he announced one day 'the dogs have overrun Czechoslovakia', it was uncertain if he meant the Nazis or a pack of foxhounds. Even in his last illness, he told me from a hospital bed, 'The toads can't make decent gravy.'

Larry was the only black person living in Leicester at that time. Schoolboys with bicycles know every inch of their territory and if it was different we would have known. In fact the only other people in the city of so-called 'ethnic' origin were a family who ran the Chinese Laundry in Evington Road. I mention this because it illustrates how difficult it is to forecast the future. Today, fifty-odd years on, there are 60,000 people from the West Indies or India in Leicester. Yet when the *Hotspur*, the *Wizard*, the *Skipper* or any of my other comics printed articles about the future, they never forecast this, the most fundamental change of all. Nobody did. The comics would say something like: 'In 1987 everyone will go around with a wireless aerial sticking out of their head. Nobody will go to school, they will just tune in to what they want to learn and it will go directly into their brains. Everyone will have their own autogyro and keep it in their garden shed. Airships will fly to New York in less than a week. Railway locomotives will be powered by splitting the atom and you will be able to get to Scotland in three hours. There will be no wars. Every country will belong to the League of Nations and an international air force will stop aggressors.'

I can't help feeling today's star-gazing is as far off the beam. Some great change is coming but it won't be something we can predict, such as a computer-dominated world. It will be something we never thought of.

CHAPTER THREE

Sheep's head and tripe

At 5 I had my first tooth out. For dental treatment the family went to 'Uncle' Aly, one of the honorary relations with which we were infested. I never knew what his name was short for. I think he was father's cousin. He had a surgery in Saxby Street (which used to be called Saxe-Cobourg Street until they changed the name in World War One because of its German origins). Today Aly wouldn't be allowed to practise because he had no hospital training so he wasn't allowed to give a general anaesthetic such as gas. Aly gave me a ride on his chair by pumping it up and down to soothe me but I wasn't deceived. He then assured me it wouldn't hurt and yanked out the tooth. The pain was excruciating. I blubbered all the way home on the Evington bus and a woman gave me a penny.

Aly was one of a whole tribe of honorary uncles and aunts, who today would simply be known by their first names. Some were distant relatives, others were friends of the family, like Aunt Amy, a school friend of mother's from Bristol, who married a Leicester man. Quite a lot were relatives of my grandparents. There was a whole house full of Grandmother Green's elderly cousins, salivating and gibbering somewhere up the London Road. They had Victorian names like Aunty Lottie, Aunty Pattie and so forth. I hardly ever saw them, but father regularly called and brought back the latest news of their health. 'Mother, Aunt Pattie is having trouble with her waterworks again,' he'd say, or perhaps 'Aunt Lottie's pipes are furred up, the doctor says.' For a young person then, no grown-up could be addressed by their first name, without the prefix aunt or uncle. My niece has called me Mick since she could talk, but when my brother was 17 he got into terrible trouble for addressing a friend of father's as Walter, instead of by his surname.

As well as Billy, son of the daring aviator Cyril Hurst, I was friendly with the English brothers who lived at the other end of Baden Road in a big house built when the area was still country. It had a rural back garden with apple trees and a pump by the sink to draw water from a well outside, although they had running water. It was Tony, the eldest boy, who shot at the R101. Mr English was a man of precarious means and no visible employment, although 'you could see he was a gentleman', as mother said. He once upset father by trying to touch him for a small loan. 'I told him never a borrower nor a lender be,' said father, who, like most of his generation, loved a good aphorism. My parents had an obsession about the evils of borrowing money. When I lost a penny on the way to the paper shop and a stranger gave me another, father wanted to identify the man so he could pay him back. They worried for weeks. Mr English had once been an engineer but there was a suspicion he suffered shell-shock in the war, where he served as a captain, and was unfit for employment. His youngest boy, Jeremy, was a special friend and together we pedalled our motor-cars and tricycles about the district and later played cricket against a lamppost or wickets chalked on a garden fence.

Mr English spent most of his time tinkering with a succession of second-hand cars which he bought for ten pounds or so from a garage at Evington. He was generous in giving rides and I remember the cars with affection, in particular a bull-nosed Morris Cowley with a dickey seat. This was a separate compartment where the boot normally is; when the lid was pulled down, two seats were revealed and you rode outside behind the car. Alas, one did not ride for long on Mr English's outings and many excursions ended with a mob of children pushing from behind while Mr English sat at the wheel juggling the ignition control and saying to his patient wife, 'Shut up, woman, I know what I'm doing, I tell you.'

Most of the trips were into the lovely patchwork country-side of East Leicestershire and Rutland, which involved going up the notorious Wardley Hill, near Uppingham. Mr English's Morris Oxfords and Cowleys usually failed this obstacle, sometimes in both directions. They had to be pushed up, steam spouting furiously from the radiator cap; on the down trip they tended to run away (despite the proud sign, 'Four-wheel brakes', on the back). Once, a wheel came off and bounded across a ditch into a field. This sort of behaviour was not unusual for cars in those days. They were expected to belch steam or run away down hills. They also had an evocative smell I shall never forget, a combination of leather and petrol, which seems to have vanished.

Sometimes my parents worried about these trips. Their anxieties were compounded by the fact that the two elder English brothers, Tony and Nigel, played cowboys and Indians with real bullets. They would go off into the woods near Evington and blaze away at each other with air rifles and pistols. Tony got a wound in the thigh and was taken to Dr Somerville in the corner house. 'I cannot treat him, Mrs English,' said Dr Somerville. 'If I do, I will have to report to the police I have treated a bullet wound.' He was nursed at home by Mrs English, a kind, generous, plump and rather vague lady.

When I was 6, mother and father insisted I went to the rugby match with them every Saturday. I think they were worried I might stop a slug playing with the older English lads. Both were rugby fanatics. Grandfather had played (of course) and was a founder of the famous Bristol club, the local side he played for being amalgamated with another to form Bristol. Father had never played but picked up mother's enthusiasm. The Leicester Tigers were then (1933) at their peak, heights not reached again until 1985, when they provided seven players for one England team.

It is difficult for an outsider to appreciate the scale of rugby union in such strongholds as Bristol, Bath, Gloucester and

Leicester. In the Midlands and West rugby was not the middle- and upper-class affair it was in London. Even 'elementary schools' had old boys' teams, and very good ones too. The big Leicester ground, with its soccer-sized crowds, was a far cry from the deserted pitches of London and their polite cries of 'Do come on, Old Millhillians.' Indeed, we despised London rugby. It was considered soft. They could not produce tough forwards like the Midlands did. There was some truth in this, for many of the great Midland forwards worked with their hands as farmers or miners. When I asked father why Leicester always played teams from Wales and the Midlands and so few from London, he replied, 'It is because the London clubs are not good enough, my boy. They are all chinless wonders and medical students down there.' It was an observation not entirely unjust at the time, although things have altered now.

The huge Leicester ground on Welford Road, where internationals were played until 1923, has changed little and this year I used the same revolting outside urinal Dad and I used to visit. The concrete is still stained green with fungus and the drain blocked by leaves. I went to the famous ground reluctantly as a boy. For mother and father, however, it was the high spot of the week. Father had a ritual pint of draught Bass in the Highfields Hotel and then we ate a midday dinner that was 'different', as it was Saturday. Sometimes it would be sausages and mash but frequently boiled sheep's head on the bone with carrots and white sauce. Thus fortified, we set out for the ground. Roger was already playing rugby at school on Saturdays so I went with them alone.

The game gave father a golden chance to exercise his wit. 'Do sit down, Jack,' mother muttered as father stood up and insulted the players in a booming voice. One of his favourite targets was a centre called Denis Morris, who had rather unsafe hands. 'Give him a yo-yo,' father would bellow as he dropped yet another pass. Fifty years later I ran a competition in my *Sunday Times* rugby column for funny stories, and Denis Morris won a prize. Once, when the referee left the field for a new bootlace father hooted at him, 'Have you gone to get your rule book?' I thought this was the funniest remark I had ever heard. But if father wasn't shouting I was bored as the great heaps of steaming humanity slithered around in the Midlands mud.

Father was not the only leather-lunged spectator. The Leicester crowd were notorious for their barracking. At one game a little man in a bowler hat on the terrace kept abusing a huge Coventry forward, one of the famous Wheatley brothers. 'Come on, Tigers, get Wheatley, that square-headed bugger,' he shouted again and again. Wheatley, a giant of a man, stood it with considerable patience but eventually lost his temper. After the sixth repetition, at a line-out, he shambled to the touchline, climbed over the fence, and began to search the crowd for his tormentor. The little man sensibly fled and caught a passing tram on the Welford Road, after which Wheatley returned to the field, nodded to the referee, and play resumed.

Many famous players turned out for Leicester and later the fabulous Russian Prince Obolensky played on the wing. In 1932 the combined Leicestershire and East Midlands team beat the South African Springboks. I was in bed with flu when I heard this strange noise downstairs. It was father, too impatient to wait for the front door to open, shouting news of the victory through the window at mother, who had given up her ticket to stay with me. He hurried up the stairs crying, 'Mick, they've beaten the Springboks,' and treated me to a blow-by-blow account of the match, which I was too ill to appreciate.

After the game, on Saturday nights, we usually had tripe for supper. This was an exception because the main meal was midday dinner and, as a rule, supper was cold meat or cheese with home-made pickles. Most meals went according to ritual and the menu never varied. On Sundays there was always a roast joint for dinner (lamb, pork or overdone beef, never veal, and chicken only on feast days). On Mondays the joint appeared cold, on Tuesdays it made its last bow as cottage pie. On Wednesday there was one of mother's enormous, thick stews cooked in her old earthenware stewjar from Bristol. Thursday was variable – it might be chops or liver or steak-and-kidney pudding; Friday was always fried fish and chips, and Saturday 'a change', anything from hearts to sheep's head. Sheep's head looked revolting as it glared from the dish but it was very tasty and the three males in the family ate it with gusto. Mother didn't like it. She cooked lots of food such as tripe which she couldn't stomach. Fortunately she had a small appetite, or so she said.

The main courses were followed by heavy puddings, perhaps spotted dick and custard or apple pie, washed down with water. Alcohol was never drunk at table except on special occasions and then it was sweet sherry. All meals were formal, except tea, with a white tablecloth and linen serviettes, everyone having their own silver ring. We all sat down together and ate as a family.

It now appears, that according to modern theory my childhood diet was a killer, being stuffed full of fat and cholesterol, and mother and father had no right to live to be 90 and 82 respectively. But the emphasis was on 'building you up', a reaction from World War One when recruits were thin and undernourished. Milk was thought to be a great restorer. Fat, now killer no. 1, was considered to be the most beneficial part of a diet. Children were forced, enjoined, ordered, cajoled or bullied into eating up the fatty bits and perhaps washing them down with milk. Meat dripping on toast was a common meal and poor people lived on it. Later, free milk was issued at schools. But even then there were murmurs of rebellion against the fat craze. 'Don't give the children too much milk, Mrs Green,' said Dr Somerville, the GP in the corner house. 'It clogs up the system.'

Like fat, smoking was also considered beneficial. 'It soothes the nerves,' they said, although father gave up some time before I was born. Doctors sometimes recommended smoking to 'nervous' patients. Smoking was also thought to be fashionable and 'manly'.

After eating an enormous meal of deadly cholesterol I might lie on the floor playing with my toys. Every one was lethal by modern standards. They were made of sharp-edged tin or lead and covered in lead-based paint, which tasted delicious. They were also racist, sexist and warlike, consisting mainly of soldiers and cowboys and Indians.

I often wonder which of today's sacred cows will be put down tomorrow. Mother, it will be recalled, was made to have all her teeth out in her twenties, because it was the medical fashion. I suppose, as she lived to be 90, the doctor could say, 'Well, it worked, didn't it?' It was touching to see mother's pleasure when plastic false teeth came in thirty years ago, replacing the giant porcelain tombstones she had lived with so long.

Along with tripe, another Saturday routine was the Great Turn Out. Like all parents of that generation, mine were obsessed with bowel performance (another passing medical fad). Roger and I were daily cross-examined as to our record – 'Have you *been* today?' Salts were put in early morning tea whether we had *been* or not and these were reinforced by vile-tasting laxatives such as California Syrup of Figs. Sometimes this was doled out as a precaution on Saturday nights, to 'cleanse the system' for the following week. The whole nation was obsessed with constipation. Every newspaper was filled with advertisements illustrated by drawings of pale, wretched people, who for some reason always held their heads not their stomachs. New brands appeared weekly. One was disguised as chocolate. Dick Martin, Roger's friend across the road, thought it *was* chocolate and ate a whole packet. He was not seen for weeks.

Like constipation, several thirties' illnesses seem to have vanished. 'Night starvation' was the classic thirties disease. It was invented by the makers of Horlicks, who, having thought up an illness which didn't exist, claimed to cure it by guaranteeing deep sleep ('ordinary sleep is not enough'). People spat more in those days, too. All public places had notices forbidding it, which have now vanished. Father spat freely. He was always hawking or encouraging us boys to 'bring it up'. The results might be subject to pathological examination. 'I think Mick's phlegm is a little green, mother.'

Men seemed to pee more frequently then. Father could never pass a public lavatory without entering and as Leicester was plentifully sprinkled with the places, his progress was apt to be spasmodic. They all had a big notice – 'Adjust Dress Before Leaving' (meaning 'Do up your trousers') – and because father had to do up his trouser buttons with one hand he took a long time. Men were permanently worried about their fly-buttons and were always checking they were done up. A few trendies wore zips but they were considered dangerous and ghastly stories circulated of men whose organs were caught in them. The general attitude was summed up by my Uncle Fred who said, 'Never pass a public lavatory after the age of 40 or you may regret it.' Today those marvellous chlorine-scented palaces of the thirties are mostly shut up and derelict, victims of economy. It is no longer a question of passing one, but of finding one. Perhaps men went more, simply because the opportunity was available.

When I was about 7, I came home from Micklefield School to find an ambulance outside the house. I naturally assumed it was for Mr Lister next door, who always looked about to collapse, poor chap. But, when I opened the garden gate, father was helped to the front door by two ambulance men. He had broken his wrist falling off a stepladder and was saying words I had never heard before. As we had no phone, mother called the ambulance from Mrs Taylor's, one of two people in the road with one.

To break a wrist for a man with two arms is inconvenient; for a one-armed person it is disaster. When father returned from the Infirmary that evening, smelling of chloroform and with his wrist in plaster, problems arose. Mother rose to the occasion magnificently. She fed father and cut up his food for him; she unbuttoned his trousers and helped him use the toilet and buttoned him up again. She dressed him and washed him and wiped his bottom. The one thing she couldn't do was shave him, so every day she put bus fare and some change in his overcoat pocket and he walked to the bus stop in Evington Road, not with his usual vigorous, rolling stride but carefully and very upright, as he had no way of balancing himself without an arm to swing. On the bus he explained matters to the conductor, who took the fare from his pocket and stuffed a ticket in it, or more likely let him ride for nothing. Father went for a shave to the hairdresser he always used, a partnership called Beard and Groves in Highfield Street. He always went to Mr Groves who regularly scalped my brother and me. There was, of course, no question of growing a beard. Father would have died rather than not shave every day.

Once, when he got on the bus it started suddenly and he was thrown off balance, lurching into a woman. In an effort to be sympathetic, she told him, 'Why don't you go to the British Legion? They have special homes for people like you.' Father returned muttering to himself and brooded for days. It threw him into a black depression and he suddenly burst out, 'I wish that German shell had finished me off, mother. I am no use to anyone like this.'

His temper, uncertain at the best of times, wasn't improved by this experience and it was a hard time for all of us, until the plaster came off after six weeks.

Although Saturday afternoons in winter were sometimes restricted by having to watch the Tigers, there were plenty of other opportunities to cut loose. Often we went to the children's matinée at the Evington Cinema on East Park Road to watch the Flash Gordon serial. These always ended on a cliff-hanging note, with the hero plunging over a cliff perhaps. Next week they cheated and it appeared he'd hung on to a tree.

The first signs of a distressing cynicism appeared in me during these excursions. I found myself sympathising with the villains and disliking the heroes and heroines. There was one Shirley Temple film in which her mother was killed by a car while running across the road to greet her with a birthday cake (close-up of birthday cake under car wheel, the tyre crushing the words 'Happy Birthday to My Daughter'). I was glad she'd been run over. The mother had bored me beyond words and I loathed her pert little daughter.

When the weather permitted, my brother and his friends Dick Martin and David Shuff, with myself and Jeremy and Mick English, would join together in a gang and roam East Leicestershire on bicycles, building dens in the woods, lighting camp-fires and tearing clothes on barbed wire. Sometimes we caught minnows and sticklebacks in the stream near Little Stretton. To get there we cycled through Great Stretton, which doesn't exist any more except for a tiny church all by itself in the middle of a field. Cromwell destroyed the village in the Civil War.* The countryside was much easier to reach then – you could milk a cow 800 yards from our house, in the fields of Mr Johnson, who ran a dairy up the Evington Road and whose son went to school with me later. And it was more sparsely populated. When you got there it was real country, with earth closets and pumps and old ladies in red-brick cottages. 'Real' country began two miles away, just beyond the village of Evington, on the footpath to Thurnby, which had a village pump still in use.

Mother and father took me on a picnic by bus to Thurnby once and we called at a cottage for some boiling water to put in our teapot (an odd request, even then, but I've remembered it correctly). While we waited, the old lady recalled the building of the railway in 1876 and how the village was besieged by drunken Irish labourers until the line from Leicester to Grantham was completed. Not that we boys bothered much with old ladies. We enjoyed a running battle with farmers and labourers who objected to us trampling over their land, and on one occasion we were actually shot at. At least, a man waved a shotgun at us and shouted something about young buggers and as we ran we heard a shot, although he may have been aiming at wood-pigeons.

We ourselves were great ones for weapons, too, always shooting with home-made bows and arrows, using ash-tree branches for the bows and dowel rods for the arrows, tipped with feathers and with nails inserted for points. Or else we had catapults made, using the thick elastic from model aeroplanes. How we all survived is a mystery. Fortunately we also used less deadly weapons such as potato-guns (which fired bits of potato) or water-pistols.

When the country palled, we were driven back on the fields surrounding our suburb and in particular the local golf course, the Leicestershire Golf Club. We regarded this as an adventure

* Local legend blamed Cromwell, but historians say it was the plague.

playground kindly provided by a lot of elderly gentleman in plus-fours for our convenience. All golfers in the thirties had red faces, wore plus-fours, smoked pipes and appeared extremely old. Golf courses were less crowded then and we might last quite a time before being driven off by a green-keeper. If that happened, we would lurk in the woods by the 18th hole. Then, just as the first golfer was in the middle of his backswing, we let out terrible retching and vomiting noises. The effect was alarming. Sometimes the man missed the ball altogether; on other occasions it curved across the fairway into the woods or even into Evington Lane. We didn't wait to see what happened after that; we fled through the woods to reappear further along the fairway. Sometimes we tried to be helpful, but this was even worse. Finding a ball in the rough we might walk back to the tee and give it to the golfer. We could never understand why this made them so angry.

I often think *The Art of Coarse Golf* was born then. How sad that I can never recapture that early pure and innocent approach to the game. If today I found children behaving like that I would roast them over the clubhouse fire, proclaiming, 'The trouble with modern kids is that they've no discipline. We wouldn't have behaved like that. We were too busy studying and trying to pass our exams.' Am I really like those angry old men of 1934, except for the plus-fours and the Swan Vestas?

CHAPTER FOUR

At school with Richard Attenborough

I left the little local school when I was 8 and joined my brother Roger at the Wyggeston Grammar School, in the junior department. The elder English boys were already there. The 'Wyggy' was the best school in the city, one of the old maintained grammar schools, with more than 1,000 pupils. Fifty per cent of the boys were fee-paying (three guineas a term) and entered at 8. At 11, we took an exam and transferred to the senior school, to be joined by an equal number of 'scholarship boys' from the elementary schools. This produced a social mix and high standards although today it would be considered élitist. The Wyggy had a good academic level and sent a few lads to university each year, but its main function was to produce clerks for banks, insurance offices or local government. Whole counters would be staffed by young men in the yellow-and-black tie of old boys.

At that time (1935), our most famous old boy was E. Phillips Oppenheim, a detective novelist who flourished at the turn of the century. He'd lived in a big house at Evington called The Cedars, which was turned into a pub. E. Phillips Oppenheim was always held up to us as an example of what we might achieve. I read one of his books once. It was about a fictitious New York detective with the unlikely name of Philo Vance and it lost credibility when the hero announced, 'This is my phone number. New York One.' It gradually dawned on me the book was rubbish.*

* Sorry, I've since learned Philo Vance was the creation of S.S. Van Dine. But dear old E.P.O. wasn't much better.

The only contemporaries of note at school were the famous Attenborough brothers, Richard, the film producer, and David, the TV zoologist. Dick was older than me and I hardly knew him, although I sometimes heard of his exploits, as he was said to be rather wild. Mother told me another parent complained Dickie was leading her son into bad ways but the Headmaster said he could do nothing as Dickie's father had a senior academic post at the University College, next door to the school. But Dickie's exploits were harmless by today's standards, mere bravado such as smoking behind the cricket pavilion. In any case he redeemed himself by starring in the school plays, playing Hamlet on one occasion. Later he got a scholarship to the Royal Academy of Dramatic Art in London, although I think the Headmaster would have preferred a £30 a year exhibition in classics at some minor Cambridge College.

David was in a form below me and much quieter. Even then, though, he had the natural charm which was to help him make such a success of his TV career.

The First World War followed us to school, which was housed in what had been a military hospital in 1918. There were two blocks of two storeys and the rest was single-storey brick wards spread out over an area of some 20 acres and impossible to heat properly. In times of extreme cold the system packed up altogether, lessons were cancelled and we gathered in the newly-built Great Hall to be lectured by the Headmaster on Bernard Shaw's simplified spelling, one of his obsessions. Occasionally old military equipment was discovered in a forgotten corner. The cycle sheds still had annexes marked 'Ward Kitchen' or 'Sluice Room'. We found some wooden drill-rifles there and marched round the playground with them.

More reminders of Passchendaele and Ypres were provided by the masters. Most had suffered in the war. At the drop of a hat, Latin lessons would be given over to reminiscences. 'Caesar's reference to Gaul reminds me of November 1917, boys. It can get filthy in France at that time of the year. I tell you, I have seen men drown in flooded shell-holes. The barrage was so intense the muzzles of the guns peeled back like bananas.' Thus Mr Date, who took Scripture and Mathematics. A favourite ruse when lessons palled was to raise the subject of the war with an artful question like, 'Is it true, sir, that the Germans boiled down dead bodies for soap?' and sit back and wait for the flood of stories.

One teacher in the junior department had been blown up and still suffered from shell-shock. He would be seized with a terrible jerking and quivering while writing at the blackboard and his arm writhed uncontrollably, scrawling strange letters. When this happened he stood shaking and trying to control himself until the fit passed. We knew all the masters' histories, of course. Those who had not been in the war were looked down upon. They all appeared incredibly old to me. It seemed impossible to imagine them kissing girls or playing games, although they could only have been about 40. But everybody aged more quickly then. 'Phyllosan fortifies the over-forties', said the advert, showing a gentle hand stroking the heads of a couple of old crones, presumably about 45.

At Wyggy we wore school uniform of black blazer, cap, grey flannel trousers and grey socks, with blue gaberdine mac. Shirt and pullover were also grey. Everyone wore uniform. Class dictated the way people dressed. Special working clothes, such as donkey jackets, were rare, and people tended to toil in the remains of what had once been a good suit. So labourers digging up the road would wear suit trousers, held up by a wide leather belt, shirt without collar, and a waistcoat. The muffler and cap were as much a badge for the working man as the bowler and umbrella for his social superiors. On Sundays working men wore a suit with a shirt and no collar or tie while for the middle classes brightly-coloured old school blazers were popular. Children of poor parents – and that included quite a few at our school – wore clothes many sizes too big to allow for growth and were clad in huge flannel shorts that came below the knees. One of the bigger changes in modern life is the blurring of barriers in a flood of jeans, sweatshirts and anoraks.

Soon after joining school I had my first proper fight. A boy with the interesting name of Archibald Onions punched me in the face in the playground, knocking me down with a cry of 'That's for what you did to Ken the other day.' I couldn't remember having done anything to Ken, who was a pal of his, but perhaps I'd insulted him. Archie was older and much heavier and taller, but seized with a wild rage I fell madly upon him with flailing fists shouting, 'I'm not going to take that from a rotter like you,' which was a phrase I must have got from the *Magnet* or some other school comic. He was rather taken aback at my ferocity and although he made my nose bleed I managed to cut his lip before being dragged apart.

It's a pity that this first fight wasn't with somebody my own size. The whole thing rather sapped my self-confidence. I didn't know then that nobody ever challenges anyone of the same build. The idea that bodily combat is manly is rubbish. People who pick fights almost invariably choose weaker opponents. On this occasion I wouldn't have fought at all if not seized with maniacal fury. In later life I discovered I have no middle gears. Peaceable to the point of cowardice, if provoked I can fly completely off the handle, which may cause difficulty in polite society. An author who shouts 'You mean bastard' at a publisher is not going to be popular. However, I do have the satisfaction of having been rude to some of the most famous publishers in London.

Fortunately the combat with Archie had a happy sequel as I later became close friends with him and his sister, who lived near Baden Road.

One of my earliest class teachers caused a scandal. A little Scotsman with a red nose, he was also music master, which involved playing the organ for assembly every morning in the splendid new Great Hall, completed in my second year at school. One morning, when the hymn was announced, the organ gave out a series of hideous grunts, wheezes and discords. The Head, a fearsome figure with a mane of white hair, glared savagely up at the balcony where Scottie sat in splendour, surrounded by pipes. He was slumped over the keyboard, apparently trying to play 'The Day Thou Gavest Lord is Ended' with his nose. Assembly was brought to a hasty close amid a buzz of excitement and the Head moved swiftly to the gallery, where a strong smell of whisky greeted him. Scottie never reappeared in the classroom and was even denied the traditional farewell gift and speech for retiring staff. Two terms later there was a discreet note in the school magazine, the *Wyggestonian*, that he had been appointed to the staff of a county grammar school.

It turned out Scottie had suffered a drink problem for a long time. Being innocent, I paid no attention to his habit of coming into form red-eyed every day and slumping in his chair. I thought all grown-ups must be like that. Apparently, however, his drinking was common knowledge. Even mother knew.

'He once threw his boots at Mrs Scott in a drunken fit,' she told me. 'That poor woman.'

For all his drinking, Scottie was a popular teacher, drunk or sober. One couldn't say the same about the Rev. Lewis, MA, who took us for English. He always wore a clergyman's collar and we often wondered why he wasn't in the church any more. Wild rumours circulated. 'He hit a choirboy and killed him with one of them things smoke comes out of.' These stories were prompted by his nasty streak. He delighted in picking out a weak boy and reducing him to tears with sarcasm and encouraging the class to bully him. 'Look at him, boys,' he'd thunder. 'Look at him. He doesn't even know Christmas is coming.' We would titter sycophantically.

Under Lewis's glowering eye we chanted our way through Victorian poetry from 'The Brook' to the 'Charge of the Light Brigade'. No modern verse, of course, and most of it came from Palgrave's *Golden Treasury*. Not that I complain. It gave us a sound basis in the best of English classic poetry and learning it by rote enables me to quote yards of verse to this day, an achievement which has silenced many a conversation. I feel sorry for today's children, unacquainted with so much splendid stuff.

Although caning was reserved for the headmaster alone, most teachers had their own brand of assault, apart from the routine slap across the face. The Rev. Lewis delighted in beating his knuckles on a child's skull. Since he wore a large signet ring this could be painful to a nine-year-old. Once more rumour was rife. 'He hit Smith with his ring and he fainted. Smith's dad says he is going to sue Mr Lewis.' One master beat pupils over the head with a large key, chanting, 'This is the key of knowledge which unlocks all learning.' Another swiped boys across the face with his mortar-board. It was expected teachers would hit you, it was part of their stock-in-trade like degrees and gowns and smelling of tobacco.

The torture was not all one way. Compared with today's children we were ground-down and humble but, even so, any master who showed weakness would be pounced upon. We even took advantage of the fact that A. L. Greene (known as 'Wiffles'), the history master, was almost blind. The usual rumour said he'd been hit with a cricket ball at university but I think it was just poor sight. He wore pebble glasses half-an-inch thick and walked through the playground with one arm held stiffly in front in case he ran into anything. He could keep order of a sort. When taunted beyond endurance he struck out blindly at the first object he could discern, whether pupil or wastepaper basket, with his walking-stick. One never knew when he would erupt, so boys trod warily. Anything silent, such as reading a book under the desk, could be carried out safely, and I remember a group of four playing cards in the back row for a whole lesson, when I was older.

His eyes were an easy target. When he took us in the senior school we played a vile trick and covered the door-handle of the classroom with jam. He couldn't see it, of course, and got his hand covered when he opened the door. The class roared with laughter as he smeared it all over his dusty gown in an effort to get clean. Then he got a heap of essays stuck to his hand and papers scattered on the floor. Wiffles retaliated by taking his walking-stick and blindly swiping it in a circle until we were all cowering round the walls while he blundered about like a bull.

A bachelor, he lived in a seedy private hotel near the London Road, groping his way there after school and waving his stick at the trams, which were only vague shapes to him. He died alone in his small hotel twenty years later. 'He gave up the struggle towards the end,' wrote a member of staff to me at the time.

Common to all staff was a conviction they could have done better outside education. The teachers believed in a mysterious world beyond school called 'business', where money was handed out freely. As our Greek master said, 'If I'd gone into business, boys, I could be earning four hundred a year with a Morris Minor and half-a-crown a day expenses thrown in.' None of them ever left for the Great Outside, though, and why they wanted to was a mystery. Outside, 20 per cent of the work-force was unemployed, people were lucky to get two weeks paid holiday a year, and few had pensions of any sort. Businessmen were going bankrupt by the dozen, although the economy was beginning to improve.

In many ways education at the Wyggy was Victorian. One junior school master often made boys sit with folded arms, although he was an exception. As juniors we spent hours learning copper-plate handwriting with steel nibs and ink-wells. Fountain-pens were banned. 'You can't write a good hand with one of those wretched fountain-pens, boys,' said the junior school Head. There was a heavy emphasis on Latin and Greek in the senior school. Our geography was unrecognisable by modern standards. We learned about mysterious regions called savannahs and deciduous belts. In geometry we ploughed through the theorems of Euclid (something else that has now vanished from schools).

Sociology, of course, was unheard of, although we did have a form of Afro-Asian studies which consisted of colouring bits of the map red to show the British Empire. It would be trendy to sneer but I won't. It was a good education and, when I came to the Open University in 1971, I found what I'd learned gave me an excellent start. I was the only person in my tutorial group the first year who could scan an iambic pentameter or parse a sentence, and that included the tutor. Furthermore, thanks to my grounding in English and history, I was an expert at *The Times* crossword puzzle.

One thing our education did give was a sense of period and space. We began in geography and history with Leicester and worked onwards to Britain, Europe and the rest of the world. When I was a teacher for a short time in later life I found modern children have little sense of period and can't relate one era to another. Thanks to the way history is taught now they exist in a vacuum. Anything over twenty years ago is just 'the old days' and they think Napoleon and Hitler were contemporaries. A schoolteacher friend told me that when he set his class a project on Christopher Columbus he found half of them didn't know who he was.

It is said that young people feel insecure today because of the state of the world, with the possibility of global destruction hanging over it. My generation also knew nothing else. Almost as soon as I could walk there were crises as Hitler and Mussolini began the run-up to World War Two, an event we were convinced would see the destruction of everything. Italy invaded Abyssinia in 1935 and instead of Germans v. British boys started to play Abyssinians against Italians, complete with imitations of being choked by poison gas. The first trickle of Jewish refugees from Germany began to arrive and a few came to our school. I got very pally with one family, who had a boy at my school and a girl at the sister foundation. I shall never forget, though, the look on the boy's face when I made a silly schoolboy remark about Jews, something like, 'Well, what can you expect from a Jew.' For just a moment an expression of sheer, stark terror flickered into his eyes.

The constant crises and the increasing threat of war made much more impression on me than the abdication of King Edward VIII. Not long previously we had celebrated the Silver Jubilee of bearded old George V with buns and lemonade. We plastered the blackboard with union jacks and a loyal message to stop masters writing on it. Scottie was at his best, doubtless topping up his lemonade with Scotch, and beamed approval and we all got a medal. Then came the King's death and preparations for the coronation of Edward in 1936. As he reigned only ten months before retiring with his American fiancée, Mrs Simpson, they were able to keep the coronation arrangements, although the cardboard coronation set which Woolworths sold for sixpence contained only one person in the royal coach. I saw a woman demand her money back. 'It's that Prince of Wales, not the King and Queen,' she said. Edward was always thought of as Prince of Wales.

On Coronation Day in 1937 I went with the English family to watch Leicester's parade pass up London Road. We had rides in an old horse-tram brought out for the occasion and I think there was a decorated tram, covered in fairy lights, which toured the city. The owner of Leicester's only TV set, in Highway Road, quite near us, was featured on the front page of the *Leicester Evening Mail*. 'His Majesty the King was distinctly visible, but only as a faint blur,' said the report.

The Italians had brought peace to Abyssinia with mustard gas but the civil war in Spain between Franco's fascists and the government was in full swing. Germany and Italy joined in on the side of Franco and people talked openly of the next war.

'Mark my words,' said Mr English, up the road. 'The last one will be nothing compared to the next. Rocket bombs weighing fifty tons, whole cities wiped out by mustard gas, civilisation destroyed in a week.'

He enjoyed terrifying poor Mrs English who with four sons dreaded another conflict. The Leicestershire Territorial Army Regiment was converted to an anti-aircraft role and lit the winter sky with archaic and useless searchlights. Sometimes an elderly biplane could be seen giving them target practice but although it flew slowly and straight so as to help them, they rarely picked it up. 'The bomber will always get through,' became the catchword.

If youngsters had any doubts about the cost of war, Armistice Day dispelled them. It was the supreme festival of the year. The current Remembrance Sunday is only a pale shadow of how we honoured the dead. There was no nonsense about commemorating those killed in all wars. There was only one and that was The Great War, ended by Armistice at 11 a.m. on 11 November 1918, the eleventh hour of the eleventh day of the eleventh month, which endowed the whole thing with a mystical significance. The effects were all round. Hardly a family had not lost someone and many had been virtually wiped out.

At the precise hour when the Armistice was signed, explosive signals known as maroons were fired from the roof of the police station and town hall and and life in Leicester ceased. Traffic stopped. Trams and buses halted. Bus drivers climbed from their cabs and stood in the road with bowed heads. Conductors and passengers remained silent and motionless inside. A passenger who failed to observe the silence would be rebuked by the conductor. Factories stopped work for two minutes. Shoppers paused in the street. Police held up traffic (there was only one pair of traffic lights in Leicester).

At school we gathered in the Great Hall, whose lobby contained a Book of Remembrance listing pupils who had fallen. A page was turned every day by Poole, the cadaverous caretaker. Solemn music was played on the organ by Scottie's successor. (That organ seemed to have a bad effect on people. Another organist later appeared in court for assaulting little girls whom he was teaching to play the piano.) We sang Armistice Day hymns and a prefect would recite the famous lines, 'They shall grow not old, as we that are left grow old', by Laurence Binyon. Suddenly we would hear the boom of maroons from the police station and a deathly hush fell. It was complete. Nobody so much as coughed. Then, as the maroons fired to mark the end of the silence, a torrent of sneezing and hawking broke out.

At home in Baden Road, father always went to Birmingham on Armistice Day to visit the grave of an old Canadian Army comrade, Lou Hannah. Lou was wounded in the head in 1916 and sent back from the front line to hospital in Birmingham. There he seemed to be progressing until one night he cried out, 'Oh, nurse, my head does hurt so.' She went over and he was dead. The story was told frequently at home and lost nothing in the telling. Lou was buried in Birmingham and father gave me his gold cufflinks, which I still have today.

For his visit to the cemetery father did not need to change his everyday clothes. His normal winter gear was dark suit, black bowler, black overcoat and black hand-knitted silk tie. He never wore any other sort of tie. Mother gave him a new one every Christmas to the end of his life. With much shouting and banging of doors and pulling of chains, he left early to catch the train to Birmingham, wearing a small poppy. In those days poppies varied in quality according to how much the donor gave. The penny one was a miserable affair of paper and wire but sixpence purchased something much grander and for five shillings you could have an enormous poppy, complete with leaves, almost like a bunch of flowers. They were hand-made by disabled soldiers in Richmond. Businessmen would ostentatiously stick five-shilling poppies in the radiators of their Austin Twelves, but although father gave generously he would accept only the cheapest poppy. He had a horror of ostentation. To be a 'smart Alec' was his greatest dislike.

After visiting the grave and putting flowers on it, father adjourned to the Exchange Restaurant by New Street station at Birmingham, and lunched on draught Bass and a steak from the silver grill, probably the only meal he ate in a restaurant all year. He always brought home presents for me and Roger on these trips, so we looked forward eagerly to his return, which usually coincided with tea and toast.

Not that we needed Armistice Day to remind us of the war. Leicester was full of men who, like father, had returned maimed. The Market Square always had a few cripples, playing mouth organs while they swayed on crutches or sat legless against a wall with their caps in front of them. One legless man sold newspapers, his son towing him along the pavement on a home-made trolley consisting of roller skates screwed to a plank. Most wore medals but father didn't approve of this. He disliked outward forms of militarism. Sometimes he passed men with medals without dropping anything in their caps. Then he would repent and mutter, 'You go on ahead, mother, I've forgotten something,' while he slipped them a coin. He did not like to be seen doing this and waited until nobody was looking.

At school they suddenly promoted me to the next form in the middle of the school year. This was policy if pupils showed promise. The result was I found myself struggling with Latin and algebra at the age of 10 and trying to catch up on five months' work. I don't think I ever caught up, and remained near the bottom of the class for the rest of my time. So much for forcing kids. Shot into the senior school at 10 I learned rugby, also. There was no mini-rugby then. We played from the start with great black leather balls nearly as big as the smaller boys. For some reason the balls slowly lost their oval shape and went round as they got older. I took to rugby quickly, but cricket was my real passion. A friend down Evington Drive, John Bradshaw, had a father who'd actually played as an amateur for Leicestershire, not a great distinction as the county was stuck permanently at the bottom of the championship, alternating in last place with neighbouring Northants. Mr Bradshaw got a pair, a duck in each innings, at Gloucester, a fact he didn't like being reminded of. We played every evening on the playing fields near our house, but not with W. G. Grace's ball. Mother wouldn't hear of us using that.

A terrible tragedy happened to my cricket at this time. I read an article in the *Hotspur* (my favourite comic) which gave a diagram of How to Bowl a Googly. Forgetting I was left-handed, I followed the instructions literally, but of course everything was reversed and my hand performed incredible contortions on the end of my wrist. The result was a ball which hovered in the air for hours and which friends called the Wrist Breaker. It became a habit and I couldn't bowl anything else. Fifty years later, I am still bowling it and my cricket career has been largely spent watching the umpire signal yet another four. I must be the only bowler in the history of cricket to land a ball on the head of the square-leg umpire. Furthermore, the unnatural action has left me with rheumatism in the wrist and tennis elbow. That *Hotspur* article has a lot to answer for.

About this time I had an operation. Like most middle-class boys I'd been circumcised but apparently something had gone wrong and I developed a sore place. A small piece of skin had to be cut away. There was no nonsense about going into hospital. Dr Somerville, the local GP from up the road, conducted the operation on our dining-room table, covered in a blanket. In honour of the occasion mother dusted the room and polished the table until it glowed, but that was the only antiseptic precaution. There was a nurse and another doctor gave the anaesthetic. This consisted of putting a mask like a tea strainer over my face and pouring chloroform on to it. I woke up in bed upstairs, to be violently sick (as one always is with chloroform) and with two stitches in my John Thomas. Why I didn't die of septicaemia I shall never know, but operations at home were quite common. A school friend with an abscess on his foot was operated on in the kitchen by a local doctor while a pot of stew simmered on the cooking range.

Memory plays strange tricks, but there seemed more 'mad' people about then (I use the word mad as we used it, to indicate anyone not normal). Is treatment better or are they put into residential homes today? Up the road lived Ralph, 10 years older than me but with the mental age of a child. 'He can cut lovely bread and butter,' said his mother defiantly, as Ralph staggered at her side down Baden Road, his thick glasses peering blankly ahead. Poor Ralph. After his mother died when he was 50 he lived on alone in the draughty Victorian villa, surviving there for several years thanks to the local doctor, who looked in every day and refused to let the council take him away. But of course They got him in the end and the social services removed him to some institution about 1975. My mother, still alive at the age of 84, was horrified.

'They came and took Ralph away yesterday,' she said. 'Doctor was very upset. He did his best to save him. To think, the poor boy had lived in that house fifty years. I remember when his mother used to hold his hand as they walked down the road.'

Another local boy was in the starkly-named Humberstone Lunatic Asylum after a traffic accident. From time to time he'd break out to try and see his mother in our road and had to be returned. Eventually the bus conductors got to know and headed him off. They were used to patients trying to escape by bus.

'Your mum told me she wouldn't be home today,' they'd say. 'But she's coming up the hospital tomorrer.' Then they'd give him a sweet and deliver him back to the great Victorian gates of the home.

As I cycled to school with Jerry English in the morning we'd be greeted at the road junction near St Philip's church by a cheerful man of about 60, dressed in plus-fours, directing the traffic. Rumour said he'd been knocked down by a tram in his youth and his mind affected. Whatever the cause, he spent the mornings standing in the middle of the road and waving his arms madly. Had any vehicle followed his directions there would have been the most appalling accident. Luckily traffic ignored him, although it was said he caused two buses to collide head-on, with dreadful loss of life. I think that may have been an exaggeration. The bus crews always treated the happy lunatic with great courtesy. Drivers slowed down and called out, 'Hullo, mate, is it safe for me to proceed?' The reply would be alarming. 'Don't go along East Park Road whatever you do, there's a gas main blown up. Fifty dead.'

'Thanks, mate. I'll tell the inspector,' and the bus drove on, the conductor winking at passengers. I am always struck by the consideration of ordinary people then. Today a bus driver who stopped to talk to a lunatic would find a dozen motorists hooting at him. One day the plus-foured madman was not there. I never knew what became of him. Perhaps he suffered the same fate as Ralph.

CHAPTER FIVE

Death in Lutterworth

We had our first radio (or 'wireless') about 1935, when I was 8. People often wonder how families amused themselves before radio and TV and the answer is they didn't. They read or played cards or talked or went to the pictures or were bored, usually the last. In many homes, father was a substitute for TV. Paternal influence has declined as TV has increased. Nobody wants to listen to dad laying down the law when 'Match of the Day' is on.

But provided the black depression was not on him, my own father was better than most wireless programmes. After a nightly glass of White Shield Worthington, carefully poured so the dregs did not go in the glass, he would put down the *Leicester Evening Mail*, from which he read extracts to mother every evening as she sewed, and tell us of his days in Canada, where he emigrated when he was 21 in 1910. He took a one-way passage for £4 on one of the emigrant ships plying between Hamburg, Liverpool, Ireland and Canada, picking up the hopefuls of ten nations on the way. 'There were the scum of the earth on board that boat, my boy,' father said, sipping his Worthington. 'Huns, Krauts, Eyeties, Wops, Frogs, Dagoes, Paddies, Micks, Murphies, Dutchies, Taffies, Ivans, Jocks – the throw-outs of Europe' (father naturally did not include himself in that category).

Father went to Toronto, but found work difficult to get. One day he heard a fellow-lodger abusing him to the landlady.

'That English bum Green will never pay you, Mrs O'Brien,' he said. 'I know that sort. He'll walk out without paying a cent.'

Stung by this reflection on his honour, father tramped the streets desperately and got a job, only labouring, but enough to live on. 'When the foreman paid me on Friday,' father told us, 'I took all my wages to Mrs O'Brien and paid off the rent which was owing. There were only a few cents left over and I spent that on half a cucumber. I was very fond of cucumber and being poor had not had any for a long time.'

At one time father worked making early motor-cars in Detroit, USA. He was also one of a survey team prospecting the route of the Canadian Pacific Railway. On reporting for work he was sent to a remote station in Alberta to take a train to the railhead. They gave him no pass but said the guard of the train knew about him. It was midwinter and the station was the only shelter for miles around. As the temperature fell that night it began to fill up with vagrants looking for warmth. Father sat dozing by the stove in the waiting-room with the tramps until midnight when the door was flung open and two Canadian Mounted Police came in. They went to the first tramp and demanded, 'Where's your pass, bud?'

'I ain't got no pass, mister.'

At that, the police picked him up and slung him outside into a snowdrift. They went to the next man and the same procedure was repeated but this time the man answered back and a policeman crashed a fist into his face. Father became worried because the police were accepting no explanations without a pass and becoming increasingly violent.

'Just as they reached me,' said father, 'the door opened and a man in uniform shouted, "Is there a guy here called Green?" I stood up and he said, "You're to come on the train with me to the railhead." I was never so relieved in my life. I passed the poor bum they'd thrown into the snow and slipped him a dollar but I think he was too cold to notice.'

Father was an eloquent yarn-spinner and with stories like that who wanted wireless? Sometimes he played the mouth organ, American ragtime of the early part of the century mostly, such as 'Lily of Laguna'. And we had a wind-up gramophone with 'Love is the Sweetest Thing' or 'All by Yourself in the Moonlight'. But the gramophone passed when the wireless arrived. Despite the excruciating dullness of most of the programmes, which seemed to consist of fat stock prices and hymns, we boys became avid listeners, especially to Henry Hall's dance music at 5.15 p.m. every day. Mother and father rarely listened to anything except the Palm Court Orchestra from the Grand Hotel, Eastbourne, and the news, broadcast only at six and nine every evening. But they would tune in for a rugby match. These were distinguished by a sepulchral voice behind the commentator whispering heavily, 'Square Four' or 'Square Three' to identify where the action was. Thus: 'And Oxford University have the ball ("Square Two") and it's gone along the line to the wing ("Square Seven") and he's fallen over ("Square Nine").' The key to the squares was printed in the *Radio Times* and daily papers. Sports commentators spoke gravely and slowly as if announcing bad news. They never became excited. The news announcers always wore evening dress and one felt the sports people at least had MCC ties.

On Saturdays the family listened to Music Hall on the wireless at 8.15. Some of those turns became classics, such as Rob Wilton or Murray and Mooney (the men with the catch-phrase 'I don't want to know that, kindly leave the stage'). Recalling others, I think we were easily amused. Percy Edwards used to come on and do animal imitations. 'And now we are entering the farmyard . . . bow, wow . . . down, Rover . . . moo, moo . . . hullo, Daisy, time for milking, I see . . . hee-haw . . . poor old Dobbin, haven't they fed you . . . baa, baa . . . nice lot of sheep you've got, farmer Giles . . .' etc., etc. Baritones sang 'The Road to Mandalay'; people imitated anything. Radio had spawned a new art form.

Roger and I were fascinated by father's use of old-fashioned American slang in his stories, the words sounding even stranger for being said in an English accent. In particular he used the word 'bum' to describe a layabout, something which caused embarrassment if we had visitors (one polite lady was greatly distressed when father described a neighbour to her as a bum). When a friend of the family died, father announced the news by saying, 'Mother, I've just met Joe Wright in the Market Place and he tells me George Hopkins has handed in his dinner pail.' Mother, who was mashing potatoes at the time, looked puzzled. 'What do you mean, Jack?'

'Woman, do I have to explain everything twice? He has cashed in his checks. Qualified for a wooden overcoat.'

'Oh, you mean he's dead?'

'Haven't I been saying so for five minutes?'

Mother said, after they became engaged in 1916, father promised her 'a half hoop of ice'. She had no idea what he meant until he gave her a diamond engagement ring and said, 'Here's the ice. Make the most of it, because I can't afford any more.'

Sometimes father related his life as an engineering apprentice in Leicester at the turn of the century. Once, walking round Bristol dock on holiday, he found a crane which he'd helped to build. A plate on the base gave the date and the name of the maker. He started work at 7 a.m. The pubs opened at six in those days and many workers breakfasted there on coffee and rum. A man five minutes late was docked an hour's pay, so latecomers waited in the pub until eight. The pubs didn't close and inevitably they would still be there in the evening when angry wives came to drag them home. It had given father a horror of drunkenness.

'Never be a booze artist, my boy,' he intoned, usually while sipping a glass of Worthington or Bass. This summed up his ambivalent attitude. He could stand neither drunkenness nor teetotalism. When Roger came home and described a temperance lecture at school he was furious. The lecturer had described the terrible effects of giving rats alcohol, 'They have no right to waste public money on that sort of filth, my boy,' he boomed. 'No doubt the alcohol did affect the rats. Human beings are not rats. A pint of Bass never hurt anybody. Tell that to your headmaster. Not that he would know the difference between Bass and Everards.'

Yet his favourite story was about a drunken friend who died horribly in his Toronto lodgings. 'His last words were, "Oh, my God, what will become of mother?" and then he died. That is the way a booze artist goes, my boy, regretting everything, achieving nothing. Pass me the bottle-opener from the drawer, please.'

Father's contempt for the headmaster's ignorance of beer was sincere. Like most of his generation he had a keen nose for it, quite as fastidious as a Frenchman's taste for wine. His favourite was Bass or Worthington, provided they were well kept. All beer then, of course, was in wooden barrels. Badly-kept Bass or Worthington was little better than poison, something I found out for myself when I grew up. The effects were not unlike those of cholera. The local brewery was run by the Co-op and had the unusual name of The Leicester Brewing and Malting Society and the beer was awful. Father always referred to it as The Leicester Spewing and Revolting Society. When I was older he saw me from the top of a bus entering an LBM pub and questioned me anxiously at midday dinner.

'I saw you going into the Dover Castle, my boy. That's an LBM house! I wondered what you were doing there when you could have got a pint of Bass in the Royal Standard or the Grand.'

Father was always telling jokes, but like most of his generation he didn't bother to acquire new ones and simply repeated his old stories. 'A Welshman and a Scotsman went to church. When they announced a silver collection the Scotsman fainted and the Welshman carried him out.' Of a stupid neighbour he commented, 'If he had any more brains he'd be half-witted.' No matter how often he repeated these sallies they never palled on us boys but mother remained unmoved. Jokes were made to earn their keep in those days.

Mother had little leisure. She simply worked all the time. By modern standards her life was incredibly restricted but she found it quite fulfilling. The days were spent cooking and cleaning, the evenings mending, darning and looking after her children. The petty economies of her life seem impossible today. Sheets were turned sides to middle; socks darned again and again; clothes patched until they hardly held together, and when they did fall apart the pieces carefully saved for further

56

patches. No food was ever thrown away unless it was actually putrid (which as we had no refrigerator sometimes happened). Even then mother hesitated to waste it. Stenching pieces of flesh would be brought out of the larder for inspection in hot weather and sometimes father, who had an iron stomach, volunteered to eat them. Stale bread reappeared as bread pudding, or baked in the oven as a snack for boys. Bones went on for ever in stock; the very bacon rinds were pressed into service, carefully cut off and fried crisp later for their fat and then served as a separate dish. One result of this economy was a wonderful variety of dishes such as bubble-and-squeak made from left-overs. Many of the great European dishes are the result of people being forced to use spare scraps. So we knew pleasures children never know today. Despite the reputation of their cuisine I feel sorry for the French who never know the delights of such great English dishes as dripping on toast or rissoles.

Apart from an occasional library book, mother's only relaxation was on Sunday evening, when she played the piano for an hour or so while father mowed the lawn, cursing as he dragged the mower about with one arm. If not using our Hornby trains, Roger and I played table football with halfpennies in the front room. A lot of games were home-made like that. We built vehicles out of cotton reels and elastic bands and raced them on the table, or played carpet cricket with tops for fielders, a marble for a ball and a ruler for a bat. Later we had a miniature billiards table as a reward for Roger passing his matric. The game had been father's passion and he watched with undisguised frustration, his stump twitching as he played the shots in his mind.

We were not allowed out to play on Sundays, apart from a walk in the mornings. That was the way Sunday went in most suburbs and the air was melodious with a dozen twinkling pianos playing 'Tiptoe Through the Tulips' and the whirring noise of a hundred lawn-mowers, all hand-operated (not many ran to motor mowers in our district). Much of the music played by mother was by minor German and Austrian composers who seemed to have an obsession with peasants.

There was the 'Harmonious Blacksmith', 'The Merry Peasant', 'The Jovial Woodcutter' and so forth. It had been passed on from grandmother in Bristol. Sometimes she chose modern stuff of the sort Henry Hall was making popular on the wireless, 'Red Sails in the Sunset', 'Home on the Range' or my particular favourite, 'Since Charlie did His Courting in a Chalk Pit, He's the Whitest Man I Know', from sixpenny sheet music from Woolworth's with squares and dots for the ukulele accompaniment. She occasionally played the inter-mezzo from *Cavalleria Rusticana* and her eyes watered as she thought of the dying soldier in Bristol. But she despised weakness and would slam down the piano lid and do some ironing.

There were not many visitors. Sometimes mother's uncle, whom I knew as Uncle Albert, looked in on his travels. Aunt Amy, mother's old schoolfriend from Bristol, had tea once a week and then father retired to the back room and relived the battles of the Somme. At Christmas, our Bristol grandparents came down and these visits transformed father, who got on well with Grampy. For a day or two, he forgot the horrors of 1916 and the black depression would leave him. But it came back soon enough. It needed only a chance remark to set it off, or a small incident such as breaking something because of his one-armed clumsiness. Sometimes he wished he was dead; then next day he might be all smiles again.

My parents hardly ever went out in the evenings. Every Wednesday, father took me to Vestry Street baths and taught me to swim, something I've always been grateful for. Occasionally mother went to a whist drive at St Philip's church hall. Otherwise they stayed home, apart from a stroll, and were disappointed when their children didn't want to do the same. 'What do you want to keep going out for?' they demanded all our lives.

Once or twice a year the whole family ritually got together. Usually it was at Easter, when we went down to stay with Gran and Grampy at Bristol. I loved the old house in Cobourg Road, with its Victorian furniture, brass bedsteads and lino-covered passages, but it had no bathroom or running water; mother washed me in a tin bath. George and Nan, mother's brother and sister, were still in Bristol. George had two children, while Nan had none, but was married to a wealthy fruit wholesaler and lived in state near Clifton Down. The other brother, Uncle Will, sometimes came down from West London with his wife Mabel and their three children. The uncles and aunts were always kind and generous to their Leicester nephews. On Easter Monday we set out on a vast family picnic in the Mendip Hills, travelling in a convoy of cars, and played games all afternoon. The uncles showed us some of their own childhood games from Cobourg Road, long-since forgotten, such as tip-cat. You whittle a thick, short piece of wood to a point at each end, put it down and hit one end with a stick. It rises spinning, to be hit again and sent whirling away. I introduced it to Baden Road on my return and broke several windows.

The life and soul of the party was always Aunt Nan's husband, Uncle Fred. Fred's conversation was considered a little daring in front of the children. When he wished to say something would last for ever he'd declare in a mass of burred vowels, 'It'll last as long as there's a hole in my arse.' Thus, 'You'll always have unemployment in this country as long as there's a hole in my arse.' Fred's blunt manner of speech was probably the result of his rural background. His father had been one of seven brothers fruit-farming in the Mendips. The land couldn't support them all, so one day all seven walked to Bristol to seek work and Fred's father built up the fruit business he'd inherited.

By then Fred was a prosperous businessman, the only one of the family to make real money, and a member of Bristol Merchant Venturers' Company. Fred drove a Morris Twelve, while Uncle Will, a commercial traveller, made do with a Y-front Ford Popular. Fred had great faith in Morris cars. One Easter a man committed suicide after a quarrel with his girl-friend by driving over the cliffs of the Avon Gorge near Clifton and crashing to death on tennis courts 600 feet below. Although the vehicle was smashed to pieces, by some freak the headlights were still burning.

'That was because it was a Morris,' Uncle Fred declared. 'If it had been one of them damn Fords his lights would have gone out before he reached the edge, never mind when he hit the bottom. They're made of tin, I tell you. Only a Morris could have survived an impact like that.'

One remark of Fred's always puzzled me. He used to say bitterly, 'A gold-mine is a hole in the ground dug by a bloody liar.' I never realised what he meant until 50 years later when he died. Among his bequests to me were 200 worthless shares in a South Africa goldmine, which had run out of gold. The company report was headed '----- Mine (Defunct)'.

Sometimes on these excursions an AA Scout on his motor-cycle would salute Fred's car smartly. Fred said it was a signal all was clear. If they failed to salute it meant a police speed trap was nearby. In the evenings the family gathered at Grampy's house for a big jaw. I lay on the floor with a book while the First World War thundered overhead or some hideous tale of sickness was recounted. War, death, disease and disaster were favourite topics. Aunty Mabel would tell how she went to Charing Cross station every evening to give wounded soldiers cigarettes when the ambulance trains arrived from France. Father's experiences, of course, dominated, but the others made a pretty good effort. Uncle Will, in particular, had an alarming story of serving against the Turks in Palestine. The first time he went into the front line he was posted to a platoon full of Irishmen, whom he found sharpening their bayonets on grindstones. 'Are ye any good with a bayonet?' asked the sergeant.

Uncle Will was a gentle soul, just a sales rep from Ealing, but he didn't like to appear unmanly and said he was. 'Good,' said the sergeant. 'You can come with us on a raid tonight. Ye'll get a chance to use one this time, I can promise ye.'

Horrified, Uncle Will miserably sharpened his weapon with feigned enthusiasm. Then an officer came along on a horse and asked, 'Do any of you men know the Morse Code?' Will instantly stuck up his hand and they took him away to a signal post behind the lines where he transmitted messages with a lamp in comparative safety.

'Bad luck,' said the sergeant. 'I think ye would have enjoyed yourself. It's your own fault for volunteering.' Soon after, the patrol set off to do battle with the Turks. 'I don't think I would be here today but for that signal lamp,' said Uncle Will.

Father was slightly contemptuous of this experience. 'What sort of war do they call that,' he demanded, 'with an officer in the front line on a horse? You couldn't have got a horse within two miles of our trenches at Ypres. They'd have been blown to pieces.'

I can remember a string of disconnected phrases from those evenings.

'The doctor said he'd never seen a lump like it.'

'I knew she was going before the nurse told me.'

'When they opened him up they found half a pound of nail bitings in him. They won't pass through the system, you see.'

'I only hope I never go like that.'

'They said he was living on borrowed time.'

'She said, "I didn't believe God could be so cruel." '

'All four brothers killed.'

'Of course, we all knew there was no hope, but . . .'

'He cometh like a thief in the night, as the Good Book says.'

Father, who enjoyed anything morbid, was in his element, and his own contribution was suitably depressing. It concerned the time when he was working for his father and called regularly on a shop in Lutterworth, Leicestershire. 'I can't give you the order until my husband comes back,' said the woman in the shop. 'He's been over to Leicester Infirmary for an investigation. But the bus will be here in a minute.'

Father waited and then the husband came in.

'Well, how did you get on?' asked the woman.

'Mother,' he declared in a sonorous voice, 'I am a dead man.'

There would be a hush among the relatives at this dramatic juncture and Aunt Mabel would ask, 'What did you do, Jack?'

'I closed my suitcase,' said father, 'whispered I'd call again next month and tiptoed from the shop. I tell you it upset me so much I had to have a couple in the Denbigh Arms to settle me down. I went back six weeks later. He was already dead.'

'Was it . . .?'

'Oh, yes. The X-rays showed it.'

This would put a stopper on conversation until Fred chimed in with another story. 'It reminds me of a man who actually died while signing his will . . .'

Fred's stories were usually punctuated by Aunt Nan contradicting him.

'He wasn't signing it, you old liar, Fred, he was drawing it up.'

'Well, that's the same thing, isn't it?'

'No, it isn't. It's not legal until he's signed it.'

'Well, I've signed mine, woman, and that's all you've got to bother about. And I've left it all to the dogs' home.' At which there would be much mirth, and mother, who took everything literally, might say, 'You shouldn't say things like that, Fred. Somebody could believe you.'

Illnesses were rarely mentioned by name in these conversations. Minor ailments might be publicised but anything more serious had to be whispered or mouthed. Cancer could not even be mentioned. Conditions involving the private parts or what father called 'the plumbing' would be referred to with a nod and a wink, thus: 'Of course, he'd been having trouble with his you-know-what for some time. Marjorie said he used to spend hours in the toilet.' Occasionally I would look up from my copy of the *Hotspur* and ask, 'What's a you-know-what, Aunty?' and be fobbed off with a vague remark.

Although only about 45, my relatives seemed old, like my teachers. They thought of themselves as old, too, and made jokes about middle-aged spread and being too ancient for golf. They behaved more like people of 60 today, when the frontiers of age have been pushed back, and seemed actually anxious to give up youthful ways and embrace middle-age early.

As well as the major excursions, father took mother, Roger and myself around Bristol on the old open-topped trams to explore the docks or Clifton Down. Sometimes the family took the same Campbell's paddle-steamers from the quay at Hotwells that mother had used in her youth and sailed away to Barry Island or Cardiff.

Apart from a couple of years at Skegness, which was called Leicester-by-the-Sea, holidays in summer were taken on the south or south-west coasts – Burnham-on-Sea, Weston-super-Mare, Sidmouth, Bournemouth, Torquay. Sometimes Uncle George, who worked for ICI in Bristol, would drive over and bring Granny and Grampy for the day, or Uncle Fred would come as well and the family would reunite once more. Going abroad was never considered. That was 'not for people like us'. The family stayed in boarding-houses with HP sauce on the table until a depressing experience at Bournemouth, after which father vowed he would use a hotel no matter what it cost.

Weston-super-Mare was our favourite resort. Grampy used to go over there from Bristol on the printers' outing; so did mother with the Sunday School. The pier had a collection of ancient slot-machines which could not have changed since then. There were the original What the Butler Saw peepholes, with photographs of Victorian beauties in *déshabillé*. When the handle was turned, the photos flicked over. Other machines had lead footballers in knickerbockers, one leg stiffly kicking the ball when a lever was pressed; there was a similar device for cricket with an underarm bowler whose metal fist punched the ball at a batsman whose bat, due to some defect in the design, would never hit the ball. Roger always sportingly played batsman to let his younger brother win.

Another machine represented an execution. On the insertion of a penny the condemned cell lit up, a lever propelled the chaplain forward, the prison governor jerked about and the condemned man glided into the execution chamber. The doors shut behind him and with a loud click all the lights went out and the figures went back to their starting places. However, I believe there were slight signs of progress even on the pier, because I seem to recall a newer machine presenting execution by electric chair. Nothing much happened except that when a penny was put in, the warders stiffly raised their arms and the unfortunate prisoner lit up for a few moments.

The luxury of having a whole family together on holiday lasts only a few years and our last two breaks were marred by the threat of war. In 1938 the Czech crisis exploded while we were at Torquay. The crisis was resolved, as the previous ones had been, by giving way to Hitler and Neville Chamberlain signed the infamous Munich Agreement handing most of Czechoslovakia to the Germans. At the time few people criticised it. The horrors of the previous war were too close for anyone to want another. Most people regarded the pact as having merely bought time.

So the threat of war became real. Air Raid Precautions (Civil Defence) were started and men in gas masks and overalls could be seen exercising in Leicester streets. They started to build air-raid shelters in parks and schools. At the Wyggeston, boys were called in to help dig them. We spent many a happy hour hurling earth over each other or chasing through the trenches. For every yard of trench dug, we caused two to collapse. Gas masks were issued to everybody. Tony and Nigel, the two older English brothers, joined the RAF as ground crew, although less from patriotic reasons than because they couldn't find work locally. They sent back lurid details of our preparations for war and told us of the new Bristol Blenheim bomber, which could travel more than 200 m.p.h.

Meanwhile, Roger left school at 16 and started work, having gained the goal of all grammar school education, a matriculation. In the great Wyggeston tradition, he entered local government service as a junior clerk, working in the education department. Father insisted he study accountancy, which he hated. However, he didn't expect to be in the job long. For the first time in Britain, peacetime conscription was brought in, and Roger expected to go when he was 18. 'He will be one of the first,' said mother tearfully.

Mrs English up the road echoed her fears as regards her two remaining sons.

'Don't worry,' said Mr English. 'This time everybody will have to go, even sixteen-year-olds. It'll be worse here in Leicester than at the front. At least they give you a rifle there to defend yourself. We'll be pounded to pieces from the air without being able to lift a finger. These days they just pick a city and systematically destroy it, like Guernica.' At the thought, he became almost cheerful.

The last year of peace was a good one. When not playing rugby at school, I watched Leicester City, and they got promoted to Division One. There was no violence then, of course, and soccer grounds were safe for children. Home and away supporters mingled freely. For some reason people were always fainting and passed over the heads of the crowd to the ambulance men on the touchline. Fainting at football grounds simply seems to have vanished. Perhaps it's not safe to fall over any more. I joined the Boy Scouts, a craze which lasted three months. The main effect this had on my life was to read the original version of Baden-Powell's *Scouting for Boys* with its strictures against mysterious things such as 'incontinence' and 'beastliness'.

I can still remember this warning. 'Men may tolerate smoking and drinking because they are men's vices, but they will despise a boy who practises incontinence.' I didn't know what incontinence or beastliness were. I'm not sure even now. One glorious aphorism I recall clearly. 'Opportunity is a tramcar with very few stopping-places.' It is a resounding phrase which still commands silence in a saloon bar. Roger had been a Scout and frequently vanished on camping expeditions, to return covered in boils. I borrowed most of his old uniform, including that ten-gallon hat they used to wear, but the craze didn't last long.

Cricket was still my biggest sporting passion and I spent the summer practising the googly I'd learned from the *Hotspur* and damaging every tendon in my wrist. It's a wonder the hand stayed on. The Australians had toured England the previous year and I got Don Bradman's autograph at the county ground when they massacred Leicestershire. We went to Shanklin, Isle of Wight, for our holidays, crossing from Portsmouth to Ryde on the paddle-steamer and puffing to Shanklin on the little steam train. At 18, Roger was growing up and went to his first proper dance at the hotel, on the second Saturday. I can still hear the strains of 'Deep Purple' as I lay in bed waiting for him to come up to our room. No question, of course, that he might be allowed to pick up a girl. Mother proudly watched the dance along with other parents. But he was showing a distressing interest in girls and grown-up things and we no longer spent the day playing on the beach and swimming together as before.

Roger prowled lasciviously among the young female flesh in their daring one-piece swimsuits while I flew model aeroplanes with a boy from the hotel or played biff-bats (the latest craze). At breakfast, Roger took to staring across the room at chest level. I now realise he was looking at a girl called Pat, who had her name stitched across her lovely bosom, the latest 1939 fashion. Her father dressed in plus-fours to show he was on holiday and sometimes had a drink with my father. He, too, wore his casual dress – flannel trousers with braces, open-neck white shirt and light jacket – but at the least excuse he would climb back into his suit.

The remnants of Czechoslovakia, partitioned after the Munich Agreement the previous year, had been occupied by Germany in May and now they threatened to invade Poland. Hitler raved and vowed terrible vengeance unless his demands were met (although he had, we now know, already decided on invasion). Negotiations between Russia, France and Britain for a three-power guarantee broke down when the Russians signed a pact with Germany. That made war inevitable. At the end of August the government decided to evacuate school-children from London, because of the threat of bombing and all teachers were recalled through an appeal on the radio. Two were staying at the hotel and left immediately. They were both women, holidaying together, and I remember the contrast they made with modern teachers – thirty-fivish, bespectacled, hair screwed back, severe expression, one gin-and-lime all evening. They could be recognised as teachers by their appearance. But in those days women were not allowed to remain teachers if they married, so those that stayed tended to be spinsterish in every way. They received two-thirds of the male salary.

At any rate, off they went, and most of the other guests too.

'Are you leaving, sir?' the waiter asked father at lunch on 31 August. 'No, we're not quitters,' he replied, 'I'm not leaving for those German toads.'

But by dinner-time we were alone in the dining-room. Even father had to admit defeat and we left for Leicester next day, Friday, 1 September. At night Roger and I watched the searchlights sweeping the sky over Portsmouth and I shivered with fear and prayed for peace.

Portsmouth was a mad whirl of sailors dragging kitbags. As we waited for the London train to start at the Harbour station, a woman in the carriage spoke to mother. 'I expect you will be worried about your two boys,' she said, nodding at Roger and myself. Mother asked why.

'Don't you know? The Germans have invaded Poland. They've bombed Warsaw already. It was on the wireless a few minutes ago. Of course, they don't declare war now, do they? They just start.'

'Bombed Warsaw, have they?' said father. 'The dogs.'

The woman spoke to father. 'Excuse me asking, but your arm – was it in the last war?'

Father grunted an affirmative and made an excuse to go down the corridor. He hated being questioned about his arm.

'This one will be worse, I'm afraid,' said the woman. Mother looked grim and nodded.

I don't know about Roger but I was scared stiff. For years, we had been impressed with the fact that immediately war was declared there would be mass bombing attacks on all cities, mostly with poison gas. Gas was the most feared weapon. We knew all the smells of each gas, so we could identify them. Phosgene smelt of burnt almonds, chlorine of swimming baths. Only a few weeks before, I'd seen a film about air raids with people clutching their throats and dying horribly when the gas bombs fell. And now, here we were, just about to pass through London at the start of the greatest war in history, and we had no gas masks. They were back in Leicester. I remembered a wet handkerchief made a substitute for a gas mask and then found I'd forgotten mine. I asked mother for one. She had no spare. 'They're in the luggage in the guard's van, dear. If it's urgent, borrow mine.' But how could I watch mother die of chlorine gas while I saved myself with her hankie?

'No, thanks,' I said. 'It doesn't matter.'

'Don't use your sleeve, dear.' But what effect would a sleeve have against German phosgene? Perhaps Roger and I could share his hankie, taking alternate breaths?

London was in chaos. People were putting sandbags in front of buildings, armed sentries in khaki stood in front of important offices, the railway stations were filled with bewildered crocodiles of kids being sent to the country. Most of them didn't know where they were going until they got there. Even then a Billeting Officer had to go round knocking on doors to get accommodation. People without a good excuse found evacuees foisted on them willy-nilly, to the mutual distaste of themselves and their guests. But I envied the evacuees; they all clutched cardboard boxes containing gas masks.

We got a taxi from Waterloo to St Pancras, to find the train service haywire. The only train to Leicester involved a change at Kettering. 'Take the advice of an old hand and get it,' said the ticket-collector at the barrier. 'You may never get another chance to get out of London. They'll start dropping bombs any minute.' I stared up at the sky through holes in the station roof. Please let's get to Leicester and get my gas mask and I will never sin any more.

So father took the train and the family got back home to find a city desperately trying to black-out its lights against German bombers. Thick wrapping paper was a favourite method but every stationer's and newsagent had a chalked notice, 'No more black-out paper.' Mother took out all the bulbs from our front-room light-fitting except one, and pinned blankets up to the windows, and we sat down to supper in gloom and misery, listening for the air-raid warning. But I had found my gas mask. I put it on the sideboard, ready for instant use.

CHAPTER SIX

War

Britain declared war on Germany two days later, on Sunday, 3 September 1939, after its ultimatum to Germany to withdraw from Poland was rejected. We listened to Neville Chamberlain's broadcast on the wireless at 11 a.m. 'German dogs,' said father grimly. But apart from the black-out, war proved to be fun. Word went round the schoolboy grapevine that volunteers were needed at various places and, with my friend John Bradshaw, I cycled round the city. At the fire station dozens of children were helping to fill sandbags to protect the building from bombs. We filled three sandbags each before starting to fight, trying to bury each other in a heap of sand. Soon it was a heaving mass of kids. Evicted by a harassed fire officer we moved to the police station, where gangs of boys were needed as bicycle messengers if bombing interrupted communications. The police rejected us as too young, although more likely because we were covered in sand. So we went to school and played in the half-dug air-raid shelters, throwing clods of earth like hand grenades. I even forgot about my gas mask.

The inhabitants of Baden Road reacted in various ways to war. Mr English was in his element when I went to see Jerry. It was one of my last visits because they were moving out to the village of Thurnby soon.

'Mark my words,' said Mr English, 'the last one will be a flea-bite compared with this. All civilisations have to come to an end some time.' The prospect cheered him up.

The war seemed to give my own father a sense of purpose and he felt less useless and discarded. Cyril Hurst, our daring aviator from Evington Drive, actually rejoined the RAF, although he was well over 40 and fit only for ground duties. The news flung father back into his depression. 'If I had both arms I would join up,' he said.

Official misery was the keynote of those first days of war. All theatres and cinemas were ordered to close and rugby and soccer abandoned. The Tigers didn't reappear for six years, but cinemas and theatres opened after a short time. The most immediate impact was the black-out. Car headlamps were masked and tram windows painted over so they glided by like ghostly galleons. At home, arrangements were makeshift and people had to reduce their lighting. We sat in 40-watt gloom at Baden Road which made reading almost impossible. Air-raid wardens and police patrolled the streets bellowing, 'Put that light out,' at houses showing the smallest chink. The wardens were part-time volunteers and one or two old scores were settled. But, as it was September, the days were still long and we could go out to play energetic games of soccer on the forecourt of the lock-up garages or on the playing fields near Evington Drive.

We went back to school but all was changed. Another school, deemed an air-raid risk, had to share the buildings on a shift basis. So we started either at 7.30 a.m. or 1.30 p.m., changing every week, until the guest school's air-raid shelters were completed.

One of the most remarkable events was the transformation of my schoolboy comics, the *Hotspur*, the *Wizard*, the *Skipper* and the rest. Most of them had at least one World War One serial, featuring a hero who disdained firearms and incapacitated Jerries by knocking their heads together. One such was a boxing champion named Rockfist Rogan from a comic called the *Rover*. An RAF pilot in 1917, he frequently settled aerial combat by inviting Germans to land and have it out with boxing gloves on. Overnight, these heroes were transformed into the current war. Rockfist Rogan abandoned his Sopwith Camel biplane and appeared in a Hurricane fighter shouting,

'That's for Warsaw, you Nazi scum!' as he fired his eight machine-guns. In the *Hotspur*, which specialised in school stories, their famous Red Circle School was immediately immersed in spy mysteries involving unpopular prefects with foreign names and the masters all became air-raid wardens. It was a feat of journalism which the world has passed by and which I gladly bring to light.

My own favourite hero, Biggles, the RFC ace who was hero of the famous books by W. E. Johns, continued in World War One, however, dodging the ack-ack bursts and sending the Fokker triplanes spinning to their doom, the pilots mouthing curses at him in bad German. The only phrases they seemed to know were '*Gott im Himmel*' and '*Donner und Blitzen*'. It did occur to me to wonder how Germany had lasted so long when its aircraft were manned by incompetent fools and I hoped maybe they would surrender more quickly this time. Certainly there was no lack of optimism. Britain began the war confidently. A speaker on the wireless boasted, 'We have the finest navy in the world, the Royal Navy, and the finest air force in the world, the RAF, and the finest army in the world, the French army.' Besides, were not the Germans shaven-headed bullocks working by the textbook and unable to use their initiative?

'That's the difference between the British and the Germans,' said Mr English, sipping a bottle of Whitbread light ale when I went up to see Jerry. 'When the British attack, the officer goes in front, leading his men on. When the Germans attack, the officers are at the back, driving the men in front of them like cattle with drawn revolvers. I have seen German soldiers chained to their machine-guns to stop them retreating.'

Despite this unfortunate handicap, the Germans conquered Poland easily enough. Warsaw became the first in a long line of martyred cities in the war, bombed, besieged and largely blown to pieces. The Poles were eventually finished off by the Germans' Soviet allies, who themselves invaded Poland and divided up the country with the Nazis. That darling of left-wing intellectuals in those days, the Russian dictator Stalin, proved a natural ally for Hitler and gave him a huge tract of

Polish land for a hunting forest as a gesture of goodwill. It was not known then that Stalin had murdered some eight million of his own people, any more than we knew the full horror of Hitler's atrocities. After that the War went into stalemate, except on sea and air. In France, the armies faced each other, waiting. An early French advance into the Saar petered out. Mr English said it was because of the German booby-traps.

'They used to nail up puppies by their tails in the trenches before retreating in 1918. When you went to release the poor dog a bomb exploded,' he explained.

The expected air blitzkrieg never materialised and gradually life returned to something like normal. Theatres and cinemas reopened and we learned to cope with the black-out, groping through dark streets and avoiding the mysterious shapes of darkened trams. As a wartime measure the last bus and tram left the city centre at nine o'clock every evening, but that didn't worry me. Anyway, we could walk home in twenty minutes and mugging was almost unknown.

The War brought a family crisis. My cousin Joan Smeath, daughter of Uncle Will, mother's brother in London, had been working as a translator with Coca-Cola in Berlin. They posted her back to England because of the crisis but not before she fell in love with a German boy named Werner and became engaged. Now all communication between them was cut off. In his last letter Werner said he expected to go into the German army if war came. Joan's position was made worse because her brother Arthur was in the British army from the first day of war. He'd been a Territorial member of the City of London Yeomanry and was called for full-time service immediately. In my wilder moments I imagined them bayoneting each other and discovering their identities as they died. Mother, too, was worried they might come face-to-face but father pooh-poohed the idea.

'Rubbish,' he said. 'Arthur's in the artillery and the artillery never come face-to-face with anyone.'

Even so, father was quite concerned for Werner. 'I hope he doesn't go in the infantry,' he said. 'The Germans use their infantry as cannon-fodder, mown down by machine-guns. I know, I was a machine-gunner myself.'

Aunt Nan, in Bristol, was less sympathetic. 'What does Joan want to get herself mixed up with some wretched German for?' she demanded. 'Aren't there enough English boys around or something? How can I tell anyone my niece is engaged to one of those awful Nazis?'

The fact of having a potential relative in the German armed forces gave me a certain pride. I boasted at school about it and the tale lost nothing in the telling. Werner became a Luftwaffe general very quickly. Unfortunately, nobody believed me. They thought it was just another Green fairy-tale.

As with everything else, the war's impact was only gradual at the Wyggeston, once we'd got rid of the school which shared our premises. We had air-raid drills and trooped to the shelters dug in the playing fields, but there were no real air-raids. A couple of masters disappeared into the forces and one or two sported ARP steel helmets strapped to their gas-mask cases (everyone had to carry their gas mask). Classroom windows were criss-crossed with strips of brown paper to minimise blast damage, but otherwise we carried on as usual.

One person, however, didn't. That was the German master, a Swiss named Dr Meyer. No matter how often boys were told Dr Meyer was not German but Swiss we refused to believe it. Did he not speak German? Was not his English accent appalling? Poor Dr Meyer spoke like Eric von Stroheim in a Hollywood film or the Germans in the Biggles books. Worse, he looked like a parody of a German and had an uncanny resemblance to the schoolmaster in *All Quiet on the Western Front*. His hair was shaven and he wore a monocle. The back of his head was quite flat. He dressed in black frock-coat with black striped trousers and wore a winged collar. To crown it all he had absolutely no sense of humour whatsoever (a sure sign of the Hun). He was already a figure of fun because of his accent and his earnest manner. He could never understand why boys laughed when he dictated '*Wo is mein Vater?*' the '*Vater*' being pronounced farter, of course. His nickname was Bog, a pun on Meyer.

From the moment he returned to school after the declaration of war in the holiday, his life was a misery. Swastikas were chalked all over his classroom, inside and out. Boys greeted him in class by standing to attention and shouting 'Heil Hitler!' Followed about the playground by pupils goose-stepping and giving the Nazi salute, he became incoherent with rage and his attempts at discipline, never very good, were howled down. Eventually the noise, principally the chanting of 'Sieg Heil!' was so great other masters complained to the head, who spoke sternly to each class, threatening a flogging if the baiting went on.

'Dr Meyer is Swiss and Switzerland is neutral,' he said. 'In any case, even if he was German, I cannot see what good would be done by this ridiculous posturing round the playground.'

So the ragging ceased and Dr Meyer stuck it out until he retired a year or two later, a sad, puzzled man.

That first winter of war I contracted religious fever in quite a big way. Although my parents rarely went to church they were quite religious. Mother said her prayers kneeling by the bed every night until the day she died and she trained us boys to do the same. For some years I'd been a member of the Crusaders' Union, an earnest youth organisation of evangelical Christians, but now I began to take it up enthusiastically. Every Sunday I bellowed the choruses such as:

> Trust and obey
> For there's no other way
> To be happy in Jesus
> But to trust and obey

Like the Salvation Army, the Crusaders knew a good tune and knew what appealed to youngsters. Attendance was baited with games and outings and camps, usually followed by prayer meetings. Roger had introduced me to the Crusaders some years ago; then he left for the Scouts with his friend David Shuff. I stayed on but my enthusiasm rose dramatically in the winter of 1939–40. The group's enviably simple faith divided everybody in the world into those who had been saved and those who hadn't. We were urged to confess our sins and pledge our conversions. Sometimes boys were encouraged to sign forms to this effect. Heaven was occasionally used as an inducement to make the decision.

Despite my remarks, I have to confess that as I get older I hope my signature is still valid.

'Boys, I stood here only last year when a boy failed to sign the form we shall give you after the service. Three weeks later he was dead, killed by a bus in the black-out. Are you, too, going to throw away the chance of eternal life?' So said a speaker at one of our rallies.

These appeals were reinforced by Victorian moral homilies. 'The famous evangelist Moody was a great sinner before his conversion and frequently went to the theatre. One day, after purchasing his ticket, he went through the wrong door and an attendant cried out, "Sir, you are on your way to the Pit." The realisation suddenly came over him that he was indeed on the way to the Pit, to that everlasting Pit of damnation and hell, and he turned and staggered out of the theatre like a broken man and sought salvation.' I knew dozens of stories like this.

It was the war which made up my mind, I think. I had not forgotten the fear I felt without my gas mask in London. I was delighted to sign. I wanted to go to heaven. There were too many threats of death. Not merely the war, which was still pretty quiet, but dozens of illnesses which had not then been conquered. TB was a death sentence. When a boy at school vanished with 'consumption', he never returned. The news was whispered around like cancer today. Parents anxiously enquired whether you had been in touch with him. We were not likely to get syphilis (another killer) but scarlet fever, meningitis, diphtheria, polio, whooping cough and blood poisoning lurked all around. And the boy killed in the black-out? They didn't like to say it, but it was strongly hinted he had gone to the Other Place.

In 1940 the Phoney War woke up. Russia invaded Finland and when that was over Germany invaded Norway and overran most of that country in a few weeks. We didn't feel quite so confident now. Then the big German offensive began in France. Holland and Belgium were invaded; British troops were evacuated from Dunkirk; within six weeks France had capitulated.

'Mother, those French dogs have thrown up the sponge,'

father shouted to the kitchen when news of the French surrender came through on the wireless in June 1940.

It was perhaps a little hard on the French, for nothing seemed able to stop the onward march of the Germans, who swallowed nine countries whole. Britain was now alone, the only country left fighting them, and the war began to bite. John Bradshaw, my cricketing pal, had a sister whose boy-friend was at Dunkirk. He was a typical young man of the time with his chalk-striped suit, thin moustache, brilliantined hair, BSA motor-cycle and Craven A cigarette dangling from his mouth, but he looked older and haggard now. His unit was machine-gunned by German planes while mixed up with a column of refugees and a young French girl torn to ribbons in front of him.

There was no more cricket on the playing fields, or at least, only with difficulty. They had been mutilated with huge trenches dug across them to stop Nazi troop-planes and gliders landing. Later all the iron railings were taken away for scrap-iron to make steel and the city looked naked. The front gardens of Victorian houses gaped open to the pavement, the parks appeared strangely wild, like heathland.

Baden Road had its first casualty. Curly, the milkman, was killed in the army at Dunkirk. And cousin Joan, who'd been writing to Werner through mutual friends in Denmark, was quite cut off from him. He was now a German soldier.

The threat of invasion loomed. Churchill, who had taken over from Neville Chamberlain, made his famous 'we shall fight on the beaches' broadcast. Perhaps it sounds a little corny now, but it reflected the mood of the country then. He was a statesman with the courage to stand up to Hitler when others, headed by Stalin, were cringing and fawning. Many people took him literally. Mr English crooned over his old service revolver and talked of taking a Nazi with him when he went. Father made mysterious journeys upstairs to the drawer where he kept his Canadian Army Colt. Aunt Nan wrote from Bristol, 'Fred says the Germans will never conquer this country as long as there's a hole in his arse.'

Roger joined the Home Guard, the part-time army of civilians hastily organised for defence against parachute troops, the new form of warfare used so successfully by the Germans in Holland. He joined the platoon at Thurnby, where the Englishes were now living. They had no rifles but the local squire provided two shotguns. These, however, were taken back when somebody broke one. But they constructed a vast store of Molotov cocktails (petrol bombs), which were said to be fatal to tanks if you got near enough to throw them. They'd been invented by the Finns in their brief war against the Russians six months previously.

Leaflets telling people what to do in an invasion were pushed through the letter-box. The general advice seemed to be to sit in the air-raid shelter and do nothing. The Home Guard, however, were taught optimistic ways to stop the Germans without weapons. The most interesting wheeze was to hang a couple of blankets on a line across a street. Unable to see past, the German tank would stop and open its hatch to investigate. When the commander put out his head the defenders would leap on to the tank, hurling petrol bombs. Night after night Roger vanished on his bicycle to practise these desperate manoeuvres and returned smelling strongly of beer.

At school, more masters vanished into the forces. Even the Head, who had pacifist leanings, joined the Special Police. The first bombs fell on Leicester in the late summer. It was a daylight raid and the air-raid sirens went in the middle of the morning. I was at home so it must have been a holiday. John Bradshaw cycled round to say his father, a special policeman, heard they'd bombed the gasworks in Ayetone Road, near the county cricket ground. We rode quickly down there and stared in awe at the smoking wreckage of several red-brick terrace houses of the sort which dominated the city, although the gasworks were intact. The ARP were still digging in the wreckage. It was probably two miles in a direct line from our house to where the bombs fell but we never heard the explosions. Father was not surprised.

'I never heard the one that got me on the Western Front in 1916,' he said.

It was not very pleasant to be a citizen of Britain in the winter of 1940. True, the immediate threat of German invasion was ended by the RAF's victory in the Battle of Britain, but the

Germans now concentrated on night bombing, against which there was little defence. The first bombs I heard at night came down with no warning (or if there was, I didn't hear it). I simply awoke with a sudden apprehension of danger for no reason at all and then there was a series of explosions getting nearer and nearer, as if a giant was marching across the city to our house. They finally stopped with a blast that rattled the windows. Leicester was not badly bombed compared to Birmingham, Coventry or London but we had enough. Every raid on Birmingham or Coventry meant a warning at Leicester and raiders often dropped a bomb or two on the city at random (aircraft frequently got lost in those days). When the sirens began their unearthly wail in the middle of the night the family gathered in the front room downstairs, where we ate and lived. Roger and I slept on the floor under the big mahogany table. Mother and father dozed in armchairs either side of the fireplace. Father approved of this arrangement.

'At least we shall all go together if we are hit, Win,' he told mother. I did not find this very comforting. I was 13 and, despite the guarantees of the next life offered by the Crusaders, I did not wish to leave this one yet.

Sleep was difficult, punctuated by the thud of bombs and the droning of German aircraft overhead as they passed towards Birmingham and Coventry. They had a distinctive engine noise, especially the Dornier 17 bomber, which gave out a peculiar wow-wow sound, said to be due to the fact that one engine was tuned differently from the other. There was no opposition. Night fighters lacked radar and blundered blindly about the sky. The whole of Leicester boasted exactly two anti-aircraft guns, which were in a field near Thurnby. Schoolboys with bicycles know these matters. They only fired three or four rounds before being moved. The Germans could have come as low as they liked. In fact, one evening a plane did come low to drop bombs near St Stephen's Road. A woman claimed the planes were so low she could see inside the aircraft when it opened its bomb doors, which was but a mild example of the wild yarns bombing created.

The biggest raid on the city was in November 1940. It was

always referred to in Leicester as 'the night of the blitz', but although a severe raid it wasn't quite in the blitz category. Even so, more than 120 people were killed and many injured. I was at a Crusaders' prayer meeting at Evington when the alert went, interrupting our discussion of an Old Testament story. After the sirens had died down there was a tense silence as we listened and sure enough there was the unmistakeable hum of a large force of German bombers overhead.

Our leader, a bank clerk named Wilfred White,* behaved commendably. Bombs were already falling and large parts of the city were on fire but he shepherded half a dozen of us to the home of a boy nearby and cycled round the district telling parents their children were safe, although he got blown off his bike when a bomb burst. It is difficult to sneer at a faith which gives a man courage of that sort. Meanwhile a dozen of us crouched in a back-garden Anderson air-raid shelter designed for six while the bombs whistled down. We got quite good at guessing which were going to drop close and when the whistle took on that urgent note that means a near miss we put our hands over our ears and shut our eyes and prayed. We may laugh at evangelists but when the chips are down we all pray.

It was a cold, wet dawn when John Bradshaw and I cycled home. Not far from where we'd spent the night was a huge bomb crater in the road and with shouts of glee we leaped into it, looking for bits of shrapnel or bomb casing. We were driven off by an irate woman with no windows in her house who shouted, 'It's been bad enough with them bloody Germans all night without you kids making it worse.' Evington Drive was roped off for some reason, so I pushed my bike under the rope and went on to Baden Road. On the way I passed a funny little hole in the road. Fifty yards on was another rope and this time I saw a sign:

DANGER — UNEXPLODED BOMB

Realising what the funny little hole was I hurried home.

All were safe at our house, but there was no gas, as a bomb

* Before this book was published, Wilfred White wrote to me, recalling he had to dive into a ditch, taking a boy with him, when the first bombs fell. At 82, he was still running a Gospel group, a testimony to the efficacy of faith.

had fractured the main. Several houses had been destroyed about a hundred yards away but 'Henleaze' was undamaged.

'Those toads failed to get us,' remarked father with satisfaction. 'They were the same in the First War. They could never hit anything from the air. I remember a German plane coming over to machine-gun us and we just stood there laughing. He was spraying no man's land.'

Mother cooked breakfast on the old coal-fired kitchen range and I got to school an hour late. On arrival I was sternly rebuked. The Head did not regard the Nazis as an excuse for lateness and it was acidly pointed out that sixty per cent of the pupils at Wyggy had managed to make Assembly. When I got home that evening mother told me the unexploded bomb in Evington Drive had gone off during the morning.

'It went off before the bomb disposal squad got there,' she said. 'It made a big bang but only shook the windows.' I didn't tell her I had cycled past it earlier.

She also told me a little boy of 6, down Bannerman Road, about two hundred yards away, had been killed. The bomb hit a small branch of the Co-op on the corner and both his legs were blown off. They took him to the first-aid post in St Philip's church hall nearby where they operated, but he died. At school next day we learned two of our own boys had been killed and all stood in silence while the Dead March was played on the organ. The day after, another death took place in hospital but the Head decided to omit any ceremony. The Dead March was becoming depressing. Besides, boys were getting to know it so well they were whistling jazzed-up versions or marching through the playground pretending to carry coffins.

Grandmother Green's house in Tichborne Street was in one of the worst-bombed districts but father reported she was not only safe but comparatively undisturbed by the bombing, thanks to her increasing deafness. 'She's better off where she is, Win,' said father. 'I only wish I was as oblivious as she is.'

Next night the Germans came again, but less strongly. They dropped only two parachute mines, huge bombs suspended on parachutes so they did not penetrate the ground and the blast was greater. Sometimes called 'land mines' they were said to have been captured from the British at Dunkirk. A boy at school's father was under one as it came down and fled for his life as the white shape slowly descended, to explode in Knighton Park Road. This time the Germans set fire to Steele and Busk's corset factory, about a mile from our house. Father and I gathered in the road with some neighbours to watch the blaze. A German aircraft was droning away overhead when a rattle of distant machine-gun fire was heard. The engine note of the plane changed and there was a peculiar distant crash, unlike the explosion of a bomb, more like two cars colliding. I think it was a night fighter shooting down one of the enemy.

'One less of the dogs,' said father.

The Germans hit no military objectives at all. It was area bombing of the sort used against Warsaw. They destroyed several shoe factories and killed many men, women and children. Among the buildings wrecked was a Nonconformist church on the corner of Saxby Street, where our dentist, Uncle Aly, practised. The church hall was a first-aid post and a volunteer doctor was killed as he operated, when a chunk of ceiling fell on him. The Germans may not even have known they were bombing Leicester. Since the war it has been revealed that British scientists had discovered a way of bending their radio direction beams and Leicester may have received bombs meant for Coventry.

With that national sense of guilt peculiar to the British, we are now urged to beat our breasts in contrition for what we did later to German cities such as Hamburg, but in 1940 it was all one-way traffic and we were on the receiving end with no retaliation possible. I do not think we can be blamed for attacking the Germans by copying their methods. Just occasionally, as Roger and I huddled under the dining-table, I wondered about cousin Joan's German boy-friend, Werner, and whether he knew what was happening to his future relatives.

CHAPTER SEVEN

The Great Sex Lecture

Things got even grimmer. Roger vanished to join the navy as a pilot in the Fleet Air Arm and found himself digging wounded civilians from bombed houses in Gosport. Rationing began to bite. Eggs came down to one a fortnight. Onions, even baked beans, almost disappeared, not to mention lemons. In 1941, all the bananas suddenly vanished. Shipping could no longer be spared to import them across the submarine-infested Atlantic. They didn't return until the end of the war in 1945 and, when they did, little children didn't know how to eat them. Some tried to bite through the skin; others broke them in half. They had to be shown how to peel them. The meat ration shrank to just over a shillingsworth a week per person (5p in modern terms). Mother spent hours in food queues to get us food and achieved prodigies with ingenious recipes but we were forced to eke out butter with margarine, the ultimate disgrace for someone trying to be middle-class. Only poor people ate margarine then. Cholesterol hadn't been invented. If we were short of food, mother just ate less herself and gave the extra to her men.

Frugality, already an essential part of lower middle-class existence, became one of the supreme wartime virtues. Men vied with each other in seeing how long they could make their precious razor blades last, sharpening them on their thumbs or on the inside of a glass full of hot water. Strange recipes, consisting chiefly of carrots and tasting like nothing on earth, appeared on tables. Everybody was asked by the government to limit their bath water to five inches, to save fuel. This made no difference to Baden Road where the hot water system had always seemed unable to produce any more.

To crown it all, my tortoise Joey died. Father buried him in the back garden, digging the tiny grave one-handed with a trowel. I suppose he's still there. I blamed the bombing for his death, but I expect it was the cold weather which killed him.

Roger's friends David Shuff and Dick Martin followed him and enlisted. David never returned – he died of a brain tumour in India in 1944. I joined the Air Training Corps. I was still crazy about flying, like so many of my generation, and the ambition of almost all the boys in class was to join the RAF. We already knew the silhouettes and characteristics of every aircraft, not only RAF but the Germans as well. Once, during a science lesson, the sirens sounded. Normally we were marched to the shelters, to sit shivering in cold concrete tunnels lit only by dim battery-powered bulbs, and made to chant Greek and Latin verbs so as not to waste time. But the science master, Horace Garside, was a genial Yorkshireman who allowed us to stay in class if in the middle of an experiment. This time he appointed a boy to watch from the window for enemy aircraft. Soon a plane flew over.

'Look out, sir,' the boy at the window shouted. 'It's a Heinkel 111.' There was a rush to the windows.

'No, you stupid idiot, of course it's not a Heinkel 111, it's a Junkers 88 with a modified nose.'

'Bollocks, it's got a low aspect-ratio wing. It must be a Heinkel, look at the dorsal gun mounting.'

'They're not using Heinkels for daylight bombing any more.'

'Yes, they are, they're putting the new BMW engines in them.'

'You're all wrong. It's a Blenheim Mark IVa. Look at the forward gun.'

'If that's a Blenheim, I'm a German.'

The argument raged while the German (if it was a German) flew serenely on, unaware of the controversy going on below. No bombs fell.

One result of the bombing was that the city was totally deserted at night. I remember walking back about eight o'clock from a friend's house a couple of miles away. It was a bright moonlit evening and enemy aircraft were droning overhead and I did not meet one single person until an air-raid warden stopped me near home, and advised me to take shelter.

At Easter 1941, while I was at a Crusader camp at Buxton, praying my friends might see the light, mother and father went to Bristol to see Gran and Grampy, who couldn't visit us because of the war. They chose a bad time. On Good Friday, the Germans launched a huge air attack which tore the heart out of the old city. Mother cried when she returned and described the damage, all the places she loved as a child in smoking ruins. She would have cried even more at what the City Council did ten years later in reconstruction. My grandparents still clung on in Cobourg Road, although Granny was showing signs of age. Grampy was now deaf and actually carried a sort of ear-trumpet, although Uncle George claimed it was a defence against being nagged and he could hear quite well playing whist. At least being deaf made the bombing easier to bear.

Mother and father stayed with Aunt Nan and Uncle Fred, who spent the air raid on duty in the street watching for fire-bombs. Every time a bomb fell he came inside for a drop of whisky. 'I don't think he cared much about the bombing by the time the all-clear went,' said mother with some understatement. 'When it was over he talked of strangling Hitler with his bare hands. Most unlike your uncle.'

Three of father's old Canadian friends turned up that year. Two were the soldiers who'd saved his life in World War One. Both had joined up again in Canada and been posted to Aldershot. Bob Kerr, who dragged father through the shelling to safety, was a white-haired captain of 49, but Cy Young, dad's second rescuer, was still a private. Once more, the shells screamed across the living-room as they talked far into the night.

'He was drunk. He'd gotten hold of a bottle of rum somewhere and got shotters. He stood on the firestep and shouted, "The Germans will never get me, I tell you." Then a whizzbang landed. When I got up I heard them call for stretcher-bearers. He'd gone. Blown his head off. Nobody wanted to touch him, so Lou put him on a stretcher. Lou was good like that. He had a kind heart, Lou. He always did the dirty work.'

They talked about Duke, King and Royal, a quaintly-named trio of brothers in the unit. Duke and King were killed but Royal survived. Next time they went up the front line, he ran back as they marched off and shook hands with the cook, a half-breed Red Indian who was his best friend. 'Goodbye, Cookie,' he said, 'I shan't see you again.' He was killed that night.

But Bob and Cy were not happy. Because of their age, they'd been given non-combatant jobs. Bob Kerr was an administrative officer and Cy, now over 50, was an officer's batman or servant. The young infantryman of 1916 felt ashamed and worried about his wife, who was looking after the prairie farm in his absence.

'I guess five thousand acres is a lot of land for one woman and a hired hand to cultivate,' he said with some understatement.

Soon afterwards they both got discharged and sent back to Canada. They were men of a vanished school of Empire emigrant, who referred to Britain as 'the old country' and believed firmly in Britain, the Empire and Canada with an unquestioning faith. When the Suez Crisis blew up in 1956, Cy wrote to father, 'Why do people sneer when the old country tries to do something? The Americans of all people have no right to criticise.' Cy made one more visit to Leicester. He came over to see father in 1969 and collapsed from a heart attack. He died in Leicester Infirmary and father buried him.

The third visitor had a lasting effect on me. A florid, middle-aged, jovial fellow called Percy, he'd been a passenger with father on the emigrant ship from Liverpool in 1910. Like father, he'd been back in England a long time but never settled down to a steady job. He eked out a living as an actor and came to Leicester because he was playing the King in *Cinderella* at the Opera House. One suspects in peace-time Percy would not have got the part. He lived in theatrical digs but often ate with us and mother looked on in despair as he consumed her precious rations with the traditional hearty appetite of the old-time pro on tour.

'I love my meals, Mrs Green,' he boomed as he consumed a week's meat-ration at one sitting. He also loved his draught Bass and he and father spent long periods talking over old times in the Gentlemen's Bar of the Grand Hotel. We had always gone to the Leicester panto as children and my parents took me along to see Percy. I can still remember the appalling dialogue. In one scene he was stopped as he tried to enter the Palace, and asked for a ticket to the Ball.

'My face is my ticket.'

'I regret I have orders to punch all tickets.'

Roll of drums and crash of cymbal as King is pushed in chest and falls over, losing his crown and groaning.

But here comes the ominous bit. 'I don't think Percy was very good,' said mother as we came out (rather a polite criticism, I now realise). But *I* thought he was wonderful. That was my idea of acting. I laughed every time he came on. Were the dreadful seeds of Coarse Acting sown in my little soul even then? I fear so.

Percy showed several characteristics of the Coarse Actor. In *The Art of Coarse Acting* I define a Coarse Actor as one who can remember the lines but not the order in which they come (among other things) and Percy fitted that like a glove. Furthermore he could always remember the previous scene better than the one he was actually in and strange *non sequiturs* floated across the footlights. He also had the desperate desire to impress, which is the hallmark of a Coarse player, combined with a firm belief that if it wasn't going well it wasn't *his* fault and the audience wouldn't notice anything that went wrong.

Encouraged by Percy's appearance I took my first step on the slippery slope the following year when the rep company at the Theatre Royal, a gloomy nineteenth-century playhouse opposite the Town Hall, put on *Goodbye, Mr Chips*, the famous James Hilton play about an old schoolmaster. They needed lots of boys, of course, and asked the school for volunteers. About a dozen were selected and I got a big part, playing three generations of one family taught by Mr Chips. I shall never forget the last scene. A boy was having tea with Mr Chips (now in his dotage) and as he left he said the title-line, 'Goodbye, Mr Chips'. He had been instructed to punch this, so he faced front and bellowed it at the audience.

'Goodbye, my boy,' replied Chips feebly, in a voice which suggested he was in the last stages of Parkinson's Disease.

No sooner was the canvas door closed behind him than the boy ran backstage to join the rest of us. We were gathered under the eye of the leading lady, a girl called Diana Muirhead, to represent the school choir. As Mr Chips suffered the first pangs of his fatal attack we broke into 'Lord Behold Us with Thy Blessing' and behold, lights glowed through little holes in the scenery which represented the chapel windows, visible in the distance through Chips' study window.

Mr Chips did not pass away either quickly or unobtrusively. It was uncertain what he died of; he appeared to suffer the All-Purpose Coarse Death described in *The Art of Coarse Acting*, when the player vaguely clutches his bowels and groans. Mr Chips certainly groaned; we could hear him above the hymn. I think the author intended Chips to die peacefully, but this was more like the demise of Lucky Luciano. He was heard tottering round the stage, clawing at furniture, until a final crash announced he had fallen down. Apart from a few final jerks and twitches all was over. Backstage there was furious bustle and activity as electricians pulled rows of old-fashioned dimmers, while out front old ladies wept in the stalls. There was not a dry seat in the house, as they say.

When I came to write *Coarse Acting* twenty-five years later, I described an incident in the show which marred my otherwise successful stage début. There was a scene where Chips expelled me from class and one night I forgot where the exit was and tried to go out of a door painted on a canvas flat. I must have looked a complete idiot clawing at the scenery with my fingernails. Chips had to go over and show me the way out. Afterwards he rebuked me severely. 'Stop trying to get into the act, laddie,' he said. 'Say your lines and get off-stage as quickly as possible and leave the rest to the real actors.'

He refused to believe it was a genuine accident. I have an unhappy tendency to panic under stress.

The atmosphere of the theatre, the smell of size used on the flats backstage, and the whole gorgeous unreality of everything fascinated me. It's a fascination that has lasted all my life and still sends me forth to inflict myself on audiences. Above all I was attracted to the actresses. Actresses then didn't go about in jeans and T-shirts, they exuded glamour and lovely smells. I thought the two girls in the show were the most beautiful women I had ever seen and I was quite distressed when I found Mr Chips necking with one of them in a dark corner. After that I went to the rep regularly as a member of the audience. Mother and father did not approve. They were suspicious of stage people, whom they regarded as living irregular lives. Perhaps Percy had prejudiced them. It is difficult not to be prejudiced against someone who eats all your meat-ration.

Evil influences must have been all around me at this part of my life, because about then I made my first entry into journalism. One of my favourite weekly comics, the *Skipper*, offered prizes for jokes. So did its companion paper the *Hotspur*. Unable to think of a joke I copied a winning entry from the *Hotspur* and sent it to the *Skipper*. Much to my surprise it was printed and a prize duly delivered, consisting, if I remember correctly, of a metal frog which jumped in the air. There was also a card from the editor congratulating me on my 'beezer yarn' or words to that effect. My beezer yarn was as follows:

Old Lady (to beggar in dark glasses): How can you prove you are blind?

Beggar (waving white stick): See that tree, ma'am?

Old Lady: Yes.

Beggar: Well, I can't.

As a special honour the joke was illustrated. There was a drawing of a man in stereotyped tramp's dress of ragged coat, football jersey, patched trousers and a battered top hat, his shoes gaping open and a toe exposed with lines round it to indicate a corn. He had a placard 'Blind' round his neck. There was nothing subtle about comics then. Tramps looked like tramps; burglars had striped jerseys and carried bags labelled 'swag'; rich people went around in top hats and spats (rather like capitalists in the old *Daily Worker* cartoons). You knew where you were.

This piece of writing had all the characteristics of my later work, namely that it was plagiarised, not very funny and in slightly bad taste. But the effect of seeing it published was traumatic to my immature mind. It confirmed the satisfaction I had already begun to feel in making people laugh. I was already a bit of a show-off. Further, it seemed an easy way to make a quick buck (or metal frog, in this case). Coming so soon after my appearance in *Goodbye, Mr Chips*, the results were fatal. The desire to write or act or show-off grew. Doubtless the motivation went deeper and I was probably a good example of someone who felt he could never measure up to his father. At any rate nobody seemed to pay any attention when I was serious, only when I was fooling about.

Other vaguely artistic feelings were stirring within me, principally sex. When I was 14, there was a sort of sex lecture at the Crusaders which proved a terrible embarrassment all round and left us none the wiser. It was so vague as to be useless and couched largely in pseudo-spiritual terms. 'A girl is being prepared for you in heaven,' we were told. 'And one day you will meet her and fall in love. Later, after marriage, you will cleave together and bring forth fruit in abundance.' There was no mention of who did what to whom and how, no indication as to which organs and orifices were involved. After the lecture was over we all stood up and sang a hymn, 'Keep Thyself Pure'. It seemed hardly necessary.

A local boy gave some of us our first real sex lesson on the nearby playing-fields. He had discovered how to 'do it' from a book his brother bought when he became engaged. The boy described love-making in some detail and, as I now know, with a great deal of inaccuracy. One of his fallacies, I remember, was that if enough seed did not go into the female, the child would be a cripple.

'That's what happened to Jones in Form Four. There wasn't enough so his leg came out all funny. That's why he has to wear an iron on it.'

The whole thing was so difficult to believe without knowledge of the female sex organ. Also, we didn't like to think our parents had behaved like that, since sex was 'dirty'. I tried to imagine my uncles and aunts copulating and shuddered. For one thing they all took their teeth out at night. From home we received no information. Everybody's parents, with a few exceptions, were too inhibited themselves to discuss sex; they were too inhibited even to tell us *not* to discuss it; it was completely taboo. Thus wild rumours grew unchecked and I daily examined the palms of my hands for the hair that masturbators were rumoured to grow there. Biology lessons began to teach us about sperms and ovaries and we saw a film of sperms swimming about to giggled remarks like, 'Please, sir, I think Brown has come.' But the great question remained: How Do You Do It?

This was supposed to be answered by the headmaster, who took it upon himself to deliver an annual lecture to the fifth form in the Great Hall. We were supposed to ask parents for permission to go to the lecture but everyone was too frightened even to ask. The Head, whose awesome appearance seemed even more terrifying on this occasion, mounted the platform, rang his bell for silence, and began in the time-honoured fashion: 'Boys . . .' The idea of giving a sex lecture to a mixed audience would never have occurred in 1942.

'Boys,' he went on, obviously embarrassed by the whole thing, 'I have called you together today to tell you how you were born.'

We stirred in anticipation. At last somebody was going to reveal how it was done. We listened in some impatience while the Head droned on about the love of man for a maid. 'One day you will meet a woman who is destined to be your companion for life. Not only in . . . in . . . matters of love and procreation but in art, literature and music as well.' Yes, we all knew that. The louts of the fifth form muttered and shuffled as they waited for him to get to the dirty bit. At length the promised moment arrived.

'Boys, you may have noticed certain changes taking place in your young bodies' (muttered remarks of 'You don't say, guv'). 'Hair may be found growing in unexpected places . . . such as the armpits . . . you may feel a vague restlessness for which you cannot account. This is because Nature is preparing you for the sacred act of procreation.'

It was like watching an exciting film. By now we were on the edge of our seats waiting for the final revelation. But at this vital stage the Head's nerve failed and he skated round the sex act by describing it in vague, mystical terms.

'You will have a love for a woman which is not like your love for your mother or sister. You will want to have with her a true union . . . the union of man and wife . . . the ultimate physical union, if I may put it that way . . . the closest possible physical and spiritual contact that can be made with your beloved wife. And Nature has ordained that she will be the exact physical counterpart of you, so that your seed will flow into her and in good time she will conceive . . .'

An audible groan of disappointment arose as we realised once more they were going to fob us off with mysticism. But having skated on what he obviously regarded as very thin ice, the Head steered into safe areas with relief. Sexual desire, he boomed, was natural. Nevertheless he treated it as something unhealthy and suggested a good way to get rid of it was to write poetry or go for a bicycle ride (a voice: 'How do you ride a bike with a hard on?'). He was more at home denouncing 'filthy practices' which he refused to specify. He somehow gave the impression the poor examination results and the defeat of the First XI by Northampton Grammar School were due to these. On our favourite hobby he was equally scathing. He referred to it as 'self-abuse' and claimed only a minority of 'unfortunate weak boys without self-control' practised it (a palpable lie). He then banged his bell and told us to file out quietly. We returned to the playground little the wiser, to continue our sexual education in furtive groups.

It must be remembered that in a school of 1,000 probably no pupil had ever had sexual intercourse, certainly not in the fifth forms, whose ages averaged around 15–16 (I was 14, owing to my earlier promotion). The same would have applied at a girls' school. Plenty boasted of heavy necking sessions in parks, but that was as far as most boys got. We were too afraid of starting a baby, of parents, of the girl telling her father, of the Headmaster (expulsion would have been inevitable), of VD and of going to hell. Not to mention the fact we didn't know how to do it. We developed later in those days, too, remaining children longer, in body and attitude. Today, many friends offer their daughters the pill at 16.

Homosexuality was practised but furtively and only by a few. It was considered the last word in filth. Ironically, racism, the greatest modern sin, was considered almost a virtue, at least as far as the Germans and Japs were concerned. Wars are not won by thinking of the other side as splendid fellows.

Despite the lack of information, my interest in girls grew. Mother and father sent me to Mrs Cooke's Dancing School, opposite Victoria Park on the London Road. Roger had been there. Learning to dance was one of the problems of growing up. Teenagers are luckier now as anybody can dance the modern way but then a boy or girl who couldn't do the formal ballroom steps was shut out of social life. Dancing was the great social get-together, the classic way for boy to meet girl as there were few teenage parties in the current sense. Wall-flowers hadn't a chance. Tea-dances were all the rage and many a romance blossomed over fish-paste sandwiches at the Palais.

I mastered the waltz and quickstep, although never the foxtrot or tango, but that was enough. The enforced intimacy of ballroom-dancing always worried me. It seemed unnatural for two people to be so close in public and rather unfair on the girl, who had to put up with her toes being trodden on, not to mention bad or beery breath, body odour and the uneasy suspicion that what was pressing into her was not just a penknife in her partner's pocket. Sometimes shyer boys tried to keep well away from their partners only to have the remorseless Mrs Cooke, a pretty little lady of about 35, say firmly, 'Closer there, closer, you can't do a spin turn two feet from your partner . . .'

It was impossible to reply, 'I'm sorry, Mrs Cooke, I've just broken wind,' or 'I'm afraid I'm getting over-excited,' so the boy complied, perhaps blushing with embarrassment and the couple hastily broke up when the music stopped.

The bombing had almost ceased now, but the war came closer as friends vanished into its jaws. Brother Roger went to Canada to train for his pilot's wings and returned a temporary, acting, probationary sub-lieutenant in the navy, flying archaic Swordfish torpedo-bombers. Now he was shore-based in Trinidad for a time. Mick English was in the navy serving on convoys to Russia. The Soviet Union had joined the war in 1941 when their German Allies attacked them and America had come in six months later when the Japanese attacked *them*.

The entry of Russia caused a remarkable turn-round by the British Communist Party. Having done their best to sabotage the war effort since 1939 they now decided it was a good thing after all. Britain was no longer alone and some of the tension went out of life. It seemed unlikely we should actually lose the war, even if we didn't look like winning it. In 1942, the Germans were overrunning Russia and the Japs marching almost unopposed through South-East Asia, but the threat of invasion receded and was unlikely to return. The Home Guard, who had been almost unarmed when invasion was likely in 1940, now received lots of weapons they would never use.

One day an Australian airman called at our house unexpectedly. He'd been a friend of Roger's who'd suggested he call on the family. He was invited to spend the rest of his leave in Baden Road and moved into the small front bedroom. Father looked forward to some excitement with the Australian and suggested expeditions to sample beer down town but he only wanted to stay home with the family and I played table skittles with him for hours. I couldn't understand why he wanted to waste his leave in such a dull fashion but mother said he had a wife and family back home, an explanation which meant nothing to me.

As the war became truly global, the streets of Leicester, normally the most insular of cities, became thronged with people in strange uniforms from abroad. In 1941, I saw what was only the second black person I had ever met, a cheerful young airman at the LMS station with a 'Jamaica' flash on his shoulder. Poles, Canadians, Australians, New Zealanders, even Frenchmen abounded, and then came the Americans, who arrived in force. There was some resentment of the Americans because of their prosperity and success with women but as individuals they were popular. They were generous, especially to children, to whom they distributed sweets freely (the sweet ration was a mere two ounces a week). They were also generous with their cigarettes and having just started smoking furtively, I was not above cadging an occasional Chesterfield myself.

The American soldiers and airmen patronised the dance-halls and pubs (where they found English beer revolting) and one or two played as guests at my tennis club. The brevity of their shorts attracted criticism from older members.

Tennis had now replaced cricket in the evenings. Thanks to the war, clubs were short of members and I was in the junior section of the Carisbrooke, a rather select club in the best suburb in the city, Stoneygate. All the men were in the forces and the club was held together by an elderly dug-out in Panama hat and blue blazer who used to go home and let us lock up ourselves. This allowed my irresponsible tendency full play and after a fight between boys with water jets from the hosepipes, which left No. 1 court awash, a curfew was imposed.

At school I was in the second team at cricket and rugby. At last I was getting more interested in rugby and showed some promise as a scrum-half. My old pal Jerry English, a year older, was stand-off for the First XV and showed every sign of being good enough to play for the Tigers when matches resumed after the war. Father and mother were keen for me to do well at their favourite game. Sometimes, as we played on the pitches near University Road, I could see the familiar black-coated, one-armed figure of father peering anxiously through the railings at me. The cemetery was opposite and he often passed on his way to put flowers on grandfather's grave. The proximity of the cemetery meant games might be interrupted for a funeral as some of the masters insisted on everyone standing to attention when a cortège passed.

There must still be a school team photograph in existence with me in it. I always remember the snobbish way the photographs were captioned. The masters were printed as 'Mr J. Smith' and the boys given their initials only, e.g. 'J. Brown'. But Bill Berridge, the groundsman, a former county cricketer in whose den by the boiler room I spent many happy hours yarning, was printed simply as 'Berridge'. However, as a former professional cricketer, he was probably used to such treatment.

At home, success at rugby was second only to academic prowess.

'Have you tried giving the ball a spin when you pass it out, Mick?' father would say at tea. 'I happened to be passing this afternoon and I saw your game and I wondered if you were ballooning the pass a bit? A pity you never saw Hayden Tanner when he played against the Tigers.'

The greatest pleasure I could give mother and father was to say I'd scored a try. Nearly forty years afterwards, when mother died, I came across a cutting she'd kept from the *Leicester Mercury* which mentioned me as a try-scorer for a local side in 1949. It was in an envelope proudly marked 'Michael's try'.

The Crusaders were being abandoned for the Air Training Corps. The school had its own flight, run by the science master 'Cissy' Cotterell, who suddenly blossomed forth in RAF officer's uniform. I was desperate to fly, like the rest of the class. We were taught simple navigation and aircraft recognition and marched around and paraded in blue uniforms. I also became secretary of the school engineering society and might have been a pillar of school society but for a tendency to play the fool. Thus when it was decided to hold a school camp in the holidays to help bring in the wartime harvest I was banned as on the entry form I entered my religion as Buddhist. Even then my sledgehammer humour was not appreciated.

In fact I did have a chance to help on a farm. A friend at the Crusaders knew a farmer in a village about seven miles from

Leicester, and the two of us spent a fortnight there. It was an old red-brick farm kept by a man who lived with his sister and was just about the meanest person I've ever met. We slept in tents in a wood until a storm flooded us out and in his charity he offered us the hospitality of his barn, rats and all. Despite the fact that food was plentiful on a farm, they fed us largely on boiled bacon, which we detested. We had a cold slice for breakfast, a sandwich for lunch and a hot slice with potatoes in the evening.

Two more of our friends were on an adjoining farm, which was a total contrast. In a merry farmhouse kitchen, the table groaning with good things, they ate huge meals under a large text on the wall: 'Christ is the unseen Guest at every meal in this house, the unseen Listener at every conversation.' Our employer hated his pious neighbour and blamed him if anything went wrong.

'Them horses from next door have broken down my fence again,' he moaned one day. Next day it was, 'Them thistles from next door have seeded all over my wheat and ruined the crop.' He even blamed the rabbits from next door for eating his cabbages. I often wondered what dreadful secret lay behind this feud. Had he been thwarted in love by his cheerful neighbour?

Despite it all, there were some experiences which are now remote history. I drove a shire horse and cart, or rather the horse went its accustomed way with me holding the reins. Any attempt to deviate from the normal route was impossible. The horse refused. The farmer had no tractor of his own but hired when he needed one and for harvest most of the village turned out to help, as in Victorian times. We had to wait for the reaping machine ('That man next door hired it ahead of me') and, while we waited, he and a labourer cleared a space for its first circuit round the outside of the field by hand, using scythes. After nearly cutting off someone's feet I learned to do this. An old village lady showed me how to plait straw to bind together the sheaves and 'shock' them, that is pile them up against each other with a passage through the middle for ventilation. When the reaping machine came, of course, the

The R101 over Leicester, 1930.

Father in the uniform of a Canadian Army corporal. before he lost his right arm

Uncle Fred and Aunt Nan, about 1930. Her cloche hat was typical of the period – so were Uncle's plus-fours and the car.

Grampy Smeath, the Man Who Might Have Nearly Bowled W. G. Grace, is on the right of the back row of this picture, taken when Uncle Fred drove him and Grandmother over to visit us on holiday at Weston-super-Mare in 1934. Fred is on the left with Roger and myself between them. Front row (left to right): Grandmother Green, from Leicester, Aunt Nan, Granny Smeath and my mother.

Father with Roger and myself (centre) on holiday at Burham-on-Sea. Note father's suit. He liked formal clothes, even on holiday, as did many of his generation.

What the well-dressed schoolbo[y]
wore in 1941. Myself (right) w[ith]
three friends from Wyggeston
School on the way home from a
Crusader holiday at Buxton. Ne[xt to]
me is John Bradshaw.

Roger in seaman's uniform
on his first leave home in
1941. He is flanked by
mother and myself. Taken
in the back garden at
Leicester.

This unfortunate youth is the autho[r, a]
trooper in the Royal Armoured Cor[ps.]
Note the shaven head, which exagg[erates]
the large ears. The sores on my face [have]
been painted out by the photograph[er.]
Taken on leave in Leicester, early in [1945.]

The 7th (Queen's Own) Hussars rugby team 1945–6, photographed outside the orderly room at the barracks at Palmanova. I am second from left on the back row.

Fooling around outside a tent near Trieste with a close friend, Trooper Mike Early, who wears a German Army leather belt round his overalls.

Self (hidden by melon) and Trooper Paddy Jackson, citizen of Eire and social member of the IRA.

Capt. Rodney Wilkinson's tank and cr[ew] somewhere between Trieste and Yugos[lavia]. L. to r.: myself, 'Mitch', Steve Henley [and] Ken Appleby.

The tank and crew again, this time cleaned up for the big parade through Trieste.

I am on the right of this group of young Education Corps sergeants enjoying themselves at the garrison swimming pool at Göttingen.

Precariously perched on an old German *Schülegleiter* before a training flight at the RAF Gliding Club. There was no fuselage and the pilot sat suspended in space.

I'm not sure where this picture of conviviality was taken, but I think it was the leave centre of Bad Hartzburg.

eniable evidence that
olism had set in
wing promotion to
ant. Cousin Joan is on
ight. The picture was
in 1947 at a party at the
rol Commission offices in
over, where she worked.

Wearing demob clothes on holiday in Devon soon after leaving the army. The expression shows what I thought of being out of khaki at last.

Buccleuch, who owned most of that part of Northampton-shire, and being chased off his land until he shouted he was a reporter from the *Northants Mercury*.

'He lowered his stick,' said Arthur, 'and shook my hand. He told me, "I have taken that newspaper for fifty years and any member of its staff is welcome here." Then he led me up to the Big House, where I interviewed him while his butler served double whiskies.'

One half-day, I took a trip on the train to London. I wanted to see Fleet Street, poor fool. My arrival in the Street of Adventure coincided with a flying-bomb attack. The flying bombs, or V1s, were pilotless aircraft launched from northern France and aimed vaguely in the direction of London. The control system was primitive and when the petrol ran out they simply fell out of the sky and exploded, so people on the ground were safe until the motor stopped. When the alert went I was impressed by the number of people scurrying around in steel helmets – things were not so urgent in Leicester or Northampton. Then a flying-bomb appeared high up in the direction of Blackfriars station. As everybody stared upwards its engine cut out and it started to plunge to the ground. The explosion sounded further away than I thought and I don't know where it landed, but the tale made a big impression when I returned to the office.

The war was looming closer in other ways. Brother Roger took part in the big Fleet Air Arm attack on the German battleship *Tirpitz*. Heavy casualties were expected but they caught the Germans unawares and only two aircraft were lost. Severe damage was inflicted. Roger, on leave, was remarkably reticent about it, except to say he'd learned that as long as you can see the tracer bullets you're all right. Only the ones coming at you are invisible. His carrier was now waiting to sail for the Pacific.

One by one the reporters' room emptied as boys went off to the forces to be replaced by even younger and spottier children. My special pal, Phil, who taught me to like Oscar Wilde, went into the navy. Roy Edgeley, with whom I used to take great walks into the countryside discussing What It Is All

About, joined the RAF (he's now Professor of Philosophy at Sussex University). In June 1944, the Allies invaded France and being 17½ I made enquiries about volunteering for the RAF, only to find there was a waiting list of stupendous proportions, most of whom never got into the air at all. The RAF was surfeited with air-crazy boys like myself. I knew the same was true of the Fleet Air Arm, so I tried the navy, but recruiting was temporarily suspended. There remained only the last resort of an Englishman, the British army.

I could, of course, have waited for call-up at 18, but that would mean no choice at all. By volunteering I hoped to have some influence on what I did. So back home in Leicester in August 1944 for my fortnight's summer holiday I went to the army section of the combined recruiting centre which was set up in a former shoe factory.

A genial, middle-aged major welcomed me with open arms. I wanted to join the Signal Corps, I said. I suggested the Signals because I knew Morse from my ATC training and it seemed less dangerous and uncomfortable than the infantry. Probably you met a nicer sort of person, too. It seems a lot of other boys had the same idea because recruiting to the Signals was closed, except for regular soldiers, who signed on for seven years. I wasn't *that* desperate. I suggested various other non-combatant corps but they were all mysteriously closed. It was impossible to volunteer for a soft job. The only choices open were the two most dangerous jobs in the army – infantry and tanks. It appeared I had a choice between being bayoneted or burned alive.

Most potential soldiers had a horror of the infantry because it was not only the most dangerous job but the worst paid and the most uncomfortable. My old pal Jerry English, now with the Rifle Brigade in Normandy, had warned me, 'Mick, whatever you do, don't go in the bloody infantry.' Not that I needed any reminding. The newspapers and cinema newsreels were full of the fighting in France. I decided to choose the tanks. They were just as dangerous but at least you didn't have to sleep in the mud or charge a machine-gun post with a bayonet. The major approved of my choice.

'Great set of lads in the Armoured Corps,' he said. 'You'll never regret it.'

They took me away for a short medical exam and then it was back to the major, who made me swear an oath to defend the King, his heirs and his successors, and kiss the Bible. Then he signed me up for the 'duration of hostilities'.

'You are now a soldier,' he said and showed me photographs of his son, who was an officer with a cushy job in an anti-aircraft unit in India. No infantry or tanks for *him*.

When I went home and told mother I'd joined the army she received the news calmly. It was a slight disappointment. But she belonged to a generation that was used to seeing its men off to war, and seeing them return in pieces, too. I think she was more worried about Roger, who'd already had longer than the average life expectancy of a naval pilot. Father approved of my decision to join the tanks. His own experiences had given him a horror of the infantry. 'Anything is better than the trenches,' he said.

Just before I went back to Northampton I saw Steve Andrews, my mathematics teacher at school. Old and worn out he was shuffling into the Coach and Horses on London Road. I told father how he'd aged and dad explained. 'His only son has just been reported killed in the RAF,' he said. 'It was in the *Mercury* last week.'

Back in Northampton to await call-up I bought my first piece of uniform – a khaki handkerchief, which I flourished all the time, hoping people would think I was a soldier on leave. Fired by my example, Michael Field, another young reporter and a special friend, also volunteered for the Armoured Corps. A few weeks later, the War Office sent me a three-shilling postal order. It was a day's pay in advance, the 1944 equivalent of the King's Shilling. There were also instructions to report to the Officer Commanding, Bovington Camp, Dorset, on 18 October 1944, and a rail warrant. I was just over 17½ and everybody expected the war to last for at least another two years.

CHAPTER TEN

14487348 Green

An old school chum, Alec Ford, who lived near us, joined up the same day as me, although he was a year older. We'd been to Miss Cooke's Dancing School together and served in many a Second XV battle at the Wyggeston. But Alec was more a credit to the school than myself, having set a new record in the mile and taken his Higher Certificate with glowing results. Now he is Professor of Economics at Warwick University and I am godfather to his children. That is the second teenage friend of mine to become a professor. Alec was posted to Northumberland and left on an overnight LMS train. As we said goodbye there was the inevitable feeling we might never meet again and in fact it was to be nearly three and a half years before we did so.

I returned to the Midland Station next morning to catch the 6.30 a.m. to London. Father insisted on seeing me off, which meant being roused more or less in the middle of the night. He was not a man to catch a train by the skin of his teeth and on most family holidays we arrived in time to get the preceding service. The habit has transferred itself to me. To this day, I never fly to Dublin, Paris or Edinburgh without arriving at the airport as the last call goes up for the flight before.

At St Pancras I took a tube to Waterloo. I'd only been to London three times before – once on holiday with Uncle Will in Osterley, the day Warsaw was bombed in 1939 and once on my day trip from Northampton. The train from Waterloo to

Wool, in Dorset, station for Bovington Camp, was crammed. Not just uncomfortably full, like a peacetime train at Christmas, but bulging with servicemen and women. They lay on luggage racks and filled even the guard's van. I felt sorry for the service girls, in particular the ATS. The stupid War Office had issued them with the same canvas kitbags as the men and it was pitiful to see them trying to drag these great clumsy things about, trailing them through the dirt and quite unable to lift them aboard the train. The men helped as best they could, but they might be burdened with full marching kit and rifle, steel helmet and gas mask.

Pressed like a sardine in the corridor, I stood all the way to Dorset, holding a little cardboard suitcase and feeling more and more apprehensive as the train got nearer to Wool. On arrival it emptied. Several hundred soldiers of both sexes poured out and either clambered into lorries or walked up the hill to Bovington Camp, which stood isolated in the middle of the heath. A small group of young men in civilian clothes were left behind – the new recruits. A corporal with a cane walked up and herded us on to lorries. After we reached camp they divided us into huts, gave us a meal, and issued everyone with a number. I remember mine to this day, more than forty years later. It was 14487348 and the 144 indicated I was a volunteer, not that the strength of the British Army had reached 14 million. A nervous cup of tea in the NAAFI (canteen), aware of the mocking glances of the real soldiers in uniform, and then we were ordered to bed.

Next moment it seemed I was awoken by somebody brutally banging the end of my two-tier bunk with a stick and shouting at me. It was the corporal. I shot out of bed, crashing five feet to the floor in my haste, fearful I'd be punished on my first day for not getting up at reveille. I needn't have worried. The corporal had roused us half-an-hour before reveille to make sure we would be ready in time. As reveille was at six this meant it was 5.30 a.m., still pitch dark and a bitterly cold, drizzly morning. We 'marched' in chaos to breakfast and returned to be divided into squads and transferred to new huts. They kitted us out, issued paybooks and blankets and made us

125

tie up our civilian clothes in brown paper parcels for sending home.

At the end of the day the sergeant-major addressed us and said, 'You've left your mother's apron strings behind. I don't want to hear any snivelling. You're men now. In six months' time you'll be fighting Jerries. Now get back to your huts and get that new equipment clean. I want to see my face in those brasses.'

Bovington was the home of the tanks, where the Royal Tank Regiment had been born in 1916, and one of the first monsters stood on a plinth in the camp. The Primary Training Wing for recruits was situated in the old original wooden huts, unchanged since 1916. They were named after animals and birds for some reason and I was in Buzzard. The day began with reveille at six. Like most soldiers I shall never forget the horror of training-camp reveilles. Tired though I was, I was usually woken by apprehension or cold about 5.30 and lay shivering in the unheated and unventilated hut waiting for the agony to begin. The long room was pitch-dark and the windows boarded up for black-out. I was in an upper bunk. For those below was the added fear of waking up covered in urine if the soldier above wet his bed, a permanent hazard in the army. In service units the man above might be drunk; in training regiments the cause was usually the youth of the recruit, who at 17 or 18 might not have outgrown childish habits.

That period so much praised by poets, the first sign of day, came about quarter-to-six when the loudspeaker suddenly became live, as the orderly sergeant switched on the public address system in the camp office. He was not pleased at having to get up so early himself and muttering, blaspheming and cursing could be heard *sotto voce*, together with persistent coughing as he lit up a Woodbine. Occasionally he could be heard groaning 'bloody hell' or 'Christ' to himself. At six he cleared his throat with a noise like somebody being sick and shouted: 'Attention! Attention! Reveille! Reveille! Get up! Get up!' With a ghastly, rasping cough he then switched over to music. This was always the American Forces Network, who played Bing Crosby singing 'Would You Rather Swing on a Star' thirty times a day.

There were no pyjamas or sheets and we slept under the regulation four blankets, ingeniously folded to get the maximum thickness between us and the cold, kit piled on top for extra warmth. For night attire we wore the uncomfortable, hairy and collarless shirts issued to rankers in those days. As soon as reveille was announced we leaped out of bed and fought for a shave. King's Regulations insisted every man must shave every morning. Unfortunately the army provided only six wash-basins between 80 men, so we crowded three deep around them, occasionally shaving someone else's face by mistake. To make sure conditions were as vile as possible the army made it an offence to shave at night, because of the risk of getting impetigo off their filthy blankets. Luckily I was too young to need a shave every day. In fact I'd had a special shaving lesson from father just before I joined up, so I'd know what to do.

At 6.30, bleeding from a thousand cuts, we mustered outside in the rain or frost and marched to breakfast. This often contained a special meat known only to the British army: liver, full of enormous tubes. I have never seen liver like it since. It followed me round the army, right through my service. Rumour said it wasn't liver but slices of something more private. This was fried until hard as leather, left to cool, and served on a cold plate with a spoonful of congealing fat. We also had porridge without sugar, bread and a scrape of butter, and tea. There was no choice of food. But it was warm in the cookhouse and we were young and for 15 blessed minutes you could put your numbed hands round the great pint mug of tea until the corporal marched you back to the hut again.

Back in the hut there was cleaning and sweeping to do. The hut might be freezing, with a coat of ice inside the windows, but we dared not light the stoves because the army insisted they must be cleaned and polished with black-lead before parade every morning. There was no time to do this, and get rid of the ash, so they remained unused except at weekends. Blankets had to be folded in a special way and squared up mathematically, with kit laid out on top, the spare boots sole upwards to show they did not need repair. Some units made soldiers polish the soles of their spare boots but we were spared this. Razor and mess tins would be examined for rust and it was an offence if any was found. At 7.30 we paraded for a day of drill, arms instruction, marching, P.T. and being shouted at.

Not surprisingly the first desertion came after only three days. A thin, dark chap named Lewis, he'd been boasting in the train from Waterloo about what he was going to achieve in the army. Alas, it was whistling in the dark and, on the second day, as the squad lined up for the first inoculations and vaccinations, he fainted at the thought of the needle.

'Drag him in here quickly,' shouted the Medical Officer as Lewis heeled over in the queue, and inoculated him while unconscious.

Lewis simply ran away, taking no kit. At the time we hadn't been issued with proper battledress and were wearing denim overalls, but he did have boots, beret, gaiters and a greatcoat and dressed in these he caught the train from Wool to seek his home in London. He never had a chance, of course. Waterloo was alive with Military Police and they asked for his pass. He didn't have one and was promptly arrested.

Back at camp, rumours about his fate were rife. He had been shot by a firing-squad for desertion in wartime ('There's a special place in the Guard's Barracks where they do it against a wall'); he was doing five years' field punishment in the dreaded Aldershot military prison; he was being given a compassionate discharge; he'd eluded them all and gone on the run. But two Military Policemen brought him back after three days and he was charged with being absent without leave.

The punishment was lenient – three days' stoppage of pay by Royal Warrant (as they phrased it officially) and a severe reprimand. It was no good, though. The wretched Lewis couldn't face the army and took to his bunk with a mysterious back disorder. He simply lay there all day, staring at the ceiling and hardly talking. The N.C.O.s ignored him. Occasionally somebody brought him food but otherwise he remained like a sick sheep, the outcast of the flock.

One day he vanished. He was lying on his bunk at first parade and when we came back an hour later to change into

P.T. kit he wasn't there. The N.C.O.s refused to enlighten us. 'He's been posted,' was all they said. We never heard of him again, although the platoon was full of theories.

'They come for you when nobody's about,' said the platoon alarmist. 'They come and take you away to a special punishment centre.' I think perhaps Lewis went to hospital. I hope.

Apart from him, nobody succumbed. The unit was specially for Armoured Corps volunteers so all were young and motivated, to use current jargon. A surprisingly large number were public schoolboys and included two Old Etonians in James Hay and Dickie Davidson. That was the unique thing about the wartime services, the mixture of types to be found in the ranks, and I met more Old Etonians (five) in the army as a trooper or private than I have met since, in more exalted circles. I also met more lorry drivers and fitters. The two Etonians made an instant impression of supreme self-confidence. They were afraid of nobody, not even the N.C.O.s. Working-class recruits were suspicious of authority but obeyed it. Middle-class lads had been brought up to both obey and respect it (it was a long time before they could stop us calling even the corporals 'sir' and saluting them). But these boys had been brought up to *be* authority. They didn't answer back. They didn't need to. The N.C.O.s, themselves experts in judging degrees of power, knew instinctively.

After an afternoon of specially severe bullying by the sergeant on the heath, James Hay once threw a clod of earth at him when his back was turned. We gasped in horror. The whole squad was petrified with fear as the sergeant raved at us. 'I know who it was and I will break him. Who was it? If I don't find out in five seconds the whole lot of you will be court-martialled. I know who it was, so don't think you can hide . . .' James remained calm and impassive.

'Weren't you scared?' we asked when we got back to the hut, having run all the way as a punishment.

'What of him? You must be joking,' came the reply.

I suppose that's why Etonians used to dominate any British Cabinet, even with a Labour government.

Our immediate C.O. was Desmond Walter-Ellis, a tall, gangling captain in the Sherwood Foresters, who was unfit for active service because of a back injury. Later he became a well-known actor, appearing in the West End and on films and TV. By a coincidence his ATS girlfriend was to be my secretary twenty years later and marry one of my chums. He spent most of his time organising the Bovington Camp Dramatic Society and playing all the best parts. A group of us went to see him in *Rope* and had to admit he was very good. He was pleasant and amiable, if somewhat aloof, but unfortunately we saw little of him. Day-to-day instruction was in the hands of a swaggering little sergeant and the corporals of the permanent camp staff. They bullied and chivvied us unmercifully but without much malice and we got to know the corporals quite well. It was Corporal Wilson, our own platoon N.C.O., who gave me my first practical lesson in sexual morality. Knowing he was married, we ragged him about being seen with an ATS girl.

'Listen, son,' he said, 'it doesn't matter who you see me with, my prick belongs to my wife. That's what the marriage ceremony means.'

While the Archbishop of Canterbury might disagree with Corporal Wilson about the meaning of the marriage service, I think it was a much better summing-up of sexual morality than the vague wufflings of my old headmaster, with his talk of mystic communions. Corporal Wilson was lucky to be alive. He'd been fired on at a range of a few feet by a German machine-gun in North Africa and hit in the arm. But he survived to be posted home and tell the tale, doubtless with embellishments, one of which was that he was so near the German he could have reached out and grabbed the barrel of his machine-gun. At least his stories made a change from the First World War anecdotes I'd heard all my life.

The chief agent of torment was the R.S.M., a huge, red-faced man from the Guards, with a row of medals on his chest. Every morning he took us for an hour's drill on the vast barrack square. His favourite phrase was, 'Strike those rifles!' It was an effort to make our rifle-drill crisp and smart by slapping the weapons sharply as we ordered or sloped arms.

130

'Strike those rifles!' he bellowed. 'If you break one I'll buy you a new one. But my money's safe. Strike those rifles!'

One of our squad, however, actually did succeed in breaking his rifle. He struck it hard, as ordered, and a bit fell off and tinkled to the ground. I think it was the brass butt-plate. It was too much for everybody and we all burst into laughter, which was quelled by the sight of the sergeant-major swelling like a turkey-cock in rage. He advanced majestically to the hapless soldier and said in a low voice, which would carry about five hundred yards, 'If I thought you'd done that deliberately, son, I would have . . . I would have . . .' words failed him – 'been somewhat displeased.' His powers returned, and he added: 'I would have cut off your balls, son. WHAT WOULD I HAVE DONE?'

This rhetorical question was one of the great stock tricks of drill N.C.O.s. A favourite wheeze was to insult the soldier, and then make him repeat the abuse, thus:

'You stupid, silly little man. What are you?'

'A stupid, silly little man, sergeant.'

'Right. Don't you forget it.'

Eventually, we could translate the shouted commands, which bore no relation to normal English. Thus, although the sergeant-major would refer to a rifle by its proper name in conversation, as part of an order it became a thing called a Hipe.

'Platoon . . . platoon . . . wait for it . . . platoon, slope Hipes! Present Hipes! Order Hipes!'

Mercifully, the R.S.M.'s bark was worse than his bite. Jim Chamberlain, who slept in the bunk underneath me, was scrubbing some steps when the R.S.M. walked up them. In his eagerness to stand to attention he jumped up and knocked a bucket of soapy water over the R.S.M.'s mirror-like boots. 'Take it easy, son,' was all the R.S.M. said.

An old regular soldier, the R.S.M. claimed to have been an intimate friend of Col. T. E. Lawrence, otherwise Lawrence of Arabia, Trooper Shaw, Aircraftman Ross, legendary figure of World War One and author of *The Seven Pillars of Wisdom*. Lawrence, in one of his periods of self-abasement, was a

131

trooper in the Tanks Corps at Bovington during the thirties, in the same way as he'd joined the RAF as an aircraftman.

''E would come on parade in the morning dressed in filthy overalls,' the R.S.M. said. 'But of course everbody knew 'e was Colonel Lawrence and said nothing. Then one day we 'ad a new second lieutenant to inspect the troop and 'e stops before Lawrence and 'e says, "What's all this, my man, you are filthy." Naturally, we was all horrified at him speaking to Colonel Lawrence like that and the sergeant tried to warn him, but Lawrence replied, "Sorry, sir, I was up late last night." "Up late?" says the officer. "And may I ask what you were doing?" And Lawrence replies, cool as a cucumber, "I was translating a chapter of one of my books into Arabic, sir."'

The R.S.M. claimed to have warned Lawrence of his death. Lawrence, who lived at Cloud Cottage, near the camp (we passed it on our route marches), was killed when his motor cycle crashed trying to avoid an errand boy. 'I told 'im, "You won't come to no good on that motor cycle, Mr Lawrence," said the sergeant-major, "not the way you ride it." But he just laughed. He was scared of nothing.'

Gradually, almost against our will, we became soldiers, although those of us under 18 were still graded as young soldiers, which entitled us to half a pint of milk every day, just like schoolboys. If somebody shouted 'You!' we would automatically snap to attention; our rifles, so difficult and clumsy to work with at first, became as familiar as a favourite cricket bat; like dogs we responded automatically to the appropriate stimulus, whether it was a shouted order or a jammed Bren gun.

Recruits weren't allowed out of camp for a fortnight and social life was restricted to a spam roll (no butter) and a cup of tea in the huge YMCA by the square, or a sausage in the NAAFI, but on the third weekend the troops were adjudged smart enough for a precious day pass. I went to Bournemouth with Jim from the bunk below. We caught a train from Wool and drank a pint of Bass in a small hotel (Jim had worked in a brewery in Birmingham and appreciated good beer). I was still under 18 and not old enough to be in a pub but a uniform was a magic passport. Then we had lunch – rabbit stew and lucky to get it in wartime. Afterwards the two of us listened to a concert by the Bournemouth Symphony Orchestra and walked miles along the cliffs and beaches, covered in barbed wire against the vanished threat of invasion. The pier was closed and blown up halfway along so enemy troops couldn't use it as a landing-stage.

Tea was taken at the inevitable YMCA and then another glass of beer before joining the packed crowd of troops at Central Station. While waiting for the overcrowded train, we drank tea out of jam-jars from a WVS stall on the platform, run by a little old lady. On the way back in the train everyone in the compartment sang 'Bless 'em All'.

I couldn't buy a day like that now for ten thousand pounds.

Although as private soldiers we earned only a guinea a week (£1.05), I don't remember being short of money. Even the pitiful wages were raided. Sixpence a week (2½p) was deducted for barrack-room damages, whether the barracks were damaged or not. Another sixpence was deducted for haircut, whether the hair was cut or not. It was shorn by the regimental barbers under a big notice, 'The barber has orders to cut all hair to the regimental style'. This meant shaving it off. They treated customers with all the consideration of a New Zealand sheep-shearer and pleas from arty-crafty recruits to leave a little at the sides were brutally ignored. Other odd sums might be deducted from pay for loss of kit, etc.

Soldiers were expected to cringe for their guinea and a lesson was devoted to teaching the squad how to parade for their pay. The soldier marched in when his name was called and banged to attention in front of the pay clerk and an officer. The clerk then doled out his few shillings. In theory the soldier was expected to check it, but in practice he was told off unless it was immediately scooped up and thrust into his pocket. He then had to bellow, 'Nineteen shillings and sixpence pay correct, sir,' salute, turn right and march out.

The army's capacity for making simple things difficult never ceased to astonish. Even a window couldn't be cleaned without shouting and stamping. At least the formalities of pay parade led to some cash in hand, although recruits seemed to have enough money, mainly because there was nothing to spend it on and we were too young to have developed expensive tastes. A pint of beer was an evening out; I had never drunk spirits in my life and in any case we weren't allowed them.

Absence of sexual desire was a strange phenomenon of these first weeks. This was put down to a cunning wheeze by the army, who were rumoured to doctor the tea with bromide to sedate troops and make them more docile. The Great Bromide Rumour was one of the most persistent of the war and the most widely believed. Yet nobody knew for certain if there was any truth in it. In hundreds of cookhouse fatigues I never saw any bromide put in tea or porridge. While potato-peeling at Bovington, I scoured the cookhouse for traces of bromide, looking for a huge bag labelled BROMIDE – OTHER RANKS FOR THE USE OF, but found no clues. The cooks, who could have settled the whole controversy, were always evasive when asked.

'There's no telling what goes into army tea, mate,' they'd reply.

The cooks probably got a kick out of being mysterious. Thus the fantasy went unchecked and plenty of men will swear they have actually seen bromide shovelled out with a spoon.

However, lack of sexual desire was real enough. An uninhibited group from one hut sat round in a circle trying to get an erection, urged on by their comrades' erotic suggestions. Not surprisingly, they all failed. The male organ is a petulant beast at the best of times and does not like performing in public. I'm sure the real reason for the sexual hang-up was hard work and fear. We were on the go from 6.0 a.m. to lights out at 10 p.m., frantically changing from P.T. kit to battledress and to denims as the occasion demanded. In the evenings we had weapons to clean, kit to polish, fatigues to do, letters to write and sleep to catch up on. There was never enough sleep.

Men lived in permanent fear of punishment. Most of the crimes were invented by the army, which had a fiendish trick of making it impossible to obey its own regulations. Typical was the rule that ordered daily shaving and provided six wash-basins for 80 men. Another lunatic regulation said one pair of boots should be highly-polished and the spare pair dubbined. Any fool who turned up on parade in dubbined boots, however, was simply asking for punishment. At times we got the impression the War Office was staffed by people who set out to make life as difficult as possible for the private soldier.

The bromide rumour was only one of many, seized on avidly by barrack-room lawyers. There was a whole series of legends about soldiers' 'rights'. There was someone in every squad who'd advise, 'Don't do it, mate, they've no right to make you do it. It's in King's Regs.' In particular I remember a rumour which said every soldier was entitled to his dinner. 'Your breakfast is a parade and your dinner is a right' ran the fairy-story. Despite encouragement from many a khaki barrister I never dared test this and missed dozens of dinners in the army without complaint. I'm not sorry. The military prisons were full of soldiers who'd stood out for their rights. One difficulty was that soldiers were refused access to King's Regulations, yet were supposed to know them. In the face of this, most of us gave up and assumed we had no rights at all and did whatever the army ordered. I think that was probably what they wanted.

Those who did penetrate to King's Regulations (perhaps some office clerk) told a fascinating story of the contents, most of which were compiled in the previous century, such as the section relating to disobedience of an order. The example quoted was of a man who threw down his rifle on parade and said, 'You may do what you will, I will soldier no more.' He was, of course, immediately to be manacled and dragged away by two comrades. There were many times when we wondered if we dare follow the mythical soldier of KRs and tell the sergeant-major, 'You may do what you will, I will soldier no more.'

The army was much criticised during the war for putting round pegs in square holes, professors of Greek cleaning latrines or skilled engineers rotting at coal dumps. In response to this, the War Office decreed psychological and aptitude tests for all recruits. The squad were interviewed by a bored officer from the Medical Corps who gave us all a bicycle pump in pieces and we had to beat the clock in putting it together. This was the mechanical aptitude test.

I'd never realised a bicycle pump was so complicated before. The room resounded to cursing and swearing as men struggled to get them working. Eventually I got mine together but it wouldn't blow any air out. Others gave off great wheezing and farting noises. A huge Irish lout named Paddy, who'd been a railway porter, broke the shaft of his pump trying to force it down the barrel. Out of thirty pumps, I doubt if half-a-dozen worked. Yet all passed the test. It was my first lesson that army tests were not designed to fail people but to pass them. Otherwise they'd be short of men all the time. Not that the army is alone in this. Thirty years later I took a teacher-training course on which 99 per cent of the students passed, including some of the worst teachers that ever disgraced a classroom.

During those early days I learned something which proved a permanent benefit throughout life. At the time, I was covering my belt with blanco, smearing a block of the filthy stuff with a wet brush to produce a khaki-coloured paste and plastering it all over the webbing equipment. This was known as 'cleaning' the belt, straps and packs, although covering it with dirt seemed a strange way of doing so. In true army fashion, the penalties for not blancoing were dire but no facilities were provided and it was forbidden in the washrooms, so I was kneeling on a path outside the hut in a thin drizzle of rain with a mess tin full of water. There were about ten of us shivering there when one of the soldiers, a tall, rather amusing chap called Mike Luton, started to sing a song. It was a rude version of a popular hit on the wireless at the time, 'Poor Little Angeline' and it was quite the most revolting song I have ever heard in my life.

I devoted the next 24 hours to learning it, all 14 verses. It served me well later, in many a tight social corner, from Bovington to Trieste and Hamburg, and in civilian life at countless occasions. It earned me free meals from grateful army cooks who asked me to sing it and once got me off a serious charge. I was found dozing on guard in Germany but, when the sergeant recognised me, he said, 'I won't say anything about this if you write out all the verses of "Angeline" for me to sing at the sergeants' mess party.' But that was in the future. Then I'd no idea how useful it would become. It just seemed a good way of forgetting the army for a few minutes.

They wouldn't trust us as sentries yet, but we went on fire picquet. The orderly sergeant read out a long list of orders which sounded as if they'd been compiled in the nineteenth century (they probably had). One clause said, 'If any Government property is seen to be blazing the fire picquet will immediately surround it' or words to that effect. The sergeant had just read out something about air raids ('When the alert sounds the fire picquet will immediately put on steel helmets and double to the guardroom') when the air-raid sirens sounded. We started to rush to the guardroom but the sergeant stopped us with a shout.

'Come back, you horrible lot,' he roared. 'I haven't finished yet.'

An aircraft, probably German, droned overhead as he ploughed through the rest of the instructions and then inspected us. By now the camp could have been in flames. Eventually he finished and we rushed off to air-raid stations just as the all-clear went.

Fire picquet provided me with the classic army dilemma. I was listed in orders for fire duty; simultaneously I was down to play rugby. I approached the sergeant, who said the penalty for not parading for fire picquet was death. I went to an officer and he said the penalty for not playing rugby when ordered to do so was also death (I may be exaggerating slightly). Eventually I think I paraded for fire picquet and went straight off to play rugby, where unfortunately the sirens sounded just as I received a pass, so I ran away to the guardroom still carrying the ball.

Meanwhile training went on. We threw live grenades and they taught us to fire rifles and machine-guns. I was a good shot with a Bren and became top marksman in the platoon. We dug trenches, cooked pitiful little meals on fires of twigs, fixed bayonets, marched 15 miles and repelled gas attacks. In these activities we were supervised by a maniacal sergeant, a strutting little bantam cock of a man, whose megalomania took a theatrical turn at times. His favourite occupation was to take us on a march in which every known military disaster was simulated.

As soon as the squad were out of sight of camp and marching through the desolate waste of Wool Heath, the sergeant would vanish. Suddenly he would reappear from behind a tree, shouting, 'Gas! Gas! I am a cloud of chlorine! What are you going to do? Are you just going to stand there? Get those gas masks out! Too late, you're all dead. You have died horribly.'

The column disintegrated into chaos as we struggled with gas masks and gas capes and, when some sort of order had been restored, we lurched on, wearing those World War One type of masks. But not for long. The next thing would be a shower of stones from behind a hedge and a maniacal shout: 'Grenades! Grenades! You have just run into a fucking German ambush! It's no use trying to take cover, you are all dead! You have been blown to pieces because you wouldn't keep a look-out!'

These crises always ended with us being 'all dead'. The sergeant would never admit anyone could come out alive from his ambushes. There could be up to half-a-dozen crises on the march and we became weary of unslinging our rifles, hurling ourselves behind the hedge and optimistically firing blanks in the general direction of our tormentor, who could simulate anything from shellfire to a Stuka attack. Aircraft were his forte and it was most impressive to see him leap up waving his arms and crying, 'Aircraft! Aircraft! I am a Stuka! You are all dead, I tell you.' With which he would vanish and reappear from some other vantage point, like a pantomine demon, with a new horror: 'I am a tank! I am a tank! No, you fool, it's no use firing your rifle at me, I am a tank, I have six inches of armour plating . . .' Sometimes men became confused and put gas masks on when attacked by aircraft or threw grenades when assaulted with gas.

Usually we returned from these expeditions with a few

genuine casualties. We were always stabbing ourselves with bayonets, burnt with blank cartridges, deafened by the thunderflashes used to simulate explosions or spraining ankles. Frequently the squad would hobble back to camp looking as if it had just returned from an attack on the Siegfried Line.

A big problem, which dogged my army career, was a tendency to burst out laughing on parade. Laughter among young men is highly infectious and soon the whole squad would be a heaving mass. (How sad that now I am older this tendency has been replaced by a predilection for bursting into tears.) It was never quite certain what would set it off – anything from someone farting in the ranks to a peculiar order.

Once a few of us were fooling around before the officer came and the sergeant-major separated the guilty men from the rest for punishment. When the officer arrived the sergeant-major addressed us: 'Men-who-were-laughing-and-skylarking-on-parade ... men-who-were-laughing-and-skylarking-on-parade ... wait for it ... slope arms. Men-who-were-laughing-and-skylarking ...' But by now we were helplessly doubled up with mirth. Not even the threat of death could have stopped the men who were laughing and skylarking on parade from laughing until the tears came. They did come later. I seem to remember shovelling about ten tons of coal next Sunday morning.

The army taught us plenty of things unwittingly, such as comradeship, or 'mucking in', as the phrase went. When I lost my purse, containing all of ten shillings, Corporal Wilson organised a search-party and when that failed had a collection among the lads to replace the money. Once my razor, laid out on the bunk for inspection, vanished. 'Some bastard has swiped it,' I thought bitterly but a friend returned it that evening. It was rusty and he'd pinched it to save the sergeant noticing. Better an absent razor than a rusty one. It wasn't all sweetness and light, of course. There were the usual tensions one would get among any group of young men and splits according to social class or character. But we rubbed along well enough. In that I was lucky. Some young soldiers were not so fortunate and found themselves in barrack-rooms dominated by bullies and thugs.

As special troops, destined for the Royal Armoured Corps, the preliminary training lasted eight, instead of the usual six, weeks. At the end, one misty day in December 1944, they marched us down to Wool Station and sent us to Farnborough in Hampshire. I never did understand why we weren't posted to the tank training unit at Bovington. Four hundred miles away, in the Ardennes, Von Runstedt was just about to begin his big offensive. A little nearer, in Holland, my childhood playmate Jerry English was in a Bren gun carrier approaching a German outpost when he was killed by machine-gun fire. He was initially reported wounded and his mother never stopped hoping he might be alive.

CHAPTER ELEVEN

'A crack at the Hun'

After eight weeks in the middle of Wool Heath, we found Farnborough highly civilised. Two pubs and the Rex Cinema were passed as we marched from the station along the A30. The barracks were next to the Royal Aircraft Establishment, the experimental airfield. I went back recently and the site is now a shopping centre, but the old convent used for wireless instruction still stands. The Rex Cinema has gone, along with Deanna Durbin and Phyllis Calvert, but the pubs are still there, much tarted-up, and the old NAAFI is now a library.

At first sight, the barracks looked more promising than the windswept huts of Bovington but we soon found that the army had managed to make them hideously uncomfortable. The proportion of washbasins was even smaller and instead of stoves there were fireplaces, but these had cunningly been painted white, so it was inadvisable to use them except at weekends when there was time to clean them. There was also an enormous coal-bunker which had to be black-leaded before breakfast every day. Instead of two-tier bunks we had single bedsteads made of cast-iron which folded in half during the day. They had three iron slats with gaps for the wind to whistle through and mattresses were the infamous 'biscuits', three separate pieces about two feet square. These came apart during the night and the draught howled up through the thin blankets. It was bitterly cold that winter of 1944 and we shivered and thought of the poor devils in action, huddled in slit trenches in Holland or France.

The commanding officer was Major Courage, a member of the well-known Hampshire brewing family. At the time I would have described him as a cheery old soul, but I suppose he was only about 40. He had one leg, having lost the other in North Africa. His artificial limb was made of aluminium and gave a lot of trouble. Occasionally it broke down on parade, and then he leaned on a sergeant's shoulder while word was sent to the workshops for a fitter, who rolled up the Major's trouser leg and got to work with a hammer. The trouble was caused by a rivet dropping out, apparently.

The Major was kind and much liked. He sometimes said, 'I know you chaps are aching to have a crack at the Hun,' but in fact enthusiasm was diminishing as the prospect got nearer.

Discipline was strict at Farnborough. They had fiendish devices such as 'double days' when everybody had to run about the camp. But it was good to be only a hundred yards from civilisation and the Rex Cinema. Two or three even enrolled at Mrs Jackson's Dancing School just down the A30 towards Frimley Green. We had no shoes and clumped around doing the slow waltz in army boots (or 'ammunition boots' as the military called them for some reason). What our poor partners suffered cannot be described. Those girls made a real contribution to the war effort. The fleshpots of Aldershot were near, too, but the town was placed out of bounds after Canadian troops mutinied. The Canadians were placed in vile, Victorian barracks and had been rotting there a long time. They had plenty of money and complained shopkeepers swindled them. At any rate, they rioted and burned part of the town and we could see the smoke from our barracks a couple of miles away, while lorry-loads of Military Police drove along the A30.

London was not much more than 30 miles away and sometimes I sneaked off on Sundays to see Uncle Will at Osterley. I would hitch a lift, perhaps switching lorries at Bert's Café at Bagshot, then one of the great military hitch-hiking junctions. Lorry drivers were good to soldiers; one even treated me to a meal at a transport café. Bus conductors were generous too, and in Leicester female conductresses rarely took a fare from a serviceman. The railways were understandably less open-handed and much energy was devoted by the military to avoiding fares. Whole cottage industries sprang up in many barracks with skilled craftsmen splitting tickets in half with razor-blades or disguising Woodbine packets as tickets.

My own feeble effort at deceiving the railways nearly ended in disaster. Taking a platform ticket at Waterloo, I travelled to Frimley, about a mile from camp, and jumped out of the carriage on the side opposite the platform, thinking to escape that way. Having been brought up among the steam lines of Leicestershire, I forgot about the electric rail until I was in mid-air. How I missed it I shall never know. This near-escape from electrocution had a salutary effect. I have never tried to cheat the railways since. The Crusaders would rightly have put it down to a Sign from Above.

One Sunday at Uncle Will's, cousin Joan took me for a walk in Osterley Park with her dog and told me of her romance with her German soldier, Werner. After war began, they managed to communicate through mutual friends in Denmark but once the Germans overran that country in 1940 all contact ceased. For four years she had remained faithful, not even knowing whether Werner was dead or alive and just hoping it would all come right in the end. Millions of others were waiting like that all over the world. Even now, the war looked like lasting at least another year and when it finished there was no guarantee they would be reunited. There was talk of 'teaching the Hun a lesson this time' and they might not be allowed to meet, assuming Werner survived or was not already dead.

Meanwhile Joan was in the women's section of the Home Guard, her brother Arthur was just about to be sent to Germany in the artillery and her sister Joyce was an officer in the Signals. It was all rather crazy.

While having lunch at Uncle Will's I heard my first V2. I'd experienced V1s, the flying bombs, but the V2s were different. These were rockets fired from Germany and arriving in England from outer space. There was no defence except to bomb the launching sites and they arrived without warning. I was just eating the last of my custard when there was an almighty explosion somewhere in West London.

'That's another V2,' said uncle. 'They can't give any air-raid warning. I thought it was time for another. There was one on Croydon yesterday. Forty dead, so someone was telling me. I should think that one fell in Chiswick, judging by the sound. They can't aim them, you know, they just fire them off indiscriminately. I think it's terrible. I hope the RAF bomb the swine good and proper.'

I wondered if Joan was embarrassed by this but she didn't seem to mind. She rode her unfortunate situation quite calmly. Although she loved a German soldier, she wanted her own country to win as much as anybody else. She made no secret of Werner's existence and as far as I know nobody ever attacked her on the subject. After the walk in Osterley Park, Joan showed me photographs of her life in Berlin, smiling happy groups of Germans, one with his arm round her, who was Werner. Tall and blond, he looked a nice chap. It did occur to me, though, that I was probably the only soldier in the British army who was spending Sunday afternoon looking at snaps of Berlin.

At Farnborough, we began to feel more like soldiers than civilians in battledress. Our ranks were changed from private to trooper and we proudly wore Royal Armoured Corps badges in our black berets. Even so, those under 18 were still given a half-pint of milk every morning.

We had our first leave and I swaggered about Leicester in my best uniform trying to impress the girls. A studio photo was taken which was so awful that mother didn't like to display it. It portrayed a shaven-headed youth, his face covered in sores, gawping beneath a beret which didn't fit. The photographer had tried to paint out the sores on my face, which made it even worse. It contrasted sadly with the picture of my brother looking handsome and smart in the uniform of a naval sub-lieutenant. Roger was on his way to the Pacific in the carrier *Indefatigable*.

We were at last trusted to do sentry-duty and part of the beat covered the perimeter of the airfield next door. This was full of secret planes, including the new jets. Strange shapes with no propellers flickered overhead as we trained. Captured German aircraft lined the tarmac. Because of our proximity to the airfield, sentries were given live ammunition. I took my duties seriously, challenging bushes and tree stumps fiercely in the dark with rifle at the ready. Eventually a dim shape approached along the road. It was a drunk corporal on a bicycle.

'Halt! Who goes there?' I cried in the approved challenge.

Instead of replying 'Friend,' he shouted 'Fuck off' and cycled past.

I cocked my rifle. 'Halt or I fire,' I screamed in accordance with orders.

'Fuck off,' he repeated over his shoulder, cycling away.

It was one of those crossroads in life which would decide whether I was a boy or a man. I decided to be a boy and stood there feeling an idiot as he disappeared into the night. I unloaded my rifle and made up my mind to say nothing. Was he a cunning German spy disguised as a drunk corporal? With hindsight I believe he *was* a drunk corporal, almost certainly a member of the permanent camp staff, judging by his contemptuous attitude. He might have been that unpleasant physical training corporal who made our lives a misery, in which case I wish I'd shot him.

There was another top-secret establishment at the other side of the camp, known as WEEVE, or Wheeled Vehicle Experimental Establishment. This was piled high with tanks and armoured cars, many German. Captured enemy tanks were shipped over from Europe for their secrets to be examined. Some still had bloodstains inside them, or else a heap of ash where the driver had been. The size and quality of the German tanks were alarming. We already knew our own tanks were no match for the Germans; the instructors, some of whom had seen action, told us that. There was no equal to the dreaded 88 mm. German gun, while our own shells literally bounced off German armour and one or two instructors had flame-scarred faces to prove it. The favourite joke in gunnery class was to parody the fire orders: 'Seventy-five millimetre – shell action!

Traverse left ... steady ... on ... 500 yards ... bushy-topped tree ... ten o'clock ... Christ, it's an eighty-eight – bale out!'

Soon after arriving at Farnborough, I saw a civilian cycling into the WEEVE whom I recognised. It was Sam Thornton, who used to captain the Second XI at school when I was playing. He was working there as a civilian scientific officer (he's now deputy headmaster of Warwick School). I often spoke to him after that or exchanged grins as the squad doubled past him down the road to the gunnery classrooms. I envied Sam. He might be far from home but I imagine he had some heat in his lodgings and if he came home late they wouldn't put him in a cell. His bosses would call him by name, not 'you' or 'dozy'. Most important of all, he could go home when he liked without being arrested by a Military Policeman for having no pass. In other words, he was like the other 40 million civilians in the country.

I tried to get this point of view over to Sam but he wasn't impressed (not that I blame him). 'Think of the extra rations you get,' he said.

Early in 1945, shortly after my eighteenth birthday, a flu epidemic roamed the camp and I reported sick for the first time in my short military career. This was an act of great difficulty for a soldier. The army did not encourage people to report sick. It is not going too far to say they did everything possible to *dis*courage it. A soldier suffering from flu, appendicitis, or pneumonia was expected to rise at 6.30, pack up every single thing he possessed, and carry his kit a quarter-of-a-mile to the quartermaster's store. He then paraded with the other invalids. This meant standing in the rain at one side of the barrack square until the orderly sergeant came to march the sick parade to the medical room half-a-mile away. Some N.C.O.s took a delight in making the sick parade march smartly, barking at men with rheumatic fever to swing their arms smartly or stop hanging on to their comrades for support.

This was effective in deterring men with minor ailments. Stomach ache was far better than the horror of reporting sick. Indeed, soldiers really ill weren't fit to go on sick parade. Thus, when I got out of bed after a sleepless night and fell over as I tried to stand up, my first thought was, 'Oh God, I can't face sick parade.' Aided by friends I somehow dragged my kit over to the stores, collapsing on the way. I couldn't eat breakfast anyway, which was just as well as there wasn't time, so I stood shivering uncontrollably on the dark, frosty parade ground waiting to be marched off.

The march that morning was especially farcical as besides three or four flu cases we had a sprained ankle and a poisoned foot. Luckily we also had a decent sergeant and we lurched along like a squad out of the Retreat from Moscow, sneezing and snuffling and stopping occasionally when someone fell over. Provided a soldier survived sick parade, all was well. The Medical Officer was sympathetic and gave me three days of bliss in the sick bay, being treated with the new wonder drug M and B.

I also had my first taste of army justice, detailed to escort a friend arraigned on a vague charge by an N.C.O. who didn't like him. This was under the all-embracing Section 40 of the Army Act, 'conduct prejudicial to good order and military discipline' which could – and did – mean anything. The mistake I made was in thinking that appearing before the C.O. was like a trial. It wasn't. The accused's guilt was proved by the fact he had been charged; the C.O. was bound to support his N.C.O.s. It was like being sent off in football – the mere fact of being sent off is a crime, never mind that the player didn't commit a foul.

Any delusions the accused might have about being innocent were shattered by the way he was marched in with an escort and told to remove his cap. The evidence consisted of a few barked words from the corporal – 'Man was dozy and idle on parade, sah!' It would hardly have satisfied Lord Denning but the officer seemed quite happy and said, 'You heard what the corporal said. Now, why were you so dozy and idle on parade?'

The only time the system was challenged was when James Hay, one of the Etonians, was charged. He insisted on cross-examining the N.C.O. 'Would you mind explaining, corporal, exactly what you mean by dozy and idle?' he asked in

147

his languid voice. The unheard of happened and the case was dismissed. That, however, was unusual and if the C.O. thought a charge not proved he simply issued a rebuke. If it was proved he awarded a spell of C.B., which meant Confined to Barracks, but there was more to it than that. The soldier under punishment had to report to the guardroom at 6.30 a.m. in his best uniform, with belt and brasses polished, report again in the evening in overalls and spend his evening on fatigues. He was allowed to use the canteen for only a quarter of an hour and forbidden to leave camp.

As volunteers were considered potential officers, so they taught us to do everything connected with tanks. All crews could do at least two jobs. Gunners could operate the wireless and wireless operators could drive. We roamed Surrey and Hampshire in armoured cars or little 15 cwt trucks with a radio in the back, exchanging strange conversations in the jargon they taught us: 'Hullo, Yoke Four, I have reached Pluto, I say again I have reached Pluto, but I have lost my Sunray.' We knew the meaning of Wilco and the difference between Roger and Out. They taught us how to fire machine-guns and the inadequate 75 mm. gun with which British and American tanks were still armed.

For one glorious week the troop went up to the ranges at Warcop in Cumberland and blazed away all week. Like most weapons, the 75 mm. is liable to do as much damage to its crew as to the enemy. In a crowded tank-turret with three men crammed in a space about three feet square, the discharge of a three and a half inch cannon was quite dramatic. The breech slammed back some 18 inches and the tank stood on its haunches. We had our first casualty, a loader who got his hand in the way of the breech. They took him away with a mangled hand and we didn't see him again (that was always happening in the army – people vanished and you never knew their fate).

I had a narrow escape myself. There was a misfire when I was loader and I foolishly bent over the breech to see why, just as the gunner pressed the firing pedal again. This time the gun went off with a bang that deafened me and the breech slammed past my face, missing it by an inch. I was trembling so much I dropped the next shell on the turret floor. The corporal instructor stuck his head inside to see what the trouble was.

'Just remember, son,' he said, 'the next time you load a gun will be against the bleeding Germans.'

They also taught us to drive. We began on trucks and graduated to Cromwell tanks. Driving a tank was fiendishly difficult, as they don't freewheel. Every time a driver changed gear the tank stopped unless he was lightning fast, and the howls of tortured gear-boxes rang through Long Valley, Aldershot, as we ploughed up and down shell-holes. One of the squad actually succeeded in getting the clutch to fly out of the engine compartment in pieces; another snapped off the huge metal gear-stick in desperation. Mercifully, there was little civilian traffic on the roads.

The easy thing about driving a tank was steering. British tanks steered off the gearbox and were controlled by a tiller-bar in front of the driver. The slightest touch was enough and they could even turn while stationary, the tracks going in opposite directions. But this meant they couldn't be steered when the gears were in neutral. I was sitting in the hull-gunner's seat beside a driver who missed a gear going down a steep hill on a public road. After playing a symphony on the gearbox he started to brake but by then they wouldn't hold. The hill wound considerably but we went perfectly straight, as the driver couldn't steer. My past life did not flash through my mind but my future life did. It seemed very short and a great pity. By some miracle the first bend followed a valley on the left and the tank carried straight up a bank on the far side of the road, stopped halfway up and slowly slid back. The corporal was as scared as I was. But then, he had a soft job and expected to survive the war unless his pupils killed him.

While out on driving instruction I saw the Queen for the first time. As Princess Elizabeth, she had just joined the army and was stationed near Camberley, learning to drive, as we were. One day we stopped to relieve ourselves on a quiet road and were lined up spraying the side of the tank when a 15 cwt truck came round the corner driven by a female second lieutenant with another officer beside her. She was going slowly with the painful concentration of a learner.

149

Someone shouted, 'Hey, it's Princess Elizabeth,' and HRH was greeted by five men with their trousers open as we turned round to have a look. It was the Princess, all right. She was a pretty girl of about 18 and we all knew her. I doubt if she saw us, however. Like all good learners, she was glaring through the windscreen with a frown on her face. Her instructor noticed, however, and delicately raised a gloved hand to her face. I rather admired the Princess. She didn't have to join the army and it must have been an awkward position for her after leading a comparatively sheltered life.

The driving course ended with a maintenance test. The student was faced with an engine on a test bed and given a fixed time to find out why it wouldn't start and get it going. Luckily, there were only two faults. One concerned fuel and consisted of placing a piece of cotton wool in the feed-pipe. The other was electrical, and was achieved in some glaring manner, such as leaving a wire off a plug. As examinees knew this, it did not take much intelligence to correct the fault. Even so, some failed to do so and took a quarter of an hour before confessing failure, despite strong hints from a sergeant.

'Look, son,' he would say, breathing heavily, 'if it ain't electrical it's bleeding well got to be petrol, ain't it? Now can you see where I'm pointing? Why not look there?' Like other military tests, this one was designed not to be failed. Re-inforcements were needed, not geniuses.

General military training also continued. Tank crews were armed with revolvers and we spent much time drilling with them, a complicated procedure which involved four separate actions just pulling the weapon out. In the Wild West we would all have been dead. But then, cowboys must have used different guns because none of us could hit anything more than five feet away. It was a terrible shock, after seeing so many films in which a gunman shot off someone's hat from fifty yards, to find it was impossible to hit anything with a revolver.

The passing-out test on pistols was spectacular. A cardboard figure of a German soldier, with a nasty, sneering face, was towed towards each of us on rails and we had to empty our six-shooters into it on the word of command. When my turn came I held back until it was only a yard away to make sure of hitting it. At this range I pumped two bullets into the heart and, carried away with excitement, turned round and put the rest through its back as it was towed past, the squad flinging themselves on the ground while bullets whistled around them.

The sergeant said afterwards one bullet missed him by inches. I think he was too shaken to be angry. 'I thought I had bought it,' he declared. 'What a way to go – shot by my own men.'

But as this was another of those unfailable army tests we all passed with credit.

The army was still obsessed by gas, which was in fact never used during the war, largely because the Germans knew the Allies could retaliate in kind. They issued a new gas mask to replace the World War One sort with its haversack on the chest and a tube. This was more compact and clipped on the belt. We tested them in a chamber full of tear-gas and the instructor made us take the masks off to see what effect it had. One whiff and we staggered forth coughing and choking. From that the squad graduated to mustard-gas and lined up while a corporal solemnly painted everybody's wrists with a splash of the deadly stuff and told us to follow the approved routine for dealing with it, which consisted of smearing the affected part with anti-gas ointment, working from the outside.

For some reason a rather simple Yorkshireman failed to do this properly. The liquid gas didn't hurt at first and looked quite harmless, but back in the barrack-room he suddenly said, 'Eee, me arm's gone all funny.' It had indeed. It had developed a blister like a balloon and he was swiftly removed to the Medical Officer, who had to look up the treatment in a book as he'd never seen a gas casualty before.

There were two more casualties. A popular extrovert called Holland (nicknamed Dutch) slammed a tank lid on his thumb and ran away screaming while his hand turned black. Remarkably, there was nothing broken and he recovered quickly. Another was more serious, a nineteen-year-old boy from a minor public school was desperately keen to be an officer. He could be a bit officious and pompous so one night when he was

151

asleep I painted an ink moustache on his face. It was the sort of barrack-room prank anybody might suffer or carry out. Soon afterwards he was killed during practice with live ammunition. A grenade was thrown too close and he stumbled and fell on it. I would give a lot of money not to have played that silly joke.

At the end of the course, they weeded out those who would go on for officer training at the RAC officers' training unit at Sandhurst, where they had taken over the military academy. About half were selected. Surprise, surprise, I was in the other half, who would be sent abroad after leave and a little further training elsewhere. It was April 1945.

And then suddenly it was all over. We had lived with the war for so long it was part of our lives and victory seemed so elusive that nobody really believed the Germans would crumble for a long time. Now they were surrendering in droves and VE Day was fixed for 8 May. It was something of an anti-climax.

For eight months we had been conditioned to do nothing but kill Germans. Their faces glared under coal-scuttle steel helmets as we bayoneted them, shot at them, drove tanks at them and even shouted at them. We had been taught how to order them to surrender ('Hände hoch,' you say, a phrase made immortal by Corporal Jones in *Dad's Army* on TV, 30 years later). We were even taught what to do when *we* surrendered to *them*. 'On arrival at the P.O.W. camp you will report to the Senior Escaping Officer and discuss ways of getting out. It is every soldier's duty to try to escape after capture.' True, there were still the Japanese to come. There was no hint of their surrender and the troop had been promised our destination would be Burma, where fierce fighting still went on. But the immediate feeling was one of let-down, mixed with relief.

The squad was actually due to leave Farnborough on the day peace was officially declared, 8 May 1945, Victory in Europe Day, but I was not with them. On parade for final inspection, my face was painted a brilliant green, the M.O.'s treatment for impetigo. An officer noticed this and I quote the conversation.

'Sergeant, why is this man painted green?'

'Don't know, sir. You, why are you painted green?'

'Impetigo, sergeant.'

'Why haven't you reported sick?'

'Did so, sergeant. The M.O. painted me green.'

'Don't try to be funny with me, son. Says he's got impetigo, sir.'

'Oh, really, we can't have green-faced soldiers marching through the streets. He looks like a bloody Red Indian. Why do people do these things? Tell him to fall out. He'll have to miss the draft.'

This had all the classic features of the way a common soldier was addressed. He would be discussed in front of his face as if incapable of answering and blamed for what somebody else had done. Obeying orders could be as dangerous as disobeying orders. The phrase 'you can't win' hadn't been invented then, but if it had it would have been extremely popular.

Thus VE Day saw me hitch-hiking to London with Dutch Holland and John Oliver (who later became a High Court Judge in Hong Kong). We toured the streets on a teenage spree, sitting on top of taxis, dancing round policemen and going to Buckingham Palace where the Royal Family appeared on the balcony. Princess Elizabeth looked lovely and appeared to have recovered from her unpleasant experience last time I saw her. Despite a green face, I finished up necking with a girl on a seat in St James's Park and caught the last tube to Osterley where Uncle Will put me up. They had extra reason to celebrate, because peace would bring Joan nearer to her Werner.

In fact, her dreams were shortly to come true. A few days after VE Day, Joan's brother Arthur was serving with his regiment in Germany when by a million-to-one coincidence he actually met Werner's father without knowing who he was. British and Germans were not allowed to fraternise then but Arthur broke the rules and got into conversation. On learning he was called Smeath, the German said he knew only one other English person with that name.

'It was a girl called Joan from London,' he said. 'She was engaged to my son, Werner.'

It turned out Werner had been captured in North Africa in

1943 and was now in a prison camp in America. The news was rushed to Osterley and Joan wrote to him, their first contact for five years.

A fortnight later, my face restored to normal, they sent me to Catterick in Yorkshire to finish training before posting to the Far East. I said goodbye to a barrack-room chum, Trooper Gerry Carr. We have sent each other Christmas cards ever since and yet in 43 years have never met again. The thought of my approach seemed to have a deadly effect on the enemy, as the week I finished the course the Japanese surrendered. The squad were up on the ranges near Kircudbright in Scotland, sitting on the grass while an officer gave a lecture on Bunker Shooting (a bunker was a group of dug-in Japanese positions). But instead of the lecture he revealed an atom bomb had been dropped on Hiroshima and the class spent the lesson discussing the news. The Japanese had not surrendered but it was plain they'd have to.

'It makes a bunker shoot rather out-of-date,' said the officer, who'd got a blackboard with some beautifully prepared diagrams. He drew a large circle round them all and then scribbled across it. 'Just drop an atom bomb there and you've destroyed the lot.'

The news was another anti-climax. The army quickly switched its training towards dealing with the Japanese and it was slit-eyed oriental faces we now squinted at through our sights. Emergencies about 88 mm. guns were replaced by Kamikaze attacks in training. Yet it was a relief, too. The Japanese were still fighting strongly in Burma and it looked as if they would be beaten only by invading their mainland, which would involve huge casualties.

There was little sympathy for the Japanese. Or rather, we had the same sympathy as they'd felt towards the inhabitants of Nanking, where the Japs killed 40,000 in 24 hours when they captured the city in 1937, most of them burned, bayoneted or raped to death. Of course, no one had any idea of the after-effects of an atomic weapon; to us it was just an extra-big bomb. I am still baffled, though, by the readiness with which some people will mourn for Hiroshima and

Nagasaki without sparing a thought for the victims of German and Japanese aggression in Warsaw, London, Leningrad and the Far East.

The army, however, still had work for us. They sent the squad on embarkation leave. It was rather ironic – just as the country was starting to return to normal I was leaving it after six years of war. But I had a great experience on leave. Leicester Tigers played their first game at home since 1939 and I played against them, for a combined local side. The organiser of the local team met Dad in a pub and told him the scrum-half had just dropped out.

'Mick's home on leave,' said Dad. 'He might like to play.'

Like? A tank wouldn't have stopped me playing on the Tigers' ground. Father came down, oozing pride in his son, and watched me from the big stand. We lost, but I couldn't have played too badly as Doug Norman, organiser of the combined side, asked me if I would be available again. I told him no –they were posting me abroad.

And sure enough, at 3.30 a.m. one chilly morning in October 1945, I was packed off with a hundred others from the little railway station at Richmond, Yorkshire, bound for Italy.

CHAPTER TWELVE

'The Hussars and I'

It might be asked why we were sent to Italy, since the war had finished there in May. But already the Cold War had begun and Yugoslavia, then in the Russian camp, was threatening an invasion of the Trieste area, which she claimed as her own. The army also seemed to find it difficult to forget the war was over and huge garrisons were maintained out of force of habit. At first sight, Italy appeared as if the war was still on. Its marks were everywhere. Bridges were destroyed or replaced by temporary structures, hungry people clamoured for bread amid ruined railway stations and abandoned tanks and guns littered the countryside. There was rubble and wreckage in abundance, some of it human. The graves of soldiers, Allied and German, could still be found in unexpected places such as back gardens or by the side of roads.

At Rieti, 50 miles north of Rome, where the draft waited in the RAC replacement depot, two German soldiers were buried by the gates of the airfield, the graves marked by wooden crosses surmounted by steel helmets. The depot quarter-master-sergeant knew how they came to be killed, from Italians who saw it happen. While they were on guard at the main gate, a Spitfire machine-gunned the airfield and they were buried where they fell. Next day the Germans retreated.

Stopping at a meal-halt on the three-day journey by train, we were serenaded as we ate by two German prisoners, one blind and the other crippled, endlessly playing 'Lilli Marlene' on a violin and concertina. Their faded grey Nazi field caps were placed in front to receive any money or cigarettes thrown their way. Many recruits on the draft ignored them, but the older soldiers, who'd fought the Germans, gave more generously.

Rieti was simply a holding unit for men waiting to be posted or for reinforcements and everybody was bored and cold, shivering in unheated Italian barracks. It's surprising how cold Italy can be in the autumn. They'd been bombed and were without sanitation or running water. However, the camp had one luxury and that was its own brothel, or rather a local brothel was approved by the unit and the prostitutes inspected regularly by the Medical Officer. At 18, I was still a virgin, like most boys of my age. My sexual experience was pitiful compared with today's youth. Curiosity drove two of us to visit the place. I went with George Edmunds, a friend of Farnborough days.

The brothel stood in a former shop in the main street, conveniently marked with a flashing red light outside. On passing through the door, we found ourselves in a large room with benches round it, like an oversized doctor's waiting-room. About 20 soldiers were waiting patiently, smoking and flicking through copies of the *Eighth Army News*, the troops' own daily newspaper. There was a large notice on the wall, saying in Italian that it was strictly forbidden for a man to spend more than ten minutes with a woman. The prostitutes worked in two rooms leading off the waiting area and, when finished with a client they wasted no time but came out for the next while the previous one was dressing. One was a slim blonde of about 30, the other a fat woman in her forties. She was jolly, though, and exchanged *badinage* in broken English with the waiting customers. Some of these would have preferred the younger woman but she stood no nonsense and dragged them bodily into her room when their turn came. A few protested but she was strong and shrieked abuse if they defied her.

Our enthusiasm began to wane somewhat, especially when a revolting soldier with scabs all over his face came out buttoning his trousers and exclaimed, 'Cor, that was some woman.' Also, the fat woman looked a lot older than some of my aunts. I could no more have made love to her than to the plump woman who delivered the newspapers at home. My apprehension must have showed because the man sitting next to me said, 'Excuse me, mate, but is this your first shag?' I modestly explained we were both novices.

'Then take my advice and don't have it here,' he continued earnestly. 'The first shag you have is very important, mate. It can make a big difference to your sex-life later. You want the right woman, you see. If you take my advice you'll wait until you can get a decent bint instead of this rubbish.'

I thought that was slightly hypocritical because he vanished inside with the fat woman two minutes later, but it was the excuse we needed and making apologies all round we stood up to go. The fat woman came out and leaped upon us with shrieks of rage, crying, *'Bambini! Bambini!'* and we shot into the street like a couple of darts.

They posted me and about 30 others to the 7th Queen's Own Hussars, stationed at Palmanova, a sleepy little town between Venice and Udine in the north-east corner of Italy. A key garrison-town for Napoleon, it was surrounded by his well-preserved fortifications. The Hussars were part of the 7th Armoured Brigade, one of the three army units entitled to wear the badge of the Desert Rat and by coincidence I was to serve in both the others later.

Life with the Hussars was very different from a training regiment. They were much more like a community. N.C.O.s were usually addressed by first names while officers rarely bothered the men and left day-to-day running to the sergeants. Troopers were expected to be able to do their job and, as long as they did, nobody bothered much. Every morning the men paraded and marched down to the park where the Sherman tanks were, made a pretence of maintenance and marched back. The afternoons were free – the regiment had experienced a hard war and won a good reputation and was treating itself to a holiday. There was the minimum of bullshit, as troops called spit-and-polish, and no lights out or reveille. For the first time in the army we were treated as adults.

No beds were provided in the former Italian barracks and for a few nights the recruits slept on the stone floor until advised that if they wanted beds they'd have to find their own. The rest of the regiment were sleeping on an incredible mixture ranging from stretchers propped up on bricks to a huge brass bedstead looted from a shelled farmhouse. I bought a mattress from an Italian peasant and laid that on the floor. It turned out to be stuffed with dried grass which slowly leaked out until I was back on the floor after a few weeks. But by then I had inherited a stretcher from someone.

The veterans had already made themselves comfortable. The wartime British army contained every type of craftsman and they'd soon got to work. It was said, with some truth, that any regiment could build a block of offices and then run them, thanks to the rich variety of skills available from civilian life. Beds and tables were constructed, home-made radios built, and electric lights festooned round the walls. One fitter nearly burned five people to death with his home-made electric immersion heater, which was basically two wires stuck into an old oil drum full of water. The electricity supply was constantly failing due to illegal apparatus plugged in. Whenever the lights flickered everybody knew a disaster was occurring somewhere. There'd be cries of 'Switch the bloody thing off, can't you?' all down the corridor or maybe shrieks of pain as soldiers danced around wringing their burned hands.

Three of us were in a room with eight old sweats who'd fought their way up Italy. Apart from referring to us as 'those bloody civvies', they were kind and helpful. They spoke in a strange language, a mixture of slang from three continents. Indian slang was still strong in the army from pre-war days: the use of words such as 'coggage' for paper, derived I was told from a Hindu word, 'jiltie' for quick, or 'charpoy' for bed. To this had been added Egyptian words such as the universal 'bint' for woman; and finally a sort of bastardised Italian was spread on top. 'Aspet, mate,' they'd say, meaning 'wait' (from *aspettare*, to wait). 'Momento' was universal, so was 'dopo' and 'lente' and 'poco'.

Sometimes all three languages would be combined with English to produce a result such as, 'I sat on my charpoy and had a cup of char while I aspetted and I thought of this bint and how dopo I'd be having some amore.' To which a comrade might reply, 'Piu, mate.' A rough translation would be, 'I sat on my bed and had a cup of tea while I waited and thought of this girl and how later I'd be making love to her.' And the reply, 'Smashing, mate.'

Almost the first advice given was 'Get yourself a casa.' A casa was an Italian house with a family who'd look after you and do the washing for a few cigarettes or lire. I was shown one in a back street of Palmanova, with a mother in black and three of the most beautiful girls I have ever seen. Father had been killed as a soldier in the war, probably by the British. The three lovely girls beat my washing in the river in the traditional Italian way and returned it spotless and with knife-edged creases. Outside their house was an open drain in which rats crawled up and down.

George Edmunds and I had quite a distinction. He was the youngest soldier in the regiment and I was the second youngest. However, I had a further claim to fame. I had the second-largest feet (large elevens). The largest pair were owned by a trooper from Portsmouth, nicknamed Pompey, who took twelves.

'But only a *small* twelve,' he protested. 'I told the quarter-master, "I'm not deformed, Q, I just want a small twelve."'

Many of the new arrivals acquired nicknames. Army tradition was cast-iron about certain surnames, of course. Miller was always Dusty, Clark Nobby, White was Chalky, Bell was Dinger and somebody else was always Knocker (I've forgotten whom). Not to mention Taffy, Paddy, Mac and so forth.

The chief impression of the regiment was the German influence. One of the first things to greet the new draft was the sight of a huge German army bus, complete with camouflage, eagles and swastikas, parked behind 'B' Squadron. Captured earlier, it was now used for expeditions to the seaside at Grado. Many men wore German belts round their overalls. Most had a piece of German equipment somewhere, such as jackboots or a Mauser pistol. It was odd to see a British regiment parading in overalls held together by the traditional German army leather belts, with their motto *Gott Mit Uns* on the buckle. The favourite song was 'Lilli Marlene', followed by the infamous Nazi 'Horst Wessel'. Sometimes a group would march down to the cookhouse singing 'Horst Wessel' or else '*Wir fliegen gegen England*', banging tin mugs and plates together for cymbals.

So life was much more informal and in some ways quite comfortable. The stoves in each room did not have to be black-leaded and could actually be used for their proper purpose. Steve Kent, one of the Hussar veterans, had an American field cooker and made tea every morning from inside his blankets, while anybody on guard was expected to bring back tea from the cookhouse for his mates. Morning was no longer marked by banging and shouting from the orderly sergeant but by a cup of tea and a joke. The atmosphere was domestic rather than military and on Sunday mornings it was like a pre-war LCC housing estate, except for the absence of children.

One man in the troop was a cheerful little Old Etonian called Johnny (strange, how I kept meeting Old Etonians in the ranks). He told lurid tales of life at the college, which he alleged was riddled with homosexuality, the favourite spot for a tryst being behind the wall where the famous Wall Game is played every Autumn. Homosexuality then was a subject for derision or worse and no one would admit to it, so the troop verdict was 'those rich bastards must all be queer' after a session of Johnny's stories. Although Johnny was still a trooper after five years and habitually went round dressed like a shambles, his family owned a stately home in the country. Before being posted abroad Johnny returned on leave to find the army had commandeered the house as a hospital. Deeming the sanitation inadequate they dug up the 500-year-old lawn and built latrines on it.

'I do wish you'd do something about it, dear,' Johnny's mother had asked. 'Your father would not have liked it.'

Johnny demanded audience of the colonel in charge of the occupying troops. Dressed in civilian clothes with an Old Etonian tie, he told him it was a disgrace to desecrate the property and unless something was done he would take up the matter at the highest level, where he had connections. The colonel shrank under the threats and promised to have the damage put right. Next day Johnny's leave expired and as he walked down the drive in his trooper's uniform he passed the colonel, whom he saluted smartly.

'His expression,' said Johnny, 'was one I would not like to see on a human face again.'

Johnny claimed the 7th Hussars' adjutant had been his fag at Eton. 'And to think I used to beat his arse when he was a snotty-nosed kid,' he wailed after some rebuke on parade. However, there may have been some truth in the story. Johnny certainly took liberties denied to others. Yet for all his high connections he remained in the lowest rank of all and felt the disgrace keenly, since most of his contemporaries at Eton were officers, many Brigadiers and Generals, and quite a lot in the House of Lords.

Whether it was his influence with the adjutant we shall never know, but he was suddenly promoted to acting, unpaid lance-corporal. He celebrated the promotion with a wild booze-up, involving gallons of vermouth and Asti spumante. It went on in the village most of the night and at one point the revellers included a couple of officers. The end came with Johnny crashing a jeep into the wall of the barracks. 'I was aiming at the main gate but I missed,' he explained later.

Next day regimental orders contained this sentence: 'With reference to regimental orders of Dec. 2nd, delete all reference to Trooper ——.'

Johnny was shattered. 'I waited five years for it,' he moaned. But after a quart or two of Asti, topped up with some vermouth, he recovered his usual good humour and returned to his old ways, lurching back to barracks at night with some cronies singing 'The Eton Boating Song'.

162

One of my first tasks was to guard German prisoners of war at a camp at Villavincentina, a few miles away. They were privileged P.O.W.s, employed as mechanics at a vehicle depot, and guards were supplied by different units in rotation. The guard consisted of half-a-dozen troopers and a sergeant, armed with tommy-guns. The guard lived in squalor in a tiny hut, fed on scraps by a German cook who stole the rations and sold them to the Italians, who were short of food. The camp was equipped with a wooden watch-tower in the approved *Stalag* manner and the first night the sergeant sent men up it with torches. About 11 p.m. there was a jingling on the perimeter wire and we saw six Germans, not breaking *out*, but breaking *in*. They were obviously drunk. By the time we'd climbed down the tower and rushed into their hut they were all underneath blankets, snoring peacefully.

Worse was to come. Two troopers were sent out to escort the Germans for a walk one Saturday afternoon. There must have been fifty, wearing their field-grey German uniforms. We tried to keep an eye on them, marching behind with a tommy-gun at the ready but every time they turned a corner there'd be a few less. By the time we'd gone two miles, half had vanished, submerged into the landscape or hidden in houses and *albergos* and bars where they were seducing girls or drinking. We returned almost empty-handed except for a prisoner who said in very good English he was grateful for the walk.

'But it is rather cold for Italy, is it not?' he remarked politely. 'I expect you will be glad to get home to England.'

I suspect his job was to keep our attention diverted. I thought I'd be court-martialled but the sergeant said it had happened before and it didn't matter as long as they came back sometime. They dribbled in throughout the night.

Eventually, a *modus vivendi* was established with the Germans. As long as they kept their excesses within limits, they could do as they liked, although the sergeant insisted the hole in the wire was mended. The food mysteriously improved after this, and we got fifty per cent of the rations. It was rather pleasant being tucked away and forgotten by the army. At night, if not on duty, we strolled to a bar in the local village and drank sour peasant wine from barrels. Already my taste for alcohol was growing alarmingly.

The Germans were pleasant enough, but rather arrogant. This, however, may have been the natural condescension of an experienced soldier to a rookie. Anyway, there was no reason why they should be polite since they'd just lost the war and their home country was a smoking ruin. The sergeant, who had fought in the desert, commanded much more respect and was rather contemptuous of the prisoners, whom he said came from non-combatant units. Apparently the guard before us had found the answer to the Germans. They marched round the camp banging mugs and plates and singing the 'Horst Wessel' song when the prisoners got above themselves.

I was sorry to return to Palmanova and the discipline of barracks but it was a lucky escape. The men who relieved us went out one evening to celebrate a twenty-first birthday. Alas, the orderly officer from Palmanova chose that night to make an unexpected visit. He roared up to the gate in a jeep to be greeted by a neatly dressed German in field-grey uniform. The German saluted smartly (rumour says he gave the Nazi salute) and greeted the officer courteously. Was there anything he could do for him? The guard were unfortunately occupied, likewise the sergeant, but they would return shortly. Perhaps he could pass on a message?

At this moment the sound of singing announced that the guard were returning, lurching down the road and waving bottles.

The unfortunate men were from another squadron, so it was difficult to extract the full story. Most of the regiment's wrath fell on the sergeant although I seem to remember the tramp of men doing extra drill for some time. After this the idea of temporary guards was abandoned and a permanent squad posted there from another unit. Later the consequences would have been much worse but the Hussars were making up for six years of war and inclined to be lenient.

But not everything was overlooked. Two of the regimental hard cases, Geordie and Jock, pinched a truck while on a drinking spree, with the intention of deserting in it. They overturned after going about ten miles. The court martial sentenced them to three months in the field punishment centre (or glasshouse as military prisons were nicknamed) and I was detailed to act as escort on the way, together with a corporal and a driver.

The punishment centre was at Klagenfurt, in Austria, and the prisoners went there in a 15 cwt. truck. The corporal sat in front with the driver, leaving me in the back with Geordie and Jock. They were not handcuffed or tied in any way and, as the truck crawled through the mountain passes towards Austria, they calmly discussed how to kill me.

'We could knock the kid on the head and take his revolver and throw him out of the back,' said Geordie in a stage whisper. 'Then we could bang for the driver to stop, run round and hold up the couple in front. Then we'd take the truck and drive to Jugoslavia and give ourselves up to the Jugs.'

I didn't like this, especially as they were sitting so close. True I had a revolver, but it was firmly buttoned in its holster and I could hardly pull it out and wave it around without precipitating an incident. Anyway, they were three feet away and I couldn't hit anything at that range.

'No, Geordie,' said Jock, 'it'll no work. The kid'll give the alarm to somebody on the road. Ye've got to *dispose* of him properly. Hold him down while ah grab his gun and shoot him. Then we'll shoot the fucking corporal in the back from inside here. Then the driver'll stop the truck and we can shoot him as well and take the truck awa' to the frontier.'

They might have done it too. Jock was a psychopath and Geordie a simple, stupid person, the sort who always get led into trouble by somebody stronger.

When the truck stopped for a break I told the corporal.

'They're planning to shoot me and throw me out of the back,' I said.

'Bollocks,' he retorted. 'You've got a gun, haven't you?'

'Then they're going to shoot you and the driver,' I added.

'Oh,' he said. 'I think in that case I'd better stay in the front to protect the driver. Knock if there's any trouble.'

165

However, as Klagenfurt drew nearer, the bravado of the two prisoners oozed away. As with so many criminals, the wild talk was just fantasy and they began to whine. They'd been inside before and knew what to expect. I had an aluminium mug hanging from my pack.

'Give us your mug, kid,' asked Geordie. 'It'll bullshit better than mine.'

Most of the time at a field punishment centre was taken up with an endless round of futile spit-and-polish and he meant it would be easy to clean and shine. They were obviously scared at the thought of three months in the glasshouse. Ugly tales circulated in the army about military prisons, where life was a routine of drudgery, bullshit and discipline which didn't always stop short of brutality. There was no one for the prisoner to appeal to outside. The guards could do pretty well as they liked.

On arrival we lined up at the main gate and when it opened a sergeant-major bellowed, 'You men there! Double!' I pitied the two prisoners until he shouted angrily at me, 'And the escort as well!' We ran to the reception office and the last I saw of my two charges they were standing at attention with their faces against a wall. They told me later they were left like that for an hour and threatened every time they moved.

Christmas 1945 came and went, lubricated by enormous supplies of Canadian tinned beer, a novelty to us. The 7th Armoured Brigade padre came round and administered Holy Communion to a small congregation with pale faces and shaking hands, many of whom blenched at the sight of the wine. In the new year I turned down a chance of promotion in favour of playing rugby. They put me in to become a higher grade of wireless operator but the test clashed with a match. I didn't always enjoy sport in the army but at this period we had a good rugby side, a pleasant officer in charge, and I liked playing. I tried to compromise by rushing through the exam and leaving early but it didn't work. I failed the exam and played a rotten match, made worse by the jeers of some German P.O.W.s who'd never seen this crazy English game before.

Early in 1946, I got three days leave in Venice with a friend who came out on the same draft. The army had taken over a small hotel as a leave centre and the waiter there recalled how, despite the absence of roads, the liberating British troops managed to drive jeeps over the Rialto the previous year. Venice in January 1946 had no tourists except for a few troops and we roamed at will. There was no difficulty getting tickets for Mozart's *Don Giovanni* at the Fenice, where a friendly officer explained the plot.

I had never seen opera before apart from Gilbert and Sullivan at school and came out quite dazed. The Italians were an uninhibited audience and hissed any singing they didn't like as freely as they cheered at other times. There was an unfortunate moment when Don Giovanni, played by a short, fat man looking rather like Mussolini, trod on a small flight of steps and they collapsed. His foot went through and became wedged but with great presence of mind he continued to sing while he hopped around stage with the steps round his leg, trying to extricate himself. This was another dreadful dragon's tooth sown for *The Art of Coarse Acting*, in which 20 years later I was to describe how Coarse Actors are incurably accident-prone. As this is combined with a pathetic belief that nobody saw what happened, their favourite remark is, 'Believe me, old chap, the audience never noticed a thing.' I won't say the Italian audience never noticed a thing but while an English audience would have been in stitches they concentrated on the singing, which was sublime.

Soon afterwards came a rather painful experience. Having no clean uniform for a drill parade I dodged it by reporting sick for dental examination and a truck took me to the field hospital at Udine. My heart sank when I saw the dentist, who was still using his active service equipment and the drill was worked by a foot treadle like an old sewing-machine. Army dentists were not renowned for their gentleness and this one obviously felt his patient was swinging the lead. He discovered three non-existent cavities and proceeded to fill them with excruciating slowness. His treadle-operated drill seemed to make only two or three revolutions a minute, a slow grinding which went right through my head. There was, of course, no injection. I left with an aching jaw, determined never to return.

In fact I was back in the hospital within a few weeks, this time with suspected pneumonia. The M.O. at camp took my temperature twice a day when I had a dose of flu, discovered it was fluctuating wildly and sent me to Udine for observation. I could have told him why the temperature fluctuated. The first observation was at 7.00 a.m. when I reported, shivering with cold, to the regimental aid post. For the second, at 5.30 p.m. I turned up full of hot food and a pint of tea, usually with a mug of it in my hand.

It was pleasant in hospital, apart from C.O.'s inspection every morning when all patients had to sit up to attention as he marched round with the sergeant-major. Those unable to sit were expected to lie to attention with their legs together. I fell in love with the ward sister, a beautiful girl of about 25 in the Queen Alexandra Nursing Service, but my suit would have been hopeless.

The even tenor of life at Palmanova was rudely shattered in the early spring of 1946 by threats of war. A year previously Jugoslav partisans under General Tito arrived in Trieste simultaneously with Allied troops. Trieste had been the main port of the Austro-Hungarian empire until handed to Italy after World War One and Slav influence was still strong. Now Jugoslavia wanted it back from the Italians, who, of course, fought on the German side until they surrendered in 1943. A nasty situation at the end of the war was defused by General Morgan, commanding British troops, by persuading the Jugoslavs to withdraw to a line near Trieste while matters were sorted out, leaving Trieste and the nearby port of Pola in Allied hands.

Now Tito was becoming impatient. On the frontier, shots were exchanged and patrols clashed. In Pola someone threw a grenade at a British brigadier and killed him. Army trucks were attacked and drivers had to have escorts. In the spring, the army moved to defensive positions and the regiment was sent to hills overlooking Trieste.

The American Sherman tanks with which the Hussars had

been equipped during the war (called Ronsons because they caught fire so easily) had been taken away with the end of Lease-Lend and replaced by British Churchills. These were infantry tanks, heavy and ponderous with a top speed of some ten miles an hour, so the move to Trieste took a long time. To give Ken Appleby, our driver, a rest I drove for the first hour or two and distinguished myself by almost knocking down a telegraph pole, when I mistook an order in the headphones.

This was my first brush with the tank commander, Capt. Rodney Wilkinson, M.C. Rodney was the son of the well-known artist Norman Wilkinson, who drew the famous LMS railway posters ('The Trossachs by LMS') which adorned every pre-war station. He was popular with the men and admired as a holder of the Military Cross, although he wouldn't talk about his medal as it apparently involved something undignified. Rumour said he chased a German officer round a table before capturing him. It's a pity I should fall out with him but I panic under pressure. It only needs someone to shout at me and my mind goes blank. Unfortunately, there is a lot of shouting in the army.

Relations became strained when we arrived in the early hours of the morning at a hill overlooking Trieste. It was pitch-dark and raining and everyone was tired, hungry and irritable. On arrival, Rodney said I would have to be his batman or personal servant. The job is generally done by the hull-gunner, or co-driver, who acts as tank dogsbody, makes tea, cuts sandwiches, etc. The first task was to unload his kit, which was strapped to the outside of the turret. I had never seen anyone carry so much kit on a tank before. I clumsily threw it to the ground where a strap broke and a large sketch-book fell out on to the wet grass.

The effect on Rodney was appalling.

'You bloody idiot, Green,' he shouted. 'You've ruined my sketches.'

The pad contained sketches and water-colours. Having inherited his father's love of art he'd brought along his drawing materials.

I gathered up the wet sketches, which were showing signs of

falling apart, and put up Rodney's tent, a standard two-man bivvy. I began to erect it at the side of the tank (normal practice) but he told me to put it at the back, a move which was to have great significance shortly. Experience had taught me it was unwise to sleep at the back of a Churchill tank parked on sloping ground.

After that bad start, nothing went right. I was not a very good personal servant and when some disaster occurred (such as his tent threatening to collapse) he would bellow, 'Green – I want you.' He had a habit of doing this at night just after getting into his blankets. The crew were sleeping under the engine-sheet, a big piece of canvas slung at the side of the tank, and I received the usual encouragement to get myself a court martial.

'Don't you go, Mike,' they'd say. 'He's no right to make you his servant, you're supposed to volunteer. Don't do it, mate. You wouldn't catch *me* acting as a bloody lackey for an officer.' Brave words, which luckily I ignored.

Then fate took a hand, as they used to say in the *Hotspur*. We'd fixed up wireless earphones inside a biscuit tin to magnify the tinny sound so we could listen to Radio Gorizia from our blankets. Everybody listened to Radio Gorizia, the local American forces station, proudly announcing itself as 'Radio Gorizia – The Voice of the Blue Devils'. That was the modest title of the US 88th Division, which also styled itself The Kraut Killers. They took their duties seriously and made their wills on going to the frontier zone, or Morgan Line as it was called, after General Morgan. Not only was the music better than on the British Forces Network, since we got the latest Bing Crosby and Frank Sinatra hits, but the station announcements were infinitely more amusing. These consisted almost entirely of exhortations to avoid VD. Bing Crosby had scarcely groaned to a stop before a nasal voice was booming – 'Remember – VD walks the streets. Keep clean, keep sober.'

Sometimes we were treated to a little radio drama:

'Hullo, son.'

'Hullo, padre. Gee it's good of you to see me in hospital.'

'That's all right, son. I guess it's my job. Can I do anything for you?'

'Gee, yes, padre. I wanna get out of here. I'm due for furlough back home. I wanna see Mom and Pop and my girl again.'

'I'm sorry, but you won't be going home, Johnny.'

'Not going home, padre?'

'No. You've got VD. You'll have to stay in this theatre of operations until you're completely cured. And that might be a long, long time.'

Sound of sobbing while padre adds: 'Remember – VD walks the streets.'

Another favourite featured a ship's hooter. 'That's the boat home, Johnny. You won't be on it. You've got VD.'

With stuff like that, who wanted the British service with its repeats of Woman's Hour? Unfortunately, the sound of Radio Gorizia began to grow faint as the crew lay in their blankets, one Sunday morning. Thinking the batteries must be low Ken Appleby, the driver, climbed into the tank to start it and give them a charge. As soon as he put the gear-lever in neutral and the weight came down on the brakes, they failed and the tank began to roll backwards down the slope. Next thing, the canvas sheet had vanished. It was flying like a bizarre banner from the tank, which was bounding backwards down the hill. Then it disappeared as it passed over a ridge and the hill got steeper.

People now became aware of Rodney's two-man bivvy, which had been placed at the back of the Churchill on his express orders. It was crushed by fifty tons of metal and the marks of the tracks went right across the torn cloth. Bits of a shattered camp bed protruded fore and aft. They stood staring, too frightened to lift the canvas and look upon the mangled Thing underneath. And then was heard a familiar voice behind them, 'What the hell is happening now?' It was Rodney, preserved by a miracle.

There was an argument about how Rodney survived, since he wasn't too sure himself. Some soldiers swear he levitated himself and shot horizontally out of his tent. I seem to recall him saying, 'I saw this bloody great track coming through the wall of my tent and the next moment I found myself outside.'

The experience shook him up a great deal and when somebody started up a nearby Churchill suddenly he turned pale and sat down.

Meanwhile, there remained Ken, the driver. Everyone ran down the hill to where the tank was last seen. It had careered over a 20 ft drop and smashed its way further downhill before coming to rest at the bottom with the gun at a strange angle. Once more we feared having to extricate a mangled heap of flesh and bone but, through the driver's porthole, Ken could be seen feebly trying to start the engine, a reflex action from long training.

'Sod off,' he mumbled as he was lifted from his seat.

He turned out to be shaken, but only bruised and cut. This was almost as miraculous as Rodney's escape. Ken was covered in a great pile of 75 mm. shells which had been jerked from their racks (the tank was fully loaded with ammunition, owing to the crisis). One of them was in his lap. There were grenades, smoke bombs and belts of machine-gun ammo lying in confusion. If anything had gone off, the tank would have been blown to pieces. As it was, the force of the fall had torn off the metal bogies, snapped the tracks and thrown the gun-turret off its mountings.

Churchill tanks were prone to run away. I'd seen it happen before, training in Scotland, when a group of sleeping troopers were surprised by a Churchill tank which burst through the side of the hut. The trouble was caused by contraction of hydraulic fluid in the brakes.

The tank was a complete wreck. So was a lot of the crew's personal kit. Corporal Steve Henley had left his best uniform hanging from the tracks and now it was in ribbons. Next time there was a kit inspection he held up the pieces and said, 'I think my uniform needs darning, sir.' We emptied the Churchill and tried to erect shelter for ourselves back up the hill, while Rodney moved his quarters elsewhere. I think he believed I was trying to kill him.

CHAPTER THIRTEEN

Goodbye, Italy

Early in May 1946, Allied forces paraded in strength through Trieste, ostensibly to mark the first anniversary of its liberation from the Nazis but more probably to frighten off the Jugoslavs. They gave us a new tank and we spent a couple of days living on board a bombed Italian warship in the docks getting ready for the parade. The tanks were polished until they gleamed, although we didn't go as far as another regiment who chromium-plated their gun muzzles, using, it was said, money from the welfare fund. It was eerie living on the wrecked ship, which was only half-afloat and without lights or facilities. During the night a howl and a splash announced someone had fallen through a hole in the deck into the flooded engine-room.

The regiment spent hours practising how to dip their guns together in salute to General Morgan during the parade. The CO's wireless operator gave the instructions, calling out over the air, 'Traverse now . . . one . . . two . . . three . . .' and the gunners all tried to keep together as they swung the turrets round and dipped the guns, levelled out and straightened up. It was most impressive but the Italians were not excited. The British were tolerated in Italy but the locals reserved their enthusiasm for the Americans. They saved their cheers for the 88th Blue Devil Division. Those members of this élite corps not stricken with VD were headed by a brass band of awesome size composed entirely of men with steel-framed glasses, or so it seemed.

Soon afterwards the regiment moved back to Palmanova, but the crisis blew up again and it returned to Trieste. We would never go back to Palmanova. The first panic move saw us occupying a bombed factory near the seashore some five miles south of Trieste. We spent a long time making the position impregnable against the expected attack, digging slit trenches and erecting miles of barbed wire. The army forgot to provide enough gloves and men's hands soon resembled flayed pieces of meat. Afterwards, they said the wire was too close to the tanks, a grenade could be thrown at us, so it was all moved again.

Then the regiment were re-equipped with flame-thrower tanks. Nobody knew anything about them. They were awesome things, with a flame-gun down in the hull next to the driver, where the lap-gunner sat. Armoured trailers were towed behind to carry compressed air and the fire fluid. As troop-commander's tank we were selected for the first firing and everybody gathered round like a football match. They even cheered as we climbed into the tank.

We were shooting into an area of dry grass and under-growth. The technique was to fire a wet shot, that is, a squirt of fluid which does not ignite, and follow it up with a dry shot (flames) which would ignite the fuel already fired on to the target. But owing to faulty air pressure, the wet shot dribbled out just in front of the tank. The gunner (Ginger Fraser, if I remember correctly) could not see where the shot had gone and immediately followed it up with a jet of flame. There was a great roar and we found ourselves surrounded by a sea of fire as the liquid caught alight and ignited the undergrowth. Ken Appleby, in the driver's seat, started the engine to back away, but it stalled and wouldn't restart.

As far as our comrades were concerned it was the funniest thing since grandmother's funeral. Shrieks of mirth rent the air as we leaped among the flames, trying to uncouple the fuel trailer. Every so often someone would jump away with their trouser legs on fire, madly beating at the flames, to more jeering and witty remarks ('What's the hurry, mate, the canteen's not open yet'). Nobody seemed to worry that the trailer contained several hundred gallons of fuel. The last straw was the arrival of the local fire brigade, who had been alerted by a dense pall of smoke which now hung over the area. But by then the trailer had been moved out of range and the flames were dying down. The tank, which was full of ammunition, was quite hot but undamaged. I don't think Ken, the driver, ever left it. Tank drivers were like that. They regarded the vehicles as their personal property and stuck by them to the end.

'They say,' said the squadron pessimist, 'that the Jugs have threatened to burn alive anyone caught using flame-throwers.' This made little impression on us. We were doing quite a nice little line in burning ourselves alive.

For a time I had a dog. A sort of large dachshund, he once belonged to the Germans and strolled into British positions just before the war finished, so he had to be called Fritz. His owner, a transport driver, was posted temporarily to Bari in Southern Italy and I volunteered to look after him. At night he slept on my blankets inside the tent and during the day roamed the camp begging for food or mixing with other dogs. There were a large number of these. Whenever a unit of the British army stopped it was immediately surrounded by hordes of dogs and children. They knew the soldiers were a soft touch.

The base at Palmanova had become overrun with a vast tribe of mongrels who considered themselves part of the regiment. Some had been adopted and slept with their masters, while others preferred to keep their freedom and roamed where they wanted. Dogs queued up with the men at the cookhouse, warmed themselves at the guardroom stove and even went on parade, sitting on their haunches between the ranks and ignoring muttered threats of 'Piss off, Rover, for God's sake'. When we moved, many tanks were festooned with dogs balanced precariously on the hull or their little faces peering out of hatches. Sergeant Robbins saved the life of one which fell off under way, grabbing its neck as it slithered off and stuffing it inside the turret beside the surprised gunner.

Fritz had survived the Great Dog Cull when they'd become so numerous at Palmanova it was decided to thin their ranks. A grim notice went out: All dogs must be registered within a week and those not claimed would be executed by the Regimental Police. For days a cloud hung over the Hussars. The best dogs (such as Fritz) were instantly claimed, but there remained a hard core of canine bandits who didn't want an owner and whom nobody would claim, as owners were held responsible for their pets' misdeeds. Dogs who left camp with a joint of meat between their teeth were obviously an embarrassment. These included some of the most likeable animals, cheerful rascals whom everybody enjoyed cursing, and as the dreaded day drew near, men went round pleading for their lives, begging someone to adopt them.

When the ultimatum ran out, familiar canine faces disappeared one by one as dogs were rounded up and put in the guardroom. They went willingly, as dogs do, expecting some treat. One, however, a black and white mongrel called Brasco, had a premonition of disaster. It escaped and was pursued in a truck and caught by Staff Sergeant Lowe, 'C' Squadron quartermaster.

'It broke my heart,' he said. 'He wagged his tail and licked my hand, but I had to fetch him.' With a strange bond of sympathy, most of us stayed in barracks that evening, until a fusillade of revolver shots announced the executions were over. A truck took the bodies away.

Despite the various crises, the defence of Trieste was not unpleasant. The city itself was fascinating. It owed as much to Austria as Italy and the influence of the Hapsburgs was everywhere in the architecture, including the Emperor's former private railway station, with a direct line to Vienna. At weekends, we strolled the boulevards, ate ice-cream in the open-air cafés on the Via Venti Septembre or got drunk on vermouth in the Bar X. It was then I discovered the peculiar properties of vermouth, namely that, if you drink too much, a cup of tea in the morning sets one off again. Many a time, three or four men would be staggering on morning parade. In the evenings we sometimes walked to a village and drank the rough peasant wine with bits floating in it ('Flakes of skin from the feet of the grape-crushers' said the troop alarmist). In a desperate effort to prove my manhood I drank a litre in two minutes for a bet. Comrades carried me gibbering back to camp and I spent a rainy night under a tank being sick. Fritz came over and licked my face.

At other times, the men made tea in the time-honoured tank-crew manner, filling half an empty oil drum with sand and petrol for a fire, and brewing up on top, using the other half of the drum as a dixie. The tea was compo – tea, sugar, powdered milk all mixed together – and it came out red and strong. Then we'd sit round and talk, or rather the older soldiers talked and the young men mainly listened. There was a strict social order in the ranks, governed by length of service abroad. Sometimes we sang. Steve Henley and three others used to improvise a barbershop quartet and harmonise old songs such as 'I'm in Love with Two Sweethearts' or 'Genevieve', like my father had done in the army. But it would be wrong to give the impression we were all nightingales. Some couldn't sing a note.

There were the usual confessionals and talk of sex. But one topic soared above all others – demob. The army had given everybody a number based on age and service. Mine was 64. It should have been 63 but the system was weighted against people who volunteered young, and I was penalised for coming in at 17. The lower numbers were sent out first but twelve months after the end of the war they'd still only reached the twenties. It looked as if we'd be there for ever. Some of the troop had been in for five years, most of it abroad, and were becoming impatient, especially those with wives and girl-friends. One or two had received the usual war-time poison-pen letter, 'You ought to know your wife is going out with Americans.' Older soldiers had received one leave home after the war finished but that merely whetted the appetite.

I was rather touched by a corporal's story of his home leave. Before going abroad he'd left a letter with a neighbour to be given to his girl-friend if he was killed. It was a typical young lover's piece, wallowing in sentimentality and saying death would be preferable to a life without his beloved. 'The fact is,' he said, 'I'd rather gone off her after three years away. The first thing I did on getting home was to go round and implore them to give me that letter.'

Rodney occasionally sat round the dixie and joined in the conversations. I seemed the only person he couldn't get on with. I really do believe he thought I was slightly touched.

Sometimes we went swimming in a nearby bay, littered with bombed ships. Offshore the outline of the half-submerged Italian liner *Rex*, pride of their merchant fleet, stood out starkly as a reminder of Mussolini's fallen glories. There is no better playground than derelict ships and they echoed to shrieks as we swam round them, inside and out, emerging covered in rust and oil. An unfortunate youth who'd come out on my draft, nearly died during these games. He was always complaining about something so, when he dived off a half-sunken freighter and came up shrieking he'd got cramp, everybody ignored him.

'Help,' he shouted. 'Honest, it's true, my legs are all doubled up.'

Ho, ho, ho. Mocking cries echoed all round.

'You rotten bastards. I'm going to die, I tell you. I'm sinking. Look, I'm all doubled up. Honest, this time I'm serious. It's true, I tell you.'

Ho, ho, ho. 'That bastard's always moaning for no reason.'

'Aaah!' (He sank.)

After a moment or two we realised he might have been serious. The water was immediately alive with guilt-ridden soldiers and the wretched youth was dragged to shallow water where he recovered, shouting 'Rotten bastards!' at all and sundry.

Perhaps it was a punishment, but showing off (as usual) I dived like an arrow over the side of a listing vessel into water that turned out to be only three feet deep. To make it worse, I'd been demonstrating a dive with the hands held at the side. A foreboding of danger came to me as I hit the surface and luckily I stiffened the neck muscles. Even so, for days afterwards I went around with my head on one side and a bandage round my scalp surmounted by a black beret. This merely confirmed my insanity in Rodney's eyes.

Fritz's owner was posted back and came over from Palmanova to claim his dog. He tempted him into his truck with a bone from the cookhouse (that dog would do anything for food). I can't blame him as I'd kept Fritz long past the agreed time and ignored messages to return him, but he did seem to have a special bond with me. Soon afterwards we moved, this time up into the hills near a little village called Basovitza, or Basovica as the Slavs called it. It was a pleasant spot, up among the pine woods with a good view of the Jugoslav frontier we were watching.

I went back there recently, reviving old memories of 40 years previously. The primitive village café, which was so awful we hardly used it, is smart and modern and sells ice cream now. The pro-Tito slogans have vanished from the walls. Neat little villas are springing up all round and the deserted road to the frontier, where one might wait two or three hours at night without seeing a vehicle, is now thronged with Italians driving to Jugoslavia to get cheap petrol. No longer do peasant women walk along the road with huge bundles of washing or firewood on their heads. It was balancing these all their lives which gave Italian women such lovely postures and fine figures, we were told.

As the crisis continued, troopers found themselves more or less on permanent guard duty. There was our own camp to guard and patrol, plus a small outpost up the road towards the frontier, and Trieste garrison kept borrowing men as they were short of infantry. We did duty at the radio station up in the hills, patrolled the streets and guarded 13 Corps Rear HQ.

The headquarters of the 13 Corps Rear HQ were in a big building in the centre of Trieste, opposite the HQ of our old friends the United States 88th (Blue Devil) Division. The proximity provided a striking contrast between the two armies. We were dressed in tropical kit but with long trousers. The 7th Hussars never wore those ridiculous, baggy shorts on duty. Long trousers were compulsory. With our black berets and pale khaki tunics, we looked quite smart and stood properly at attention or ease, saluting when officers passed, presenting arms to higher ranks and marching stiffly to and fro. Changing of sentries was accompanied by the usual stamping, shouting and formality.

Opposite, I watched Americans change guard. At the appointed hour, the sentry, who was smartly if somewhat extravagantly dressed in a blue steel helmet, shouted, 'Where's that cock-sucking bastard who's supposed to relieve me?'

A corporal appeared from the guardroom and called out, 'Stow it, will ya?' A muttered 'goddam cocksucker' answered him. A few minutes later the relief appeared. He was a huge Negro with a great beam on his face and he carried a portable radio loudly playing 'Chatanooga Choo-Choo', which soon faded into the customary warning against VD. The sentry slouched inside and his relief sat down on a chair beside the gate, listening to the music with closed eyes. After a while he noticed me, rigid at my post across the street.

'Hi!' he called out, with a friendly smile.

I didn't answer. I wasn't allowed to.

'Hi!' he shouted again. 'You deaf, or sumpin'?'

I smiled desperately and mouthed, 'I am not allowed to speak.'

His lip-reading must have been good because he picked up the idea. 'Can't speak? Jeez, what sort of army you in? How do you challenge anyone if you can't speak?'

He amused himself for the rest of my stint by addressing remarks to me, knowing I couldn't reply. They were quite friendly, comments about the tunes on his radio and so forth ('Great song that: you know Benny Goodman?') and, when I was relieved with the usual banging and drilling, he stood up in awe and shook his head.

Rodney and I began to fall out again. As orderly officer inspecting the guard at camp he asked politely, 'Green, I wonder if I might look at your Sten gun for a moment?'

This is one of the army's oldest ruses. A soldier on sentry is not supposed to surrender his weapon to anybody, not even an officer. But it's one of those catch-22 situations the army delights in, because if the officer genuinely wanted it, a refusal would mean punishment. I didn't think my own troop officer would pull a dirty trick, so I said, 'Of course, sir,' and handed it over.

Rodney immediately pointed it at me with a shout of anger. 'You bloody idiot, Green, what would have happened if I'd been a Jug spy?'

That seemed a bit far-fetched, so I told him so.

'But you're not a Jug spy,' I protested. 'I know who you are. You are Captain Wilkinson.'

'I know I'm Captain Wilkinson, you bloody fool, but supposing I wasn't. You'd be dead.'

'But you *are* Captain Wilkinson.'

'Don't argue, for God's sake. You really are completely impossible, Green.'

I gave up arguing and stared into space with the bovine expression approved by the army. 'Yes, sir,' I muttered, making a private resolution to vote Labour when I was old enough, which would be 21 then. Like most men in the ranks I rightly or wrongly identified our officers with the Conservative party. The Labour landslide of 1945 came as no surprise to ordinary soldiers. It was the result of six years of petty humiliations rather than economic policies. I voted Labour only twice, I think. Then I became disillusioned.

It's only fair to say Rodney suffered from me as much as I suffered from him. The more he shouted the more I went to pieces. One day the whole troop were out exercising when a low branch removed the wireless aerial. I didn't notice. Meanwhile all communication between troop commander and his tanks ceased. Rodney frantically bellowed into his microphone while Churchill tanks lumbered in all directions. His desperate final command, 'Hullo all stations Able One, halt. I say again, halt. Stop. Stay where you are, for God's sake,' went unheeded and, as we stopped, the rest of the troop vanished into the distance towards Jugoslavia. Rodney looked at me in disgust.

'You are the most ziff wireless operator I have ever had,' he said.

Even at that moment I noted the word 'ziff'. Unusual and potent. I could use that in an article some time. 'Yes, sir,' I said unhappily. It took half an hour to round up all the tanks, who'd gathered together for a tanks' tea-party or brew-up.

Tanks are always brewing tea. We used to keep a can of water over the engine to warm up in readiness.

If this gives an impression I was the squadron idiot, it would be wrong. No less a person than the Squadron Sergeant-Major, a cheerful Irishman named Mick O'Connor, regarded me as a useful man about the unit. That was his opinion after I scored the winning run (or whatever they call it) for his softball team against 'B' Squadron. Lacking cricket facilities, the unit played a lot of softball in the country around the camp. We actually won a match against an American unit, friendly, cigar-smoking men in bomber jackets, but this was because their side had been decimated by syphilis, and the best men were in hospital.

'Yep,' a G.I. told me proudly, 'the Gen'l said we'd got the highest rate in the whole goddam US Army when he came round to inspect us.' VD was a problem for all armies, but had assumed gigantic proportions for the Americans. Obviously they didn't pay enough attention to Radio Gorizia. Penicillin was just being used as treatment and nobody was sure if it would work.

Cricket was played but under difficulties. Usually the pitch was a strip of matting laid in the wilds and the outfield was covered in bushes. The only decent pitch was organised by Corps headquarters, who'd found a beautiful level stretch of turf high up on the cliffs overlooking the Adriatic. I played there once; I forget for which side, but I don't think it was the regiment. Fielding at long-leg by the edge of the cliff I distinguished myself by vanishing over the edge after a ball. It sounds worse than it was, because it wasn't a sheer drop, just a slope getting steeper and steeper. The ball had rolled down the slope and stuck in the roots of a bush so I slithered down after it. Just as I got there, a minor avalanche occurred and the ground gave way, leaving me hanging on to a bush. I started to pull myself up but the bush began to weaken, so I shouted 'Help!' Nobody heard; they'd got another ball and continued to play. The absence of long leg is not noticed by most cricket teams and in civilian life I've known long legs who hopped into the pavilion for a drink.

182

I waited for some time, calling feebly for aid at intervals, until another ball trickled over the cliff and an officer stuck his head over the top. On seeing me, he exclaimed, 'Good God, what are you doing down there?' I told him and he went away and came back with a length of tow-rope from a truck, and they pulled me to safety. When I got to the top he asked me for the ball and was very annoyed when I'd forgotten it.

'You can't get them out here,' he complained.

Although continual guards were a strain, they had their compensations. One of the few enjoyable moments on sentry was early morning. I always tried to get the last two-hour turn as it meant four hours' uninterrupted sleep. Then I could watch the dawn come up over Jugoslavia, the sun appearing behind the mountains and flooding the tops as if a volcano had erupted. Even better, the last man on guard had to wake the early duty cook, and that meant a buckshee cup of tea.

This, however, was not a job for the squeamish. On being shaken in his tent at 5.30, the cook would get out of his blankets to reveal he was sleeping in nothing but a filthy vest. After investigating his anus and other private parts with his fingers, he would use the latrine loudly and, without washing, go straight to the cook-tent. There, putting a kettle to boil on the petrol field-cookers, he started laying out slices of cold spam for breakfast with his bare hands. When the kettle boiled, he made tea – sergeant-major's tea, we called it. This was strong enough to stand a spoon upright in, with lashings of sweetened condensed milk, not the insipid, sugarless muck the troops got later. He stirred it with his finger and sucked the end.

I always told myself not to have any cold spam for breakfast and always forgot. I was still growing and got so hungry. Sometimes I worried whether I might catch a terrible disease from the cook's fingers, having seen where they'd been, but a hundred of us ate heartily without illness. I say 'ate heartily', but we were always hungry. This was partly because the cooks were flogging food to the Italians for the black market. If we received all our rations, I can only say they must have been a small allowance.

I should really have been hardened to the horror of the

cooks, having survived a far more revolting experience. The regiment were camped in a water catchment area, so it was forbidden to dig latrines. The home-made eight-hole toilet was erected over empty oil-drums instead of the usual pit. The most feared fatigue in the camp was to remove these when full, manhandle them on to a lorry and empty them down a vast sump dug by the Royal Engineers, at a place where the water wouldn't be polluted. This task came round about once every ten days and was organised by the sanitary corporal. He had no other duties and his lance-corporal's stripe was simply compensation for the filthy job, one of those human touches the army sometimes provides. A rather shy, fastidious person with glasses, he had the look of a student about him. About the second time I was on duty, the shit waggon (as it was colloquially known) had a minor collision and the drums full of ordure in the back fell over. The working-party standing in the back of the truck caught the full flood.

On return the lads refused to let me in the tent. I stripped naked and tried to wash the overalls but there wasn't any water. It came up every morning in the water truck and men filled their own bottles, but there was none spare for a big washing job. So I tried scrubbing them in petrol, of which we had plenty. They still stank, a horrid mixture of ordure and tank fuel, and I was forced to leave them outside the tent to dry. A passing trooper lit a cigarette and threw away the match in their direction and they vanished in flames.

'It was the best thing,' said Corporal Steve Henley. 'They would only have had to be buried six feet down in lime, like they used to do when you died of plague.'

Often my partner on guard would be Paddy Jackson, a young tearaway from the Irish Republic, who slept in the same tent. Paddy was a member of the IRA, although he insisted he joined only for the women, for whom he had a fatal attraction.

'It's a great place for pickin' up bints,' he said. 'You get the best malarky in Dublin at the IRA meetings.'

Sometimes, shaking Paddy awake in his blankets to go on sentry, I thought how ironical it was that the safety of a complete British tank regiment would now depend upon a member of the IRA. Paddy drank heavily and once had such a bad hangover he was too ill to parade and reported sick. The M.O. wrote on his sick report, 'This man is boozed', which offended Paddy deeply, especially when the sergeant-major personally punished him by running him round camp until he dropped.

As summer passed, the crisis eased and Tito began to quarrel with Stalin instead. The regiment left the frontier and moved north-west to another place in the wilds, an idyllic setting with a stream meandering near the tents. Within a week, the lads had built a dam across and formed a pleasant bathing-pool. As always happened with these things, it began to become competitive. What started off as an impromptu affair of a few logs to deepen the water became a vast, complicated thing as men vied with each other in showing their skill. Someone built diving-boards; another lot constructed steps. The lads were proud of the pool. Every day we bathed naked, to the distress of a local priest who passed each evening with a crocodile of children, whom he made look the other way, while he crossed himself.

One day, I decided to follow the stream to its source and waded stark naked against the current for what seemed miles until my sudden appearance caused shrieks of alarm from two girls washing clothes by the bank and I picked my way back. A naked walk along an icy stream on a hot Italian summer day – it was heavenly, and I was only 19 and going to live for ever.

Among reasons for the move was to get in some firing practice and we blazed away a great deal, sometimes cooperating with infantry on exercises. Indirect fire was practised by rather primitive means. The CO's gunner fired an air-burst and everyone else lined up on the smoke and wound their guns down. All were then theoretically on target. But the wind blew the burst off-line and salvoes started landing around the observation post, an armoured scout-car manned by Corporal Mick Fineberg, who was a good friend of mine. I could hear his bellows of alarm in my headphones. The explosions knocked his set off wavelength and by some freak of wireless transmission only I could hear his cries for help, very faint behind the noise of fire orders. After vainly waiting for the firing to cease, I jumped out of the turret and ran to the command tank and asked them to stop.

'There were a group of Italian peasants passing by with an ox-cart,' Corporal Fineberg told me later, 'and when the shells started to burst all round them they tried to jump in the dingo with me' (a dingo was a small armoured reconnaissance vehicle). 'We had about six of us in there, packed like sardines, all the women screaming and the men praying and crossing themselves. It wasn't very funny, I can assure you.'

I wasn't on Rodney's tank then, much to his relief, I imagine. On leaving Palmanova, 'C' Squadron was split up between 'A' and 'B' Squadrons and now there was more shuffling around; briefly I found myself on the tank of 'A' Squadron Commander, Major John, who was rather alarmed at my habit of banging recalcitrant shells into the breech with a steel mug. A popular officer, he was good to serve under, though he once gave me seven days' CB for being improperly dressed. Thirty years later, we met at a rugby international at Twickenham and for the life of me I couldn't stop standing to attention and calling him 'sir'. It was highly embarrassing as he was very anxious to be friendly, but old habits were too strong. I only just managed to stop myself saluting, when we said goodbye.

There was a village nearby and in the evenings, after scrubbing and boiling out the guns, we went to the Stella d'Ora *albergo* and ate spaghetti and drank sour wine. I could have stayed there forever but they moved us again, to a small town where we were billeted in a factory. There took place the Great Mutiny. For months, meals had been getting smaller and smaller as cooks sold grub on the black market. The town was a racketeers' paradise, since we were stationed in the centre and tank-park guard was marked by a queue of Italians coming up and demanding of the sentry, '*Quanta costa benzina?*'

I resisted these offers for petrol but not all sentries were so dutiful and a guard might come off duty with a few thousand lire in his pocket. So the cooks seized their chance and eventually the midday meal was down to two army biscuits and a thin slice of corned beef. Feelings were fanned by news from the sergeant in charge of officers' mess catering, a companion on the draft from England as a trooper.

'Roast chicken today,' he said, when we stopped for a chat. 'I'm just off to buy some melons in the market.' When I told him our troubles he was sympathetic. 'Any time you're hungry,' he said, 'come round the back of the officers' kitchen and ask for me. You can have an egg. They have one every day for breakfast.'

Eggs were a soldier's delight and dream. The ration was only one a week unless we ate in an Italian café, where a plate of egg and chips cost half a week's wages.

Came the day when midday meal was even smaller than usual. The last people in the queue didn't get anything at all. Senior soldiers acted as shop stewards, going round the tables and saying quietly, 'Stay where you are. Sit at the table until they come for us.' Nobody left. We were totally united and the mood was ugly.

The days when there was no work in the afternoon had long since vanished and time for parade came and went. The orderly officer poked his nose into the cookhouse and was met with a howl of abuse. Scenting trouble he sensibly retired and Quartermaster-Sergeant Lowe was detailed to deal with the revolt. It was a good choice since everybody liked him. He stood on a table and listened to everybody's shouted complaints and wrote them down. He uttered no threats, issued no orders. When we'd finished, he simply said, 'OK, lads, you can take my word I'll do something about this,' and left. This nicely ended the mutiny, so the soldiers left, too. After a slight improvement, the food continued as bad as before.

The troop had its first case of VD about now, an unfortunate young lad, newly arrived from England. He seemed unlucky in his health as he celebrated his arrival in the regiment by being constipated for a fortnight, which must be nearly a world record. He refused to see the MO, probably because he suspected he'd got VD and was afraid of being found out, since it was a punishable offence. In vain his comrades tried to treat his constipation themselves. He was given hot tea and marched to the toilets, bent up and down, regaled with stories of how delightful bowel relief was. The simple psychology failed to move him, as did physical efforts, which ranged from jumping up and down to eating enormous quantities of spaghetti.

Then VD appeared. Deeply ashamed, he sadly examined his penis every morning, hoping it was better. He received little sympathy, only cries of, 'Why don't you get that thing of yours mended, chum, you'll spread it all over the whole bloody room.'

Eventually he reported sick, and was treated for both complaints, after which he was charged with getting VD and punished. His constipation may have been due to the Italian toilets as much as anything. They were the old-fashioned European sort with no seat, just a hole with two places for the feet, called 'stoopers' by the troops, and he couldn't get used to them. I could never properly adjust to them myself. To this day I fear going into a public lavatory in Italy.

For some time there had been rumours of another move and now they were confirmed. With the easing of the Jugoslav crisis fewer troops were needed in Italy. Word came the Hussars were to move to Germany, where the Cold War was in full swing as tensions between Russia and her wartime allies got worse. It was said to be a move to rest us after our exertions around Trieste.

CHAPTER FOURTEEN

'Have you stump, Tommy?'

The 7th Hussars said goodbye to Italy with a grand regimental dance organised by a committee from the ranks. As usual, most of the girls brought their mothers. The tanks were to travel to Germany on railway wagons with crews going in goods trucks at the back of the train. Each train took only a few tanks so their departure was spread over several days. The rest of the regiment (headquarters, fitters, transport and so forth) went by road, a long convoy snaking its way through Europe for several days, as there were no motorways and many bridges were still war-damaged.

Festooned all over tank-transporters in the sun, we drove slowly to a rail depot after loading the tanks. The huge transporters travelled slowly and I dozed on the mudguard, getting up to brew tea occasionally. Sometimes we stopped and ate maize from fields by the roadside. It took all day to get there and then came the delicate task of edging the Churchills on to railway wagons. The men's accommodation was the 'Eight horses or forty men' continental goods truck of World War One, about a dozen of us to each. They were completely bare and the wooden floors showed evidence horses had indeed been using them, although it looked more like eighty than eight. But we slung our blankets down and made ourselves comfortable amid a smell of dung.

It was a fascinating journey. To start with, I love railways, and Europe then was full of weird steam locomotives and ancient trucks and carriages with wooden seats, any one of which would have fitted perfectly into a film about the Russian Revolution. But more than that, we didn't know how long it would take, we didn't know what to expect when we arrived and we had no control over what happened on the journey. No one even knew when we'd start.

After loading the train, we waited. Nothing happened. There was no officer and a sergeant was in charge. No locomotive arrived, so after an hour or two some of the lads sloped off for a drink, promising to be back in a minute. They were still absent when the engine puffed up an hour later and was coupled to the trucks. The Italian driver assured us they would be off immediately, as soon as the signal was raised. No, it was impossible to wait. ('*E vietato aspettare. Devo andare presto.*)' A panic party went to search the town and by good fortune found the absentees in the first bar they came to. If we hadn't they would still be there, having reached the cosy stage where nothing matters.

'What's the hurry, who wants to go to Germany anyway?' they protested.

The locomotive slowly puffed out of the railway yard soon afterwards but it was something of a false start. After only a short time on the track, at an average speed of about ten miles an hour, it stopped. A signalman spotted smoke coming from the wheel-bearings of a flat-car and the wagon had to be left behind. It was a tank from my own troop and the driver, 'Slash' Winslade, insisted on remaining with it, in the drivers' tradition. They shunted him away to nobody knew where and the last we saw he was sitting on the tank looking depressed but determined. I felt a bit guilty at not volunteering to stay with him.

He told us later they took the truck to a shunting-yard and left him. There were no military personnel there, and nobody to tell him anything, and in any case he spoke hardly any Italian. He had no food and no money as we'd deliberately spent our last lire, since they would be useless in Germany. However, Slash was a man of some character, one of those dark, talkative, Cockneys you see wheeling barrows, and he refused to be defeated. He survived by siphoning petrol out of the tank and selling it on the black market. Once word got round the district that there was ample petrol at the railway sidings, he was besieged with customers.

'I could have made a fortune if I'd stayed there long enough,' said Slash when we got to Germany. As it was, he made enough for food and drink, although he had difficulty shopping because he dare not leave the tank for more than a few minutes in case the railway people moved it away in his absence. At night, he slept on the truck, underneath the Churchill. After three or four days of this they repaired the wheel-bearing and he found himself shunted on the back of another train carrying tanks from 'B' Squadron.

Meanwhile, we crawled towards the Brenner Pass and Austria. We lived, ate and slept in the horse-trucks, cooking on tank petrol cookers and sleeping soundly, despite the hardness of the floor, lulled by the clickety-clack of the wheels. The troop sergeant had thoughtfully stocked up with booze before leaving and set up a little bar whenever the train stopped, bellowing 'Bar open!' from his truck. The scenery was breath-taking and at its loveliest in October, and we sat with legs dangling out of the doorway as the train puffed and wheezed through the mountains, prisoners of the railway and cut off from the outside world.

Sometimes the train stopped for hours and then started off without warning. Once we entered a vast shunting-yard somewhere in Austria and they took the locomotive away. I took the chance to explore, clambering around derelict and bullet-riddled steam engines of that nostalgic European design with huge smoke stacks and driving wheels. Finding a row of silent trucks I decided it was a good place to attend a call of nature and crouched between two of them. As I did so, they started to move. With trousers round my ankles, running was impossible so I flung myself flat between the rails and let the train slowly pass over me.

When the train stopped, either for a signal, to change crews, or for no apparent reason, we might walk up to the locomotive and cadge a ride in exchange for a few cigarettes. The crews were friendly, but as they changed frequently they couldn't tell much about what was happening. We became adept at clambering over the trucks while the train was in motion, leaping from wagon to wagon like something from a film, until reaching the tank. Then we'd put up the aerial and listen to the radio. Alas, the old favourite at Gorizia had long since gone out of range but we twiddled and got the local Russian Forces station. It broadcast nothing but military marches, mixed with exhortations in an unknown tongue. Were they the Russian equivalent of 'Remember, VD walks the streets'?

The habit of listening to the tank radio nearly led to a nasty accident. To get better reception I erected more aerial, forgetting we had entered a section where overhead electric power was used. I was climbing out of the turret when an Austrian railway worker ran alongside the truck shouting '*Achtung! Achtung!*' and pointing at the aerial, which was waving two or three inches from the electric wires. Later, a rail official came to warn us. He said that the previous day a man from another squadron had been killed when he slipped climbing on to a tank and grabbed instinctively at the overhead wire. Years later, in London in 1959, I met a former Hussar who'd become a stonemason in civilian life and had just carved our dead friend's name on a war memorial.

At one point we passed through the Soviet Zone of Germany. I met my first Russian soldiers at the check-point. They looked very smart and well-equipped in their long brown overcoats and fur hats, with tommy-guns slung on their shoulders, although they held up the train for twelve hours while our documents were examined. It was getting colder as we moved north and we started to shiver in the horse-trucks. I rather envied those Russian hats.

Early one morning the train stopped and didn't start again. I couldn't sleep because I was cold so I got up and peered out. It was just before dawn and in the drizzle I could make out the steeply pitched roofs of a small German town. The train was in the coal-yard of the railway station. The sergeant went forward to investigate. After a few minutes he returned.

'This is it, lads,' he said. 'We're here.'

A quick reconnaissance revealed 'here' to be the little town of Soltau, near Luneberg Heath, where the German army had surrendered to Field-Marshal Montgomery 18 months previously.

Then a strange thing happened. Or perhaps I should have expected it. How the news spread at that hour I don't know, but within minutes we were surrounded by children and dogs, in the British army tradition. As the first thin streaks of dawn appeared so did the kids, accompanied by a positive pack of mongrels. About twenty little children with wan, starved faces, stood looking round at us, oblivious to the fact that for six years we had been the enemy. However, the sergeant was an old hand and knew what to do. He'd seen this happen in half-a-dozen countries.

'Right,' he shouted, 'get out all the buckshee rations. Now then, you Jerries, line up by the truck door. Children first, dogs afterwards.'

The children rushed excitedly into line, laughing at the way the sergeant was ordering them about, while a mass attack by dogs was beaten off. It was impossible to split the rations fairly so we opened all the tins and dished out food by the spoonful and slice and hunk. Strange smiles appeared on the children's faces, expressions of sheer ecstasy when they slurped down a simple treat like tinned pears or condensed milk. Life was grim for Germans in the first year or two after the war. While in England food was short, in Germany it was non-existent except for a bare subsistence ration. After the children had eaten, we fed a few scraps to the dogs, bits of old biscuit and so forth. Some adults appeared and looked on wistfully but we didn't give them anything. We weren't certain what our attitude ought to be and Belsen was not far away.

Afterwards the tanks were unloaded and driven to our new home, a former Nazi barracks at one end of the village. Compared with British barracks these were palatial. There were no unusable white-painted fireplaces or cold, polished stoves but good central heating and double-glazing. There were plenty of wash-basins and lots of hot water. Most of the regiment hadn't arrived, so for a few days we lived like lords, sleeping the autumn day away in our heated quarters with only four men to a room (in England I'd never slept less than 30 to a room) and playing endless games of cards and Monopoly in our waking moments. We explored the village and gazed curiously at the land of the Hun. In fact it looked distressingly familiar. What with the evening mist and the autumn leaves and the gabled houses it was just like Farnborough. Italy had been totally foreign, it looked nothing like England. This felt more like home. Even the toilets were normal, with huge seats. It was odd to find the land of the enemy so much like our own.

Meanwhile, the regiment arrived in dribs and drabs. Slash Winslade turned up with his strange story, begging to borrow some money. Then the road convoy arrived piecemeal after a ghastly experience at a French transit camp in southern Germany when they demanded tea with their evening meal instead of wine.

'I really thought that French cook was going to have a fit,' one of the lorry drivers told me. 'He shook a ladle and shouted something I didn't understand. I kept repeating, "tea – *comprenez*, char, tea," but I couldn't get through. So afterwards we went outside and brewed up in the trucks. The Frogs thought we were mad. They all came out to look at us.'

As occupation troops we had little real function in Germany except to be there and remind the Germans who won the war. Although there was tension with the Russians, who were consolidating their grip on Eastern Europe, there was little danger of a physical invasion. They didn't have an atom bomb in 1946, although captured German scientists were working on it. After being part of the Trieste defence force we now had little to do except what could be invented. Occasionally there were dawn road-blocks against black marketeers, when bicycles and prams were earnestly searched for contraband and arms. At other times we went out and showed the flag with patrols or stood by in case of trouble, once when a party of displaced persons from Eastern Europe were being sent back home against their will and a riot was feared. But they went peaceably, most of them to be executed or buried alive in a prison camp.

The DPs were a distinctive feature of post-war Europe. They consisted of people from dozens of nations who'd been forcibly brought to Germany by the Nazis as slave labour. There were literally millions of them and many died before liberation, especially the Russians who were treated as sub-human. Hundreds of thousands still remained, mostly those from Eastern Europe who feared to go back, a lot of them Poles and Russians. They stayed in hutted camps and, having little love for the Germans, sometimes indulged in mild banditry, so one of our jobs was to search their camps for stolen property.

This was usually a formality but once I found something. I entered a hut, heated like a greenhouse by an enormous stove, and was greeted by an old Russian lady in black and two girls with long skirts and kerchiefs over their heads. The scene resembled an illustration to Tolstoy. They beamed at me and invited me to search and offered tea, Russian style, without milk from a home-made samovar. The hut was divided by a partition but they indicated someone was asleep next door, and out of curiosity I tried the door. It was not locked and to tearful protests I opened it and went inside.

There was a horse in the room. It was standing by the bed chewing a corner of the mattress. The bed was unoccupied.

Only a sergeant could deal with this and he duly came. After a short conversation in signs and shouts he turned to me and said, 'I think we'd better pretend we never saw that bloody animal,' and we left to much bowing and smiling. Doubtless some German farmer was bewailing the loss of a horse somewhere but after what the Russians had been through I think they were entitled to it.

The main focus of life in Germany in 1946 was women. Respectable Italian girls didn't mix with soldiers un-chaperoned; a few of the more daring went to dances at the NAAFI club in Trieste but the competition was horrendous. There remained only amateur or professional prostitutes. But we'd heard enviously about the girls in Germany. It was said the country was one heaving mass of sexual intercourse and we were eager to participate.

Rumour, for once, had not exaggerated. Women in Germany had abandoned all restraint. There were many reasons, although all stemmed from the war. There was little to brighten existence except sex. There was no entertainment, little food and drink and a great shortage of men, since the war had killed many young males and not all prisoners had yet returned. There was also that instinctive human urge to breed that so often seems to follow a major war. Most important of all, sex could buy for a woman the otherwise unobtainable necessities and luxuries of life – coffee, cigarettes, alcohol, food.

There was little actual prostitution in the normal sense but a girl would aways expect to have some cigarettes, which were the universal currency in Germany then. The mark was useless and British troops were paid in tokens, so cigarettes replaced normal money. A 'nice' girl would ask for a few cigarettes 'for my father'. A more business-minded lass would demand a packet 'for the landlady, you understand'. Middle-aged prostitutes round Hamburg station were reduced to asking, 'Have you stump, Tommy?' in return for their favours. A stump was a cigarette end.

At Soltau the girls usually hung round the entrance to the camp cinema in the village, and waited to be asked inside by a soldier. If she didn't like him, she said she was waiting for somebody. But if he wasn't too repulsive there'd be a little kiss and cuddle inside. Although most of the films were about the war, with the Germans portrayed as strutting bullies or shouting buffoons always outwitted by gum-chewing Yanks or Englishmen with peculiar voices, the girls didn't seem to mind. Afterwards they'd make love, probably in the open air or perhaps at her home with parents tactfully withdrawing to bed (few girls lived alone). It must be remembered that young males were frustrated by the day's standards and jumped in with whoops of glee. Back home, women's magazines were still urging girls not to have pre-marital sex under any circumstances ('He won't respect you any more') and the majority of girls still came virgin to their husbands.

Many attributed the sexual orgy to the Nazi influence. 'The

Jerry girls have all been on them Nazi stud farms where they did it all the time to breed a master race,' said the barrack-room know-alls. I don't think that had any influence on the girls, most of whom had no interest in politics. In any case a lot of them weren't German, but DPs from elsewhere. More likely it was just the triumph of the reproductive instinct after six years of slaughter and suffering. A soldier who liberated a DP camp told me that as soon as the inmates were free they all started to have sex wherever they were, against the wall of a hut or on the ground in the open.

Many soldiers settled down and married their German girl-friends, who were regarded very highly. 'The Jerries aren't stuck-up like some English bints. They reckon their first duty is to look after their bloke and make him happy,' would be a typical opinion.

It was no surprise that I lost my innocence in the early part of 1947, during the bitter winter of that year. That's late by modern standards, of course. A healthy lad of 20 who'd never had it off would be considered inhibited today, although recently there appears to have been a shift back among the young towards chastity. The momentous event occurred after a regimental dance at the Neunhaus beer hall down the road from the barracks. I had the last waltz with a well-built blonde girl of about my age and walked her home. I never knew her name properly as I couldn't understand what she said and we had to communicate in bad German. For the same reason I never knew her nationality either, but as she sounded like something out of *Dr Zhivago*, I think it was Russian.

She lived in the DP camp outside the village and it was there the deed was consummated. We couldn't use her bunk because there were ten other people in the room, so it was performed against a post of the fence surrounding the camp and the whole thing was accompanied by an unearthly chorus of twanging wire. Unfortunately the winter of 1947 was one of the coldest in living memory. No sooner had my numbed fingers struggled with those special army buttons that won't undo when my sensitive parts were struck by a blast of freezing air which rendered them quite powerless for a moment. The girl must have felt the blast as keenly, but nobly stood her ground. At one point my feet slipped on the snow and I clawed at the barbed wire to keep upright, tearing my hands. It seemed a long way from the old headmaster and talk of 'mystic communion' between man and woman.

'Thank you, Tommy,' she said. *'Haben Sie Zigaretten?'* I noticed she didn't use the familiar *'du'* even then. 'I will need some for the hut warden.' I gave her a whole packet of Capstan full strength, a favourite among Germans, and we parted, she to the crowded wooden huts of the DP camp and me to barracks.

But not to bed. The army insisted on a rigorous programme of VD precautions before and after making love. It was as well to follow these, as it was a crime to get VD. A signature in the prophylactic centre register would mitigate matters. Before leaving barracks a soldier anticipating intercourse was expected to sign for some contraceptives and anoint his organ with anti-VD cream which got all over the underwear and hands. On return, he had to scrub the penis and anoint it with another cream. The treatment room, however, was outside the barracks' central heating system and there was no hot water. It was so cold that month that anti-freeze froze and we had to start up the tank engines every hour throughout the night to stop them from freezing up. An icicle hung from a tap in the treatment room. The effect of scrubbing my unhappy organ, already cold, in ice-cold water may be imagined. By the time I came to put on the cream it was without feeling and the end had turned blue. In the morning it was still blue so I reported to the MO He was surprisingly shy of mentioning the word penis and kept calling it by euphemisms.

'This is a bad show,' he said, 'getting your little wurlitzer in this state. Where would the army be if we all went round getting our winkies frozen, eh?' He assured me there was nothing wrong and told me to bathe it in hot water. The sergeant-major, going his rounds, found me kneeling on a chair by a wash-basin waving my winkie up and down.

'Can't you ever leave that thing alone?' he shouted. 'No self-control, that's the trouble.'

This first experience of sex was so traumatic I didn't follow it up for some time. Apart from anything else, I felt riddled with guilt and terrified of getting VD. What would mother and father have said if they knew I'd had sex with an unknown Russian girl against the barbed wire of a DP camp? As regards VD, penicillin was only just being introduced as a cure. Formerly the army had been able to frighten men with terrifying stories of the painful treatment for syphilis, screaming men with instruments stuck in their penises. I think they resented that penicillin made it so easy. They certainly went out of the way to warn us it was still unproved.

'It might just suppress the disease for a few years and then it could break out again,' we were told. 'Only next time it will be the tertiary stage and you'll die raving. Abstinence is the only real safeguard.'

A soldier who succumbed was immediately sent to hospital and charged when cured. Every day I anxiously inspected my winkie. The first act of most soldiers on getting up was to look at their sexual organs for signs of trouble.

Although we had plenty of social contact with German girls, there was hardly any with the men. A few German civilians were employed round the barracks as cleaners and we established a sort of relationship with one or two, especially with an ex-soldier called Hans who still wore the remains of his uniform. Sometimes we would taunt him, saying, 'Come off it, Hans, you were in the Gestapo, weren't you?' and the poor chap would go wild with rage and splutter, 'I have a paper signed by a senior officer to say I was not in the Gestapo.' But then, normal civilian social life hadn't resumed yet. Even the bars were empty, as they had nothing to sell except a filthy substitute beer and no food at all. Most Germans just concentrated on staying alive. In any case, troops had no German money, being paid in a special forces currency.

At Christmas 1946, just before my great sexual disaster, I caught up with my old acquaintance Geordie whom I'd escorted to the field punishment centre in Austria. He arrived in Germany in handcuffs, under close arrest for some crime or other, probably stealing a truck. It was the only offence he could think of. He'd already been waiting months under arrest for a court martial. Now some vital evidence was in Italy and the trial was postponed indefinitely. Meanwhile he stayed in the regimental cells by the guardroom. He was there so long he became part of the establishment. They let him out during the day to sit in the guardroom doing little jobs such as cleaning equipment for the regimental police and at night he sat up yarning with the guard, totally against orders, as he was supposed to be locked up all the time.

The army relax at Christmas and, on Christmas Eve, Geordie was allowed a drink. Stirred by the booze, he pleaded with the guard sergeant to be let out so he could find a girl.

'Just one shag, Sarge, just one shag, honest, that's all I want, just one tiny shag and then I'll come back,' he said. The sergeant, himself mellowed by alcohol, relented and Geordie vanished, armed with 50 cigarettes. He promised to return within the hour but by ten o'clock he wasn't back and the sergeant was worried. Those of the guard not on sentry scoured the village, looking in places where Geordie might be consummating his lust. To no avail. We dreaded the arrival of the orderly officer, who was supposed to inspect the cells. The printed guard report, which he had to sign, was written in the first person and part of it read: 'I inspected the prisoners. The boots of those charged with drunkenness were removed and their clothing loosened. They were not allowed to shave until sober . . .'

Mercifully, the orderly officer had also been celebrating Christmas. He not only failed to look into the cells but kept signing the guard report in the wrong place and holding on to the sergeant for support. He weaved away to inspect the tank-park guard, who reported he got lost and had to be shown the way out. Geordie came back at dawn with a satisfied smile on his face. By then the whole unit was in drunken slumber. That morning, in accordance with Christmas tradition, we were served tea in bed by the officers.

Months later, Geordie was court-martialled and sentenced to a spell in a military prison. When he came out, they made him a regimental policeman. The army had a theory that poachers made the best policemen and when I last heard he was doing well.

For three weeks, they made me 'A' Squadron pay clerk, when the regular man went home on leave. Quartermaster-Sergeant Lowe let me move into the clerk's billet in the stores. This was a sort of nest he'd built out of old cupboards, impregnable to the outside world. For the first time since joining the army three years previously, I had a room to myself. It was nice working on the books with 'Q' Lowe, who was an old friend from Italian days, when he'd been 'C' Squadron quartermaster. He was a little man with grey hair shaved close to his scalp.

'You can't grow hair and strength together,' he always said. 'It stands to reason, all your energy goes into your hair.' As he'd just become engaged to a sturdy ATS girl, also a quartermaster, he probably needed it. Freed from the discipline of the ordinary trooper, with no parades or guards, I turned my little home into a pigsty of unmade blankets, scraps of food and bottles of black market schnapps. But Mick O'Connor, the squadron sergeant-major, knew human nature only too well. He arrived in the stores one morning and visited my nest.

'Oh, I do like working in the stores,' he boomed, with high sarcasm, as I watched his advance into the den. 'Oh, yes, I don't have to make my bed and clean my equipment and polish my brasses, do I? And I don't have to clean the floor or tidy the room, do I? Because I know the sergeant-major won't inspect it, will he?' As he spoke, he was slashing with his stick, hurling things in all directions. He then destroyed my little home, throwing blankets on to the floor, pulling open cupboards and tearing out the contents, chucking webbing equipment on the ground and stamping on it. Finally, he carried away a bottle of schnapps in triumph (troopers aren't allowed to have spirits, so I couldn't complain).

I mention this in detail because it shows how conditioned we became to military life. If anybody behaved like that in a civilian occupation he'd be arrested. I wasn't really resentful. I rather admired Mick's rhetoric. He was, in fact, much loved in the unit for his eccentricity. At times he flagrantly disobeyed army regulations which forbid NCOs to strike men. He would beat an untidy soldier on parade with his cane, bellowing, 'Am I hurting you? I hope so because you deserve it.' Technically he could have been court-martialled but in practice nobody complained. Once he snatched the beret off a trooper on parade and threw it away because it was dirty, and then charged him with having no hat.

Yet he was genuinely liked and respected and the night the regiment's soccer side won the B.A.O.R. Cup he was chaired round the canteen. If you passed him in the street he'd always give a wink and a grin. Older soldiers respected him because in the Italian fighting he commanded a tank when he could have stayed behind with the transport.

The three weeks ended all too quickly and it was back to the barrack-room, fatigues, potato-peeling, guards and the tanks. Always the tanks. Like the cavalry we were, we tended the steeds daily. The troop solemnly marched to the tank park every morning and found something to do on them. Sometimes they were taken for an airing on the heath behind the barracks. This contained a small railway line and we distinguished ourselves by getting stuck on the level crossing. A segment of track became jammed under the rail and we couldn't move without tearing up the track. Once more, the driver refused to quit his post, but the train stopped a few feet away.

I examined my winkie with anxiety every few hours but the nearest I got to sex was when the whole regiment was paraded for identification by a rape victim, a German woman who'd identified her attacker as having a black Armoured Corps beret. She stopped rather a long time in front of me but passed on and picked out nobody. I remember thinking a man who was driven to rape with the amount of sex available in Germany in those days must have been pretty desperate.

One wintry afternoon a group of us had some fatigue near the Belsen concentration camp. I think the army had a coal depot by the railway line, the same one which brought in the prisoners and took away the valuables stripped from the bodies. It was nearly dark as we drove past the camp and the wind sighed dismally. The barbed wire and the watch-towers were still there. I felt a sickening premonition of evil. It was as if something vile was pressing down all around. The others felt it, too, and the truck drove away quickly. As Belsen vanished into the gloom, I saw an old woman in black scrabbling in the road for a squashed turnip which had fallen off a farm cart.

The routine was enlivened by an inspection from the brigadier commanding 4th Armoured Brigade, a young man with a reputation for being a fire-eater. It wasn't long after the arrival from Italy and things were still a bit haphazard. He ignored the conventions of these inspections and started poking around the barracks in an alarming way. Finding a rusty, green-painted army bicycle with no wheels in the tank park, he insisted on having all the regimental bicycles counted against the manifest. Bicycles were a sore point. They had all been neglected and cannibalised until they were just bits scattered around camp. The quartermaster desperately scoured the barracks and had the pieces hastily assembled but when they were all put together he was still one short, not to mention odd wheels and handlebars. Later there was a formal court of inquiry into 'the loss of War Department Bicycle No. 984765'.

Encouraged by his success, the brigadier suddenly rang the fire alarm, a large metal triangle with a steel bar by the main gate. There was no sign of the fire picquet but a corporal peered out from the guardroom and shouted at the brigadier, 'Who's that clown ringing the fire alarm?' When some of the fire picquet did arrive he made them run out the long hose by the guardroom, but this turned out to be only six feet long, the rest having been cut off for some unknown purpose. Altogether, it was an unfortunate inspection.

Having experienced the Great Mutiny over food in Italy, I got mixed up with another. This was over the rugby team. I'd enjoyed rugby in Italy but now the officer in charge was a little lieutenant nicknamed Pinocchio. He picked the side in descending order of rank, except that sergeants got priority because he was frightened of them. There weren't many sergeants, however, as they preferred to play hockey (a relic of the old pre-war regular army days in India) and vanished on expeditions to remote parts of Germany. But there were lots of officers wanting to play and any young second lieutenant could guarantee getting a place at the expense of a trooper. The six or so troopers in the team became fed up and said they wouldn't play again. Twenty years later, I met one of them, an old friend called Peter Sheffield, at a rugby dinner in Hertfordshire and he was still bitter about it. However, a flu epidemic left the team short and we were ordered to turn out.

'It is a parade,' said Pinocchio, pursing his little lips. 'If you fail to turn out you will be charged with disobeying an order.'

The result was that we took the field baa-ing like sheep or giving the Nazi salute. Perhaps our gentle hint had an effect because somebody higher up suggested a trial match. This proved a fatal error as various old scores were settled. Cries of commissioned anguish rang round the field. To make matters more farcical a major insisted on playing. Nobody could bring themselves to do violence to such an exalted rank and whenever he fell on the ball everyone waited for an officer to kick him off it. They were equally reluctant and Pinocchio murmured 'Excuse me, sir,' as he prodded tentatively with his boot.

Rank was the curse of service sport then. For one thing, there was nowhere for officers and men to mix after a game, so as soon as the whistle sounded the team all went separate ways. Not that officers made much effort to remedy matters. A journalist colleague told me that when he played rugby in the army they made him eat his tea at a separate table from the officers. After leaving the army, I played for a Leicester side against an RAF station in Rutland and found things just as bad. Every officer in the opposition vanished as soon as the game ended without even saying goodbye and we civilians had tea with the airmen in the NAAFI.

Later, as a journalist, I got to know a lot of people connected with services rugby and found a vast improvement, although only a few years ago the Army Sports Council issued an edict that all players must in future be called by their ranks on the sporting field, a stupid order which showed that the spirit of Pinocchio dies hard. Apart from anything else, the order hardly seemed practical. By the time someone wanting the ball has shouted, 'Quick, outside you, acting company quarter-master-sergeant,' the chance would have been lost. Fortunately, the army has had much practice at ignoring impossible instructions and I suspect the order was quietly ignored. A lot can happen in forty years.

CHAPTER FIFTEEN

Sergeant Green

Early in 1947 came the first leave since leaving England in 1945 and I returned home to Leicester. It was a bad time. The whole of Britain and Europe was frozen solid. There was a crowded crossing of the North Sea from Cuxhaven in an old Liberty steamer converted to a troopship with a seaman standing in the bows to watch for wartime mines, still around, followed by an attempt to hitch-hike home from Grantham station along roads blocked with snow. I arrived exhausted and late having taken ten hours to get from Hull.

Roger was back from the war already and working as a commercial traveller (as they were called then) for a brewery in Nottingham, so he wasn't home much. My entire generation had vanished into the services and the girls all had civilian boy-friends. Billy, son of the daring aviator, was in Indo-China with the Signals, poor Jerry English had been killed in Holland, John Bradshaw, son of the county cricketer, was in India. Alec, who joined the army on the same day as me, was in the artillery in Palestine. The Labour government were just about to shut down every factory in the country for a week to save coal and grandmother Green had moved in with us, so I had to sleep downstairs on a convertible bed.

However, my parents were glad to see me after 18 months away, even though mother kept complaining 'I'd changed', which was hardly surprising. Father looked forward to making friends with a son who'd grown up since he last saw him and delighted in showing me round some Leicester pubs now I was old enough to drink publicly with him, although I'd been in a few illegally without his knowing.

'Not that I want you to become a booze artist, my boy,' he said with that ambivalence that always marked his attitude to drink, 'but if you're going to have a drink anyway, you might as well have it with me and have a proper one.'

As usual, his list of pubs was being constantly updated.

'I don't go in the Coach and Horses any more,' he told me. 'The landlord is a toad. I've taken to using the Nag's Head in Millstone Lane, where they keep it nice and cool and the landlord cleans the pipes regularly. I've stopped going to the Bell. My last pint there had bits in it and the barmaid wouldn't change it. Of course, they don't understand beer in a big hotel.'

He took me following the hounds near Melton Mowbray and, as it was cold, we had a nip of Scotch. Having a slight headache next day, father pronounced that he had been poisoned by fusel oil. The Great Fusel Oil Theory was one many of his generation believed in. This mysterious substance was reputed to have been produced in whisky by alcohol reacting with the cork.

'That is why you will always see a good landord shake a bottle of spirits before putting it up,' father told me. 'That distributes the fusel oil and stops it concentrating at the bottom of the bottle.' Nobody seems to have heard of fusel oil these days and I often wonder how much substance there was in the theory.

On arrival back in Soltau, I found I'd been picked for the brigade cross-country run. Whether this was a tribute to my stamina or punishment for the rugby mutiny I never did find out but the news filled me with dread. In vain I cast around for a way out. Then luck took a hand. When I was on sentry, an Alsatian guard dog bit me in the ankle, leaving two tiny punctures of the skin. It was enough. I hobbled to the Medical Officer after the usual farce of sick parade, my face twisted in pain. The waiting-room was filled with members of the cross-country team and the MO was suspicious.

'It shouldn't really hurt as badly as all that.' he murmured. 'Medicine and duty.'

'But sir, I'm in the brigade cross-country. Is it wise for me to run? I mean, I might let down the regiment.'

'Oh, all right, tell them I said you needn't run.'

The man who took my place in the cross-country was carried in with a frostbitten penis. I always feel a bit guilty about that.

Times were changing in the regiment. The older men were going home, except for those who'd signed on as regulars. Paddy Jackson, of the IRA, demobilised himself by not returning from leave in Dublin. Anyone with Italian service, like myself, was an old soldier. In a mass reshuffle, a group of us were transferred to 'B' Squadron. It was pleasant and homely there, because they were based half-a-mile from the main barracks in a former hospital up the road. They had their own little bar where we played darts every night and sang rude songs. Every time I sang 'Angeline', the ditty I'd learned way back at Bovington, the cooks invited me to have egg and chips with them. They were the first chips I'd ever had in the army in three years. Fat was rationed too strictly for them to be served publicly but the cooks treated themselves to plenty. The era of 'chips with everything' came later.

The cold spell broke to be followed by the hottest summer for years. I found myself guarding a former Jugoslav partisan general, wanted for war crimes and collaborating with the Germans, who was being held in a house in the village, normally used as officers' quarters. I never did know why they took him there but perhaps he'd been arrested nearby. He was being sent home to certain death and when two of us took him for a walk he made a feeble attempt to escape, breaking away and running down the path in the woods. An out-of-condition war criminal is no match for two healthy young soldiers and there was no difficulty keeping up. It was rather bizarre. We ran alongside, urging him not to be so foolish.

'Please stop, sir,' we panted. 'We've orders to shoot you if you don't stop and you wouldn't like that, would you, sir? Please slow down, sir, and come back to the house.' As he was a general, even though only a partisan, we were unnaturally polite.

Eventually he just ran out of breath and stood there, panting. I remember thinking he wouldn't be much good in a threequarter line, but then he was going to be dead in three months, anyway.

About this time, I met the Duke of Gloucester, brother of the reigning monarch, King George VI. Half-a-dozen troopers were sent as serfs to a great jamboree at the taxpayers' expense called the B.A.O.R. Horse Show. The job was to guard the site and clear up. I met the Duke, who had come over from England for the event, walking down a path behind the V.I.P. tent. I was in a fit of deep distraction at the time, cogitating over my loins. A tiny red spot had appeared. Could this be the first sign of syphilis? Was my brain already rotting away? Dare I report sick? Dare I not report sick? I walked with head bowed, talking to myself. I would have collided with the Duke but he very decently got out of the way and politely stepped off the path as I shambled along, oblivious to my surroundings.

I was not oblivious for long. The Duke's entourage was headed by the smallest sergeant-major I have ever seen. He was also the fiercest.

'Don't you know to salute the King's brother?' he shouted. I looked up, recognised the Duke, and was smitten with fear. My right arm shot up and crashed to the temple with such force I nearly knocked myself unconscious. The Duke courteously returned the salute and passed on. The sergeant-major paused for a short speech about my future prospects and he, too, moved away. It struck me afterwards that it was the second time I'd met a member of the Royal Family under unusual circumstances, the first occasion being my unfortunate exposure in front of Princess Elizabeth.

That evening we were left guarding the deserted arena. Investigation of the dark V.I.P. tent revealed the remains of a Babylonian orgy. Caviare and half-empty bottles of champagne littered the tables. We plunged in madly, stuffing caviare into our mouths and drinking champagne from the necks of bottles. We fought with caviare, rolling each other on the ground and smearing it over the victim's face or stuffing it down his shirt. When both caviare and champagne were exhausted, a little Scotsman from another unit volunteered to take us in his truck to some barracks where there was more liquor (in the army there was always someone who knew where there was more drink and who suggested leaving in a truck). The truck entered the barracks of a Scots regiment at 60 m.p.h. Mercifully the barrier was up. The driver went straight round the barrack square and left by the same entrance some ten seconds later still doing sixty, a speed he maintained until we got back to the horse show.

'Why didn't you stop, Jock?' we asked. 'We thought you were going to get some more booze.'

'It were nae wise. Ah saw the sergeant-major.'

I am always grateful to that unknown sergeant-major, whose sudden appearance undoubtedly saved me from a court martial, along with the others. Awaking in the morning with terrible headaches, we shuddered at the recollection. The truck had a great dent in it, but nobody could remember collecting it.

That spring a letter came from cousin Joan. The classic saga of her love story was still going on. Werner, her German boy-friend, had been repatriated at last from prison camp in America and was back in Germany, living with his parents in Duisberg. To be near him, Joan had got a job in Germany as a secretary with the Allied civilian control commission. Would I like to come over and be introduced to Werner? We could all spend the weekend at Werner's cousin's house in Hamburg.

I collected every spare cigarette and scrap of food I could scrounge and took them over to Hamburg on the weekly leave truck, or 'passion wagon', as the soldiers called it. I knew Hamburg well and went there most weekends for a meal at the NAAFI and a film at the garrison cinema. I say 'knew' Hamburg, but that was difficult. Most of it was vast heaps of rubble, sixty or seventy feet high. Reconstruction after the bombing hadn't even been thought of, they were still clearing up. Werner's cousin lived in a flat in one of the huge nineteenth-century houses by the Alster lake. The district had been badly bombed and the house looked empty and uninhabitable, with the front door hanging at a crazy angle and great holes in the roof and walls. When I knocked, the sound reverberated through it as in a horror movie. Eventually a little girl of about 7 ran down the stairs and came to the door but when she saw me she ran away screaming. After a short pause, Joan came up from the basement and greeted me. She apologised for the little girl.

'The last time British soldiers came to this house was when they captured the city,' she said, 'and then they took away all the electric light bulbs for their barracks.'

She led me down to the basement flat and introduced me to the legendary Werner. He was tall and thin, with sparse fair hair, in his late thirties, good-looking and charming, one of those assured German types that make people like me feel inferior. Perhaps he was a bit on the defensive but I took to him at once and thought he would make a good addition to the family. I was also introduced to Werner's cousin Annie and her husband Fritz. Fritz was a fat, jolly little German, the sort one associates with lager beer and gemütlichkeit. His war service had been even more uneventful than mine, as he'd never left Denmark.

'You are like me, Michael,' he said. 'When I was a soldier in Denmark, I looked also like a sack. Just like you. It is the uniform. I, too, was no good as a soldier.'

Presumably he meant to be friendly but I was a bit peeved at being compared with the dregs of Hitler's army. I thought I was looking quite smart. I'd polished my Hussar cap-badge to impress them all. It was, however, difficult to look impressive in the army greatcoat of those days, which was invariably too short and bulged out at the bottom, giving a bell-like appearance.

It was a jolly weekend, with lots of schnapps. To save their rations, I ate mostly in the NAAFI club in Hamburg. Werner felt obviously lost, bewildered and rather bitter, which was understandable after four years in a P.O.W. camp during which the family business had been bombed. He took me for a walk round the Alster Lake, swept his arm in a circle to encompass the wrecked houses and said savagely, 'There,

211

Michael, there you see the new German house-culture. We live in cellars.' I stifled the obvious reply, that it was their own fault for starting the whole thing.

It was strange to see cousin Joan from Osterley settling down as a German *hausfrau*, and talking German all the time, except when she addressed me. We were still technically at war with Germany and Joan and Werner couldn't get married yet but they were sleeping together. Today, of course, it would be the normal thing, especially after six years of separation, but it was still not something to be publicly admitted in 1947, not among the English lower middle-classes. Joan took me aside at bedtime and explained.

'Werner and I will be sleeping together,' she said. 'Don't tell Mum or Dad or Uncle Jack and Auntie Win, will you?' She needn't have asked. I could imagine the effect of the news in Osterley or Leicester. Thus the difference just one generation made in attitude.

Werner and Joan eventually got married in 1950, at Osterley, after eleven years of waiting. Old Grampy Smeath from Bristol, who had moved in with Uncle Will after grandmother's death, was present at the wedding, making Werner probably the only German whose wedding had been honoured by the presence of a man who might nearly have bowled W. G. Grace, although I doubt whether he appreciated the honour. They returned to Germany and later emigrated to Canada where they had two lovely daughters and two grandchildren. Werner died in 1984, much loved and respected by all of us.

Although the majority of officers and men in the 7th Hussars were still wartime recruits or national servicemen, the regiment was anxious to get back to the piping days of peace as quickly as possible. Wives and children came out from England. Horses were imported and stables built. The cavalry tradition died hard in the Hussars, even though the regiment had tanks, and an indoor riding school was set up. Soldiers were used to serve officers' families in various menial ways. It was rather humiliating to take orders from a civilian, especially one 12 years old. That must have been the age of one little girl who told me to hold her horse.

'You,' she said, when I was on stable fatigue, replacing jumps in the riding school. 'Hold Jason for me.'

Jason looked an evil-tempered brute, stamping and rearing and showing the whites of his eyes, and I have always been slightly afraid of horses, so I hesitated. She at once complained to her father, 'Daddy, that man won't hold my horse,' so I conquered my fear swiftly.

Sometimes we took revenge. Any civilian horsewoman outside barracks might well find herself pursued down the road by a Churchill tank. But since the Churchill could move little faster than walking pace, escape was easy.

I had not volunteered in the war to hold horses for civilians and began to consider a change. The fact that after two-and-a-half years in the army I was still in the lowest rank of trooper may have had something to do with it. I liked the camaraderie of the barrack room and the good blokes who were my mates, but the pay was still only £1 8s. a week (£1.40p) and I wanted to do a bit better. And lucky though I was in my companions, it was down in the ranks that the bullies, the thugs, the psychopaths lurked, the men who beat up people in lavatories just for the fun of it, the people who would pick a quarrel after a couple of beers, the men who made their comrades' lives misery. We had none in 'B' Squadron but there were plenty about in the army at large.

The chance for a move came when they advertised for men to transfer to the Army Education Corps, which needed teachers for demobilisation programmes. Those were the days when it was believed education would solve anything. Two troopers volunteered, myself and a special chum, Frank Gardiner. We went to Headquarters of the Rhine Army at Bad Oeynhausen for interview and were supposed to spend one night there but managed to desert for a week after finding a retreat in a strange transit camp in a big house in the centre of town.

It wasn't really a camp, just a house full of bunks with a blanket on each and people came and went as they pleased. The place was stuffed with deserters and absentees and there was usually a raid by Military Police every night, which ended with struggling men being dragged off on lorries, but we were protected by a genuine movement order. For food we marched into a Royal Engineer barracks and just queued up with everybody else or else went to the NAAFI. After this little holiday, most of which was spent in the garrison swimming-pool, we hitch-hiked back to camp and explained the interviews had been very stringent and had gone on for days. Frank failed – he did not have the magic matriculation – but in June they posted me to the Army Education Corps training centre at Göttingen, the college of the Rhine Army.

Göttingen was an ancient university town, which looked like a stage-set for *The Student Prince*. Joining the Education Corps was traumatic because the trainee received instant promotion to sergeant. It was strange after being ground down for so long to be waited on at meals and treated with respect. It took some time to get used to privates standing to attention and asking permission to do something. The pay was nearly triple and, most important of all, one lived in a sergeants' mess where spirits were served. The army sensibly did not serve spirits to those below sergeant's rank, except in cold weather or emergencies. Within three weeks I was well on the way to becoming an alcoholic with brandy and whisky about three-pence (2p) a measure. Father's fears about booze-artists were being realised.

The three months at Göttingen passed pleasantly in a daze of alcohol, teaching practice and lectures. The army reminded us of its presence with occasional drills but otherwise it was like being at a civilian college. We formed a drama club and put on a play. At night, the students talked far into the small hours discussing Life and What It Was All About and Literature and Truth and drinking enormous quantities of whisky and brandy. The medieval university atmosphere of Göttingen was the final touch. The sergeants' club was, in fact, the old *Studenthaus* which had an interesting device, peculiar to Germany as far as I know, called a vomitorium. Situated in the toilet, it was for German students to be sick in after drinking enormous quantities of beer. It consisted of a bowl at waist height with a flow of water controlled by a brass stud at the top. An inebriated student pushed his burning forehead against the wall, it pressed the stud, and water flowed.

While at Göttingen, I took up flying. The RAF gliding club at Salzgitter, near the Russian Zone, advertised courses and I spent several weekends and a longer leave there. The place had once been a Luftwaffe flying school, as German pilots were trained initially on gliders, rather as seamen may be trained on sail, which also saved fuel. The German Chief Flying Instructor, a Luftwaffe colonel named Adolf, had stayed on as the British CFI. A large, jovial man, used to command, he was oblivious of the fact that Germany had lost the war and the British were in charge. As a glider has no engine, noises from the ground can be heard quite well and Adolf had a habit of abusing his British pupils by shouting, 'Come down, you bloody fool, you'll kill us all!' Staff told us Adolf used to run across the airfield with a megaphone bellowing at the Luftwaffe cadets in their gliders, terrifying them.

Adolf's position was rather anomalous. In 1947, the Germans were still technically enemies but he continued to treat British students like Luftwaffe privates. In those days, they went solo from the start, strapped into a crazy old contraption called a *Schülegleitder*, which had no cockpit, just a stick with a seat on it sticking out into space, like the original Wright brothers' plane. They started off with slides along the ground, the aircraft towed on a winch cable and graduated to low hops (six feet); high hops (sixty feet); high hops with S-turns; and finally a circuit at 600 feet. This primitive form of instruction enabled Adolf to exercise the maximum abuse on each trainee. Even on a circuit there was no escape; you could see Adolf down below, between your legs, jumping up and down and waving his arms, and perhaps catch a faint cry of 'Come down, you bloody fool . . .'

Actually, I *did* nearly kill Adolf. I came swooping in silently over the turnip field as he stood with back towards me, and, struck by a sudden downdraft, brushed his hair with the landing-skid. I expected abuse, but his reaction was more technical.

'Next time, Sergeant Green,' he said icily, 'you get the focking nose down earlier so you have some focking flying-speed and more control. Then you will not kill us all.'

There were only two members of the RAF on the station, the CO, Flight-Lieut. Gerry Winters, and his second-in-command, Pilot Officer Jock Forbes, who looked after training. Jock was a gifted glider pilot and later became British champion. Much to my surprise, when I arrived, the CO asked, 'Would you like to mess with the officers? There's only Jock and me and we're fed up with each other's company. This place is miles from anywhere.'

'What about the sergeants' mess?' I asked and he replied there wasn't one. 'We'd like to have you,' he pleaded. 'We need a third for cards. Otherwise we just go mad looking at each other every night.'

For three weeks, I had the pleasure of being an officer, only a few months after shovelling manure in the Hussars' stables. Being an officer principally consisted of playing pontoon every evening with Jock and Gerry. They drank enormous quantities of Cointreau (which was only a few pence a bottle) and I happily joined them. We used to get through nearly a bottle each as battle was joined and went on far into the night. They were impressed by my skill at pontoon, but then I'd learned in the hard school of the 7th Hussars. If I wanted a change, I was in the unique position of being able to use the other ranks' facilities as well and could go and play table tennis with the aircraftmen and privates. It was a happy, pleasant place and I could cheerfully have spent the rest of my life there.

They told me of an embarrassing visit by a high-ranking RAF officer, who presumed Adolf must be from an Allied nation by the way he was abusing the pupils. Thinking him to be Polish, he invited him up to the mess for a drink and Adolf accepted. They spent hours yarning about the war until it gradually dawned on the Air Commodore that when Adolf spoke about the enemy he meant the British, and when he said he shot down a fighter, he meant a Spitfire. He left hastily, muttering, 'Get that bloody Jerry out of here.'

Just before the end of my three weeks' leave I passed the 'C' certificate of the British Gliding Association which entitled me to a splendid pilot's licence, headed 'Federation Aeronautique Internationale (British Empire)', with an inscription asking the civilian and military police to assist me in four languages, including Russian. I once produced it to a policeman in Nottingham who was going to book me for parking and he became most helpful.

At the last moment I nearly failed. One test was to soar for 15 minutes (that is, rise above the point of release) and approaching to land I flew too near some electricity cables by the field. Adolf had an obsession about this and went into one of his rages. 'It is no good, you have failed, Sergeant Green,' he shouted. 'I do not pass bad pilots. Go near the cables and you will kill us all.' But he relented later and I got my certificate. Adolf's fear of the cables was probably based on experience, as tales of blazing aircraft dangling from them were legion.

At the end of the Göttingen course they posted me to HQ 7th Armoured Division, the original Desert Rat formation of 1942, so now I'd worn all three Desert Rat badges: the green of the 7th Armoured Brigade in Italy; the black rat of the 4th Armoured Brigade in Germany with the Hussars; and now the red of the 7th Armoured Division. All without ever seeing the desert. After a week or two they sent me to the Army Education Centre at Osnabruck, a huge mock-Gothic folly built by a rich German about the turn of the century. It was covered in dwarfs and gnomes. They peered from the ceilings, leered from the flower-beds, snarled over the fireplaces. There was a fountain in the hall, full of gnomes, of course. The staff consisted of a captain, who was C.O., and myself and another sergeant. I was given responsibility for the demob classes, groups of happy soldiers filling in two or three weeks before leaving the army.

I established a good relationship with my pupils. I slept in an attic room under a canopy of plaster dwarfs and the first class of the day would arrive by lorry at 8.30 and knock on the door. Since I invariably went to sleep drunk and fully-dressed all I had to do was to get up, light a fag, and start teaching. Occasionally the hangover would be so great I couldn't manage the lesson and then we'd all sit down and talk about life, but usually I got through and a cup of tea at ten o'clock put me right again. I would teach anything demanded by the

217

students or the C.O., but it was usually what would now be called liberal studies. I even tried poetry appreciation with some success. They liked 'The Burial of Sir John Moore at Corunna' by Charles Wolfe particularly. We spent some time discussing the lines

> We buried him darkly at dead of night,
> The sods with our bayonets turning

and arguing whether it was possible to dig a grave with bayonets.

I decided the only way to settle this was by a practical test and the class were asked to bring their bayonets next time. Capt. Greenwood, the CO, would have been surprised to see the liberal studies class kneeling in the garden tearing at turf with bayonets but the test was abandoned when I realised the old bayonets were twice as big as the modern sort. The class were most impressed when told that the Duke of Wellington complained to the War Office about the quality of British spades, which bent and were useless, so he used captured French equipment.

'Just like the army,' they said.

I also introduced educational visits. These included the gasworks (a vital part of everybody's education) and the local British troops' brewery. This latter visit was spectacular. The lads marched there smartly in columns of three and were shown the fascinating process of making beer. They then offered us unlimited quantities to sample free. We did not march back so smartly. A shambling mob of soldiery lurched through the town, led by a sergeant who had difficulty in walking straight. Unfortunately Capt. Greenwood saw us return – he could hardly miss us, the noise was heard all over the district – and put me on the mat. He was kind and fatherly.

'What is it that drives you to drink, Sergt. Green?' he asked.

I didn't know what to say. I presumed that every healthy young man of 20, who could get unlimited quantities of whisky, brandy and gin at threepence a shot, would get tight. If he didn't understand that, we couldn't communicate. I decided to hint at vague pressures on me.

218

'It's nothing, sir,' I said. 'I can fight this myself.'

'Have you any private worries?'

'No, sir . . . not really . . . it's just that . . . well, no, sir . . . not really. . .'

I thought that was rather clever, just a hint of secret troubles. Looking back, though, it was mean to take advantage of the captain's kindness, but young people do that. He sent me away with a warning.

The boozing reached its zenith on my twenty-first birthday in January 1948, which I celebrated by getting banned from the Sergeants' Club at Osnabruck. About a dozen friends joined me and after the first ten gins I remember little until I found myself alone with the civilian manager, who was asking me to leave. It was long after closing time and the place was deserted. I had collected a vast cocktail from the remnants of leftover drinks and was sipping this contentedly. I declined politely to leave until I finished my drink and he called the garrison police. By a stroke of good fortune I saw their jeep arrive from the toilet window and slipped out the back way, skulking back to the education centre and leaping into bushes whenever a truck came by. My misdeeds, however, were reported to the long-suffering Capt. Greenwood who once more called me in and rowelled my emotions by being decent. This time, though, it didn't matter. I was due to be demobbed soon.

Before going home I made a farewell visit to the 7th Hussars. It happened to coincide with some celebration at 'B' Squadron and I sang 'Angeline' for the last time. I slept with the troopers and Pete Sheffield was sick on my sergeant's stripes. Despite promotion to sergeant, I couldn't be at ease in the sergeants' mess where I found myself standing to attention every time Sergeant-Major Mick O'Connor asked me to have a drink. But everybody was very good and I left with real regret.

A new sergeant came to replace me at Osnabruck and I spent the last day or two playing table tennis with Otto, the German clerk. Otto had been a submarine officer (they made him bathe every day in the Baltic during training, he said, winter or summer). He was easily the most intelligent person in the centre and we spent hours yarning about life, women, war and submarines. He wrote to me in England when I left the army but I lost his address and didn't reply. If he should read this, perhaps we could start writing again. After I returned to civilian life, I used Otto as the basis for a character in a play which won Northampton Drama Club's one-act play competition in 1950. It was about an intelligent and cultured German reduced to acting as waiter for a lot of drunken British soldiery. Otto was only half the man. The other half was based on a waiter in the sergeants' club at Göttingen, who used to do *The Times* crossword, a feat beyond most of his customers.

The leaving party was more respectable than the twenty-first. It was held at the sergeants' mess of the Royal Engineers' unit where I had my meals. There were wives and girl-friends and dancing and a band. I provided an unusual and stimulating punch which made everybody ill, due to the introduction of condensed milk 'for smoothness'. Next day I said goodbye to Capt. Greenwood, who said he was sure I would do well in journalism. Like most people, he had a vague idea that drunken irresponsibility was some sort of qualification for newspaper work. Or perhaps that is an injustice.

A truck came and took me away to a transit camp. On the way, I asked the driver to stop, got out my revolver and some ammunition left over from Trieste and spent half-an-hour blazing away in a field at a tin can and a few birds. I hit nothing. Next morning I was on the train for the Hook of Holland and Harwich and home. The last sight of Germany was children playing around the station where the troops embarked, drawn as usual to the British army by visions of chocolate and sweets. The soldiers must have given them something at any rate, because they were blowing up french letters like balloons and hitting each other playfully. And then the train puffed slowly away from the home of the Boche, as Rockfist Rogan would have called it in the *Triumph*.

Next night I was at a demob centre in York, where hundreds of returning warriors were processed. Within an hour, all had been issued with hat, raincoat, a pair of trousers and a sports coat, three months' pay, a war-service gratuity, various credits and our discharge papers. Capt. Greenwood had given me a character of 'good'. While this might seem generous, it wasn't very high. 'Excellent' was standard; 'very good' meant not-so-bad; 'good' was really a qualified bad. I probably deserved it.

With an hour to wait for the train to Leicester I went into the sergeants' mess at the barracks and ordered my usual double brandy. It set me back half-a-crown – five times the cost in Germany. I began to wonder if I'd done the right thing as the train rattled over the old Great Central route to Leicester.

CHAPTER SIXTEEN

Home

I returned to civilian life at the end of January 1948 with some suspicion. On going into the army I thought I would never become a soldier; now I didn't see how I could become a civilian again after three-and-a-half years in khaki. Leicester presented a strong contrast to the fleshpots of a sergeants' club in Germany. Food was severely rationed and even bread was on coupons now; fuel was short, petrol almost non-existent, the beer thin. But a bonus was that the price of drink saved me from becoming an alcoholic. No more double brandies – it was back to draught Bass when flush, Everard's bitter when money was short. Once, in an effort to economise I was reduced to drinking a pint of the filthy L.B.M. beer my father had warned me against. It cost 10½d (4p) and was so awful I nearly went straight down to the army recruiting office.

There was no hurry to start work. With several weeks' demob leave and pay and allowances of about £50 in the Post Office, I had more money than ever before. First of all, I wanted to find what had happened to my old pals. Poor Jerry English would never come back, nor Ken, who'd lived by the playing-fields, nor Roger's pal David, who'd died in India. But the rest had all returned to England. I went out with Billy, son of Cyril Hurst, the daring aviator. He'd just returned from serving with the Signal Corps in Saigon, where British troops were helping the French re-establish their rule. I met his father next day and he said, 'What did you do to Billy last night? He went to sleep in the armchair with his eyes open.' I saw Alec, who'd joined up the same day as myself, and together we played a game for the Old Wyggestonians' Second XV. Alec had just returned from Palestine and was waiting to go up to Oxford University.

Roger's naval air squadron contained half-a-dozen Leicester pilots and they kept together when they came out. On return they joined Stoneygate Rugby Club en masse and it was natural for me to forsake the Old Wyggestonians and play with them. Stoneygate played on a dank meadow down near the canal at Aylestone, on the outskirts of the city. A stream was an essential part of their game. With ten minutes to go and Stoneygate leading, instructions were to boot the ball into the water at all costs. A stick was kept for retrieving it, but if Stoneygate were ahead this used to disappear. Somehow a spare ball could never be found.

It was there, down by the Grand Union Canal, that the experiences came which were to result in *The Art of Coarse Rugby* in 1960. I frequently played in the third team (although sometimes graduated to the second and firsts). This level of rugby was full of wartime casualties, gallantly struggling to keep up their favourite game. Our greatest rivals, Westleigh R.F.C., had a forward who'd lost an arm in the war. He played with incredible dexterity, taking and giving passes with one hand and fighting off would-be tacklers by flipping his stump at them, in a way that reminded me of my father when upset or distressed. Another opponent had been badly wounded in the head by shrapnel. Before the game his skipper came into the dressing-room and asked, 'Would you mind tackling our left winger gently? He's got a steel plate in his skull. The RAF, you know.'

One local player had been blown up in Normandy and would suddenly foam and gibber in the line-out. Men with one eye, desperately groping for the ball, were not uncommon (and some played cricket, too). Over at nearby Northampton, Tommy Gray, wounded in Normandy, was playing with half a foot, the empty space stuffed with cotton wool. Two years later he was to play full-back for Scotland, empty boot and all.

223

We had no wounded men, but we did have Jim Ridgeway, who suffered from epilepsy. About twice a game Jim, who'd been at school with me, would fall down rigid and staring, and roll about with foam coming out of his mouth. The opposition were horrified but we were used to it. Jim had left instructions for his team, 'If I have a fit, just carry me to the touchline, put a coat over me, and leave me alone till I'm better.' Play then continued and Jim would eventually sit up, shake his head and rejoin the fray. Often the other side complained Jim had an unfair advantage as they didn't like to tackle him in case he started foaming again. Several times the opposition thought he was dead.

On Saturdays I walked to the city centre, carrying a cardboard suitcase with my kit. Perhaps I'd have a pint with father in the Royal Standard and then catch the tram to the ground. The city was full of thousands of young men doing the same, on their way to rugby, soccer or hockey. They were usually dressed alike in demob kit of ill-fitting sports coat, grey trousers and fawn mac. Some wore the appalling pork-pie hat issued to ex-soldiers, but I sold mine to Dad for 10s. 6d. I have never worn a hat since leaving the army.

Hardly anyone had a car then so the tram was packed. The atmosphere was social and jolly. People would make joshing remarks to strangers – 'You playing on them pitches at Coalpit Lane? I thought the canal had flooded them buggers.' There was a peculiar atmosphere to those post-war days. For years life had been grim and sometimes dangerous. The city was drab; paint was peeling, nothing was shiny or bright, bombed houses remained uncleared. But now it was all over and people were starting to enjoy themselves again, even though rationing was still there. At least the beer was getting stronger.

Rugby in Leicester was a much more widespread game than in London, home of the 'chinless wonders and medical students' father despised. But Stoneygate was a bit posh and stuck-up, they said locally, and more earthy sides such as South Leicester or Oadby used to delight in trying to take us down a peg. Midland rugby always had a special flavour. It's summed up by what happened when I tackled an opponent by the corner-flag just as he was about to score. He came down with a terrible thump in touch, but as we got up he said, 'That were a bloody good tackle, mate.'

Occasionally both Roger and I would find ourselves in the Second XV and it could be rather embarrassing. Roger considered it his duty to protect his younger brother, even though I could easily look after myself, and, as his temper had a short fuse, flare-ups were frequent. 'How dare you kick my brother in the balls?' he'd shout, aiming a swipe at one of the opposition. 'Do that again, George, and I'll have you carried off.' I'd beg Roger to shut up but he paid no heed. The rather gawky lad who'd gone into the navy eight years previously had changed considerably. It brought home to me quite vividly that apart from occasional leaves, we hadn't seen each other since 1940. Luckily he was 6 ft. 4 in. tall, so he got away with it.

Saturday night meant a pub. On away games we had favourites, such as Jimmy Thorpe's in Uppingham, one of two small towns in the tiny county of Rutland. It wasn't really a pub. It had a large sign, 'James Thorpe, licensed victualler, corn chandler and insurance agent' and his beer was the best for miles around. Above the bar was his corn warehouse. Sexism was rampant and no girl expected to see her rugby man on Saturdays, at least not until the pubs shut (which was ten o'clock, and few extensions allowed). Once, returning by coach from a game at Stamford, we stopped for the customary carouse at Uppingham. One of the team had just got engaged and begged us to leave.

'I've promised to meet my girl at nine o'clock outside the Midland Station,' he said. 'She'll murder me if I'm not there.'

We were inexorable. 'You shouldn't have arranged to see a girl on Saturday night.' As nine o'clock approached he became incoherent with anxiety and then quietly surrendered and drank huge quantities of beer to numb himself. In the coach he lapsed into despair – 'She was the only girl I was ever really fond of.'

Roger was in the First XV so we didn't often play together. But he had a car with his job, which enabled him to tour the unspoilt pubs of East Leicestershire villages with his navy friends and drink and play dominoes and darts. Father, who still regarded me as an innocent young man, took me aside before these expeditions and warned, 'They are the hardest school in the county, my boy. Drink halves when they drink pints.' I agreed, but had no intention of doing anything of the sort. Mother severely disapproved of these outings. Like so many of her generation, she had a horror of drink and relief at having both her sons back from the war was tempered by fear they had become alcoholics. No matter how late it was, she always waited up for our return.

'Your grandmother's cousin died of drink in Bristol,' she said when we returned home slightly the worse for wear. 'He even asked for whisky on his death-bed. It runs in the family, you see. You boys are going the same way.'

I used to resent being treated like a child and mumbled something about 'being old enough to do what I like', but Roger was a practised liar.

'I was having coffee at a friend's,' he once said, 'and the vicar was there, so it wasn't polite to leave.' (That was the night I'd last seen him balancing a crate of light ale on his head as he left at closing time.) Mother was a simple, unsophisticated soul, and usually believed him.

If lying failed, Roger resorted to blaming his war service.

'If that Jap suicide pilot had got me I wouldn't be able to drink at all,' he declaimed, sounding like an actor from a particularly bad British war film. 'When you have been shot at for four years, you see life differently.'

This argument did not impress mother.

'Your father was shot at but he never got into the disgusting condition you're in.'

That was undeniably true and unanswerable. Father always looked slightly embarrassed on these occasions as he was not averse to a pint himself but felt he should be on the side of mother and morality.

Yet by today's standards our behaviour was almost restrained. 'Late' meant being home after midnight. The pubs shut at ten and drinking afterwards meant taking bottles of beer to somebody's house. An average young man of today would regard late as being 4 a.m. and his beers in the bar would be topped up with two or three litres of cheap wine at a party. If he met a girl, he wouldn't come home at all. Today we are all booze artists by the standards of forty years ago.

A great problem was to stop using army language, principally one word. There was a universal service word for the ranks (although not for officers). It did for adjective, noun, verb, ejaculation, gerund and expletive. It was used partly because of its convenience and its solid ground; partly to show hostility to a society that was keeping us in the army so long; and partly to pretend we were tough. It became ingrained in speech and although I survived for a few days after demob I eventually disgraced myself in front of mother.

'I'm sorry, mum,' I said when I was late for midday dinner, 'but the fucking bus was full.'

Mother, naturally, was aghast and refused to believe my excuse that I'd actually said 'shocking'.

'I have not heard that word since your father broke his arm,' she said, deeply offended. 'I can't think what would happen if you used it in front of your Aunt Nan.'

The lapse into 'the language of the gutter', as mother would have phrased it, was typical of the change in me. Respectable lads who served in the ranks tended to emerge transformed – suspicious of authority, inclined to rough language, and striking up acquaintance with people who were 'not nice.' It was a natural result of 'mucking-in' for several years. Apart from my foul language, I declared the intention of voting Communist at the next election and my attitude towards any form of privilege was contemptuous. I even held cigarettes in the style of a labourer, the lighted end upwards inside the palm, the result of many furtive smokes in the Hussars' tank park. In pubs, I used the bar rather than the saloon or lounge.

Few of these traits survived in later life. Unfortunately, the habit of bad language did and many a famous West End restaurant has resounded to a cry of 'Sod me!' when I am lunching with a publisher or literary agent. My Labour Party sympathies dwindled when I found they merely provided a bonanza for bureaucrats. But the services stopped me being a snob; I was a manual labourer in the army and I found how unpleasant it can be. I'd rather work behind a desk or in a classroom any day.

At lunchtimes I often had a drink with father, who'd become friendly with a millionaire. Gordon Roll, captured at Dunkirk, inherited a fortune while in a P.O.W. camp in Germany and started to spend it when he came home. The papers were full of the exploits of 'the playboy P.O.W.', which included throwing champagne bottles like hand grenades at Ascot races. Gordon got through his fortune rapidly and finished up in Leicester almost broke, although he tipped the hotel porter a fiver. Father met him in one of the city centre pubs he used.

'His rich acquaintances had deserted him, my boy,' said father. 'The only friends he had left were the scum of the earth, boxing managers, fight promoters, bookmakers and racecourse touts.' His prejudice against sporting parasites had not diminished over the years.

Gordon rather took to father and sometimes they had a drink together. He told him, 'The lawyers have got at what's left of my money and they've tied it up so I can't have it.' Yet he was still generous and offered father a silver cigarette-case. 'You might as well have it, Mr Green,' he said. 'It's all I've got left.' Naturally father refused but was very touched by the offer.

'He was a real gentleman,' he said, 'unlike a great many aristocrats.' (Although a Conservative, father had a healthy suspicion of the gentry.) 'What a shame to see a nice boy like that come down in the world. It is a lesson to us all, my boy.' As always, he could not resist a moral homily.

On Saturday nights the young men of the city went down town to dance. Inner cities had not yet decayed. The Bell Hotel, known locally as 'the cattle market' because of its function in enabling boy to meet girl, was the upmarket venue; the nearby Palais de Danse was cheaper in every way. I went to both but preferred the Bell because it had a bar extension to the sinful hour of eleven o'clock on Saturdays. Entrance was expensive and it became a challenge to local youth to get in for nothing. Many ingenious routes were worked out and frequently a tousled young man would be seen appearing from behind the band or trying to enter disguised as a waiter.

Leicester marriages often began at the Bell or the Palais, although social conditions restricted the courting process. Most couples had to leave in time to catch the last tram or bus home. Taxis were a luxury. The age of the bed-sitter was only just starting and most single people either lived at home or in hostels or lodgings, where restrictions were placed on visitors. A girl at a Scottish university told me male visitors were allowed only on Sunday afternoons and a condition of the visit was that the bed had to be pushed out into the corridor. Nurses' homes were particularly savage, with girls having to sign in and out. As late as 1958, I remember a friend getting married and being refused permission to have his wife sleep in his single bed-sitter until their flat was ready, and that was ten years after the time I'm writing about.

So courting would be the familiar furtive process up an alley or ginnel as they were called in the East Midlands. The day of 'Your place or mine?' had not dawned. Meeting a nice girl at the Palais one night I walked two miles to her house, grappled in an alley and then walked three miles home. Fortunately mugging was rare. Crime tended to be restricted to 'rough' areas.

The weeks passed all too quickly. My uniform lay discarded. I'd meant to sew on the one medal I was entitled to – the War Service Medal – something I'd never got round to, but I never wore khaki again, except for the greatcoat, later used for motor-cycling. The army gave me a form to claim back my job and I sent it to Bill Cowper Barrons, the editor at Northampton. He wrote a terse letter saying he could not guarantee employment for more than the statutory six months for which he was legally forced to give me work. I thought that was rather a grudging way to welcome someone returned from the war.

Going over to Northampton to find digs I got fixed up with a railway fireman and his mother in a terraced house not far from the station. After looking at the cold room with its iron bedstead I realised I'd made a mistake, especially when the landlady said, 'The geyser's broken so you won't be able to have any hot water or baths, but if you really want hot water for shaving I'll boil a kettle.'

But I didn't like to offend the old lady, who was a widow and not well off. It was 25 bob a week with breakfast and Sunday dinner. Wages had increased enormously since I joined up and I was going to start on more than £4 a week. With beer around a shilling a pint I would survive.

Taking the familiar train to Market Harborough, I changed to the Northampton branch line and called in the office, to find the reporters' room full of strangers. Old Frank Reid, the chief reporter, was still typing his fat stock news, but he wasn't in charge any more. He welcomed me with all the enthusiasm of somebody greeting a typhus carrier and complained bitterly.

'They've kicked me out,' he said. 'I was too old. They don't want experience and dedication any more, they want youth all the time. You'll find everything's changed now. Let's see, you were in the navy, weren't you?' He fiddled with his typewriter and added, 'Drat this ribbon. I've only had it six months and it's gone faint already. They don't last like they used to.'

He took me over to the new chief reporter, an immensely tall bundle of energy called Piggott (he insisted on pronouncing it Pygote) who'd served in Burma with the Intelligence Corps during the war. One of his colleagues had been Alice Hope's husband but she'd left now, off on the trail that was to lead to Fleet Street. It was the dead hour of day, just before one o'clock, and the office was deserted, but he introduced me to one or two people, including a spotty-faced sixteen-year-old youth with glasses and brilliantined hair.

'This is Alastair Foot,' he said. 'He's just joined us from the grammar school.'

A little over 20 years later, Alastair was to become joint author of the world's longest-running farce, *No Sex Please, We're British*, but at the time he looked an unlikely candidate. He told me he was writing a revue for the local Boy Scouts. I asked after Arthur Steff, the last of the Victorians, at Kettering, but he'd died. My old friend Phil Osborne was over there in his place.

The editor had not become any more intelligible over the years and the interview with him was rather one-sided. He began by nodding quietly to himself for a few minutes. Then he rose and walked to the window overlooking the Market Square.

'Borch,' he said quite distinctly, with his pipe in his mouth.

I didn't know what to say, so I agreed.

'Aye,' he grunted. 'Wahah.'

He sat down at his desk and began to type on an old portable, completely ignoring me. Suddenly he looked up and gave a loud hoot, like a surprised owl.

'Feely beely oot,' he remarked, waving a skinny hand towards the door. I assumed he wanted me to leave.

'Monday?' I asked as I rose.

'Aye. Wahah Mundah.'

I had intended to ask all sorts of leading questions about conditions of work and wages and prospects of promotion but it all seemed a bit futile, so I left. 'He gets worse as he gets older,' said plump Miss Toyer, his secretary. 'It's got so only I can translate now.' I asked after the beautiful Beverley sisters, but they had left.

Thus Sunday found me walking once more to the Midland Station at Leicester with my suitcase. It was only thirty miles to Northampton but the train service was awful and it was two hours before we puffed into Castle Station after changing at Rugby. Packing clothes away in the room at my digs I found the landlady had lined the drawers with old copies of the *Chronicle and Echo*. There was a familiar look about one headline. Like most of the *Chronicle and Echo*'s headings it was banal to the point of imbecility and said something like this:

A G.O.M.
Remembers
—

Days of Boer War
Recalled

It was the story about the one-legged veteran who lived in a village near Towcester. The term G.O.M. was short for Grand Old Man and frequently used in headlines because of its brevity. Indeed, old people were known as 'Goms' in reporters' room slang. I read the story again, standing over the drawer with my socks in my hand, and decided I could do better in future.